MEN OF HORLEY 1914–1918
Lest We Forget

Reveille Press is an imprint of
Tommies Guides Military Booksellers & Publishers

Gemini House
136–140 Old Shoreham Road
Brighton
BN3 7BD

www.tommiesguides.co.uk

First published in Great Britain by
Reveille Press 2014

For more information please visit
www.reveillepress.com

© 2013 Doug Cox

ISBN 978-1-908336-45-3

Cover design by Reveille Press
Typeset by Vivian@Bookscribe

Printed and bound in Great Britain

IN FLANDERS FIELDS

In Flanders fields the poppies blow
Between the crosses, row on row,
That mark our place; and in the sky
The larks, still bravely singing, fly
Scarce heard amid the guns below.

We are the Dead. Short days ago
We lived, felt dawn, saw sunset glow,
Loved and were loved, and now we lie,
In Flanders fields.

Take up our quarrel with the foe:
To you from failing hands we throw
The torch; be yours to hold it high.
If ye break faith with us who die
We shall not sleep, though poppies grow
In Flanders fields.

by

John McCrae   near Ypres   3 May 1915

ACKNOWLEDGEMENTS

This book was written with the help and encouragement of members of Horley Local History Society who also provided many of the photographs used. The Society also loaned a number of maps and other local records.

Particular thanks are due to Brian Buss who, because of his extensive knowledge of Horley's past, provided much of the information about the town and consistent help and advice.

Thanks too to Chris Baker of fourteeneighteen research for permission to quote from his excellent website www.1914-1918.net. This site provides links to a number of sources which will answer many questions for serious researchers and those simply interested in the Great War.

Much of the research for this book was completed with the help of resources at Ancestry.co.uk and the Commonwealth War Graves Commission. The CWGC provides a wonderful service worldwide by its dedication to the memory of Commonwealth servicemen who died in the two world wars. They care for cemeteries and memorials at 23,000 locations, in 153 countries and have done so since 1917.

Several surviving descendants of our WW1 dead – or their close families – have also given information and photographs which have been incorporated into individual stories where possible, and for these I am most grateful.

INTRODUCTION

Although we could hope that this plaque and the similar memorials in other local churches referred to above should bear some relevance to where the men listed actually lived, this is not always the case and in some instances this brings forth even further questions.

Before arriving at a comprehensive list of the Men of Horley who gave their lives in World War I, two other significant sources of fact need to be considered. The first of these is the Roll of Honour produced for use at the Dedication of the Horley War Memorial in February 1922. The second is a memorial plaque which commemorates former pupils initially erected inside Horley's first Infant School. The names recorded on both of these are at variance with the War Memorial.

Preliminary investigations have revealed that these variances have not been considered before and the main purpose of this book is to attempt to do so.

Therefore the book has several aims:-

- To describe what Horley Village was like in 1914 and explain what happened in it during those four years of war.

- To ensure that the present and future generations of Horley residents will know more about the 122 men named on the Horley War Memorial than simply their names carved in stone.

- To give some idea of life in England immediately following the war.

- To identify what memorials exist within the broad boundary of Horley Parish in World War I and to record the names of the men listed on them.

- To determine how names were selected for placement on the Horley War Memorial.

- To determine whether there is any duplication or omissions of names.

- To examine other sources of information and build a list of men missing from local Horley memorials.

- To arrive at a suggested list of men connected with Horley who lost their lives in World War I and to determine where possible their correct names, units and locations, dates of death and their place of burial or commemoration.

- To set out, in an Appendix, details of British Army casualties in World War 1 in order that readers can judge local losses against those of the whole country.

To assist in achieving these aims Chapters 1 and 2 will describe what Horley was like at the outset of war in 1914 and during the years 1914–1918.

Chapter 3 sets out some of the principal events throughout the conflict and lists the deaths of the men named on Horley War Memorial in a timeline, whilst Chapter 4 gives the individual stories behind each man's name.

Chapters 5 and 6 deal with the years immediately after the war and the construction of Horley War Memorial, whilst Chapter 7 examines, in some depth, the other local memorials and tries to identify who is commemorated where and why.

Chapter 8 lists the names of men assembled from all sources who are known to have connections with Horley and gives details of where, if at all, they are buried and commemorated.

Finally, Chapter 9 explains how the research was carried out and draws some conclusions about this proud chapter in the history of Horley.

An Appendix is included, which gives some detail of National losses in order that the full scale of sacrifice can be appreciated.

It is hoped that this book will add to the knowledge of what took place one hundred years ago in Horley Parish and ensure that the Men of Horley who gave their lives in World War 1 will never be forgotten, whether they are commemorated on a memorial or not.

CHAPTER ONE

HORLEY VILLAGE WITHIN HORLEY PARISH IN 1914

The weird triangular shape of the ecclesiastical area of Horley Parish in 1914 was about 8000 acres. It stretched from South Earlswood in the North to almost a point where Radford Road met Balcombe Road, some 5¾ miles to the south. Its western edge tended to follow the meandering line of the River Mole flowing north bordering the Parish of Charlwood, and its eastern boundary stretched to the edge of Smallfield Village, some 4½ miles to the east.

It consisted mainly of heavy clay-like soil and the whole, almost flat, area was part of the South-Eastern Division of Surrey. It was in the Southwark Diocese, Kingston Archdeaconry, Reigate Rural Deaconry, Reigate Petty Sessional Division and Reigate Union and the Redhill County Court District.

A large part of its area was bought by Christ Hospital in 1602 and much of it was still under the same ownership in 1914. Although there were still several ancient properties, some built in the 13th century still standing, there were no vast estates owned by the landed gentry. The Parish then was considered predominantly rural, still with many farms that once were around the edge of the huge open common that was enclosed in 1812. The railway that came to Horley in 1841 was laid north to south across the common with its station placed well away from the three small ancient settlements known collectively by that name that had survived for

CHAPTER TWO

THE HOME FRONT 1914–1918

THE INTERNATIONAL SITUATION

Before examining the situation in Horley when the war began, it is worth setting out in brief terms the international background to the crisis in July 1914.

Why did the murder of Archduke Franz Ferdinand in Sarajevo on 28 June lead to a general European war within a few weeks?

The answer briefly is this:

1. The assassins were Serbian. Serbia, supported by its ally, Russia, was engaged in terrorist activities to promote its expansionist plans in the Balkans. Russia hoped to score a foreign political success; its ultimate goal was to open the Dardanelles to Russian warships.

2. Austria–Hungary was worried about the dissolution of its empire and loss of face following the assassination. It was allied with Germany. The Germans wanted Vienna to wage war on Serbia in order to prevent the breakdown of the Habsburg Empire. The Germans feared, moreover, that the modernization, population explosion, and industrial growth of Russia would transform their eastern neighbour into a superpower that would sooner or later crush Germany.

3. On 28 July, with German support, Austria declared war on Serbia and, as a consequence of its alliance, with Russia.

4. On 1 August Germany declared war on Russia, which was also allied with France. The French attitude in July 1914

was mostly defensive (wait and see). The headlines of the French press in July were preoccupied with a murder committed by the wife of a minister and rarely discussed the Balkan crisis.

5. On 3 August Germany declared war on France and invaded that country via Belgium. Britain was pledged to guarantee the neutrality of Belgium and issued an ultimatum to Germany that was rejected. Britain was primarily concerned about the rise of German naval power and feared German predominance on the Continent.

6. On 4 August Britain, supported by its Commonwealth, declared war on Germany. The British Expeditionary Force (BEF) was despatched to France and saw its first actions near Mons on 23 August.

AUGUST TO DECEMBER 1914

Horley was last affected by war some 14 years earlier during the Boer War (1899–1902). Horley Village itself lost three men out of about 4000 inhabitants within the Parish and their names can still be seen carved in the timbers of the Lych Gate leading to St Bartholomews Church. In August 1914 it found itself on the threshold of another war that most claimed would be over by Christmas that year, but it was not to be.

Between those two wars, the Victorian era had come to an end when Queen Victoria died in 1902. Her death came at a time when the country was ostensibly one of the most richest and powerful in the world. However, the new 20th century ushered in the start of several changes. Imperceptibly, at first, the social class structure began to shift away from one where the lower classes continued to work hard for middle and upper class employers who had the money. Already there were signs of a decline in agriculture as towns grew when new industries and technologies came about and rural communities wanted to be part of them.

Horley Parish and Horley Village in particular, was still developing as these changes were slowly taking place. Horley had few upper class inhabitants in the latter part of the 19th century, but a good number of middle class families that still required domestic workers in 1914. It was probably fair to say that out of the working population in the Parish, approaching half were employed in the activities of what we know as the town centre and the other half were mainly connected with agriculture, and smaller businesses around Mill Lane/Lee Street and Horley Row.

So after war was declared on 4 August 1914, very little in the Parish changed in the first months except for Reservists and Territorials who had to report for duty to their regimental depots. Recruiting Centres were set up in all the major towns and these would also arrive periodically at smaller locations such as Horley. The County Regiments were the principal recipients of volunteers and the recruiting sergeants of The Queens (Royal West Surrey Regiment) at Guildford and The East Surrey Regiment at Kingston did brisk business. Thousands of men enlisted, happy to exchange the poor conditions in agricultural labouring and similar jobs for a chance to participate in a great adventure, where victory was assured and which, no doubt, would be over by Christmas.

The immediate effect of this mass exodus from the civilian labour pool was that women steadily began to take over men's employment for the first time. In some cases these jobs were in addition to their existing duties but for many the taking of a job, which until now had always been a male preserve, was simply to ensure that they put bread upon the table of their families.

The Defence of the Realm Act was passed in August 1914. This gave the government powers to commandeer economic resources for the war effort, imprison people without trial, censor the printed or spoken word and greatly control the lives of ordinary people.

As well as rationing, public house opening times were restricted. This was as much to keep the nation fit for long hours at work, as to satisfy Lloyd George's anxieties over alcohol. Originally allowed to open anytime between 5.30am and half-past midnight, pubs were now to be limited to opening from midday to 2.30pm and 6.30pm to 9.30pm daily. In addition, the practice of 'treating' or buying drinks for others, was forbidden.

TROOPS IN HORLEY

The first indication of how irksome wartime was to be for inhabitants who lived on the east side of the railway was the closure of the recently erected new foot bridge.

When the railway company wished to lay two fast tracks through Horley in 1904, it undertook several major alterations. It had to reposition the station from its original location adjacent to todays Factory Shop (then a goods building) to its present location. It also had to remove two manually operated level crossings. One was at the eastern end of today's High Street (then called Station Road) along with its adjacent foot-bridge that had, of course, to straddle just two tracks. The other was to the south where it crossed Victoria Road, (where Waitrose car park is today). It also had to construct a subway to allow horses to pass under the railway from where they grazed alongside the White Swan pub (where St George's Close is today), in order to reach the Fire Station in Albert Road.

Obviously many residents on the eastern side of the railway did not favour the subway and for several years forcibly agitated for the return of a footbridge, which then had to straddle four tracks. After years of wrangling, it was agreed to reinstate one but just before it was officially opened, war was declared and the authorities decided it was too dangerous to allow this and it was boarded up for fear that enemy spies or agents may use it to drop explosives onto passing trains.

Three soldiers of C Company 6th KLR patrolling the tracks, believed to be north of the Balcombe Road bridge. Note the outside two have railway handlamps while the centre one is in shorts without a lamp and different belt.
(Photo courtesy of Horley Local History Society.)

The line was important for the transit of war supplies between London and Newhaven and to ensure its safety, soldiers of the King's Liverpool Regiment were billeted in Horley in order to patrol the tracks.

It is interesting to see this photo and the one below. For who was the photographer? Obviously a local person who could print and sell them as post cards, as both were posted from Horley during October 1914. Clearly security and censorship were not observed then and the soldier's message home to Liverpool talked about his *"Communication duties"* as well as the imminent movement of his Battalion and that it was still in training.

Members of the 6th Kings Liverpool Regiment relaxing on Horley Station. The NCO's are obviously regular troops whereas others appear to be to be young recruits. The message on the post card sent from Horley on 4 October 1914 told the soldier's mother that most of the men were overcoming their vaccinations.
(Photo courtesy of Horley Local History Society.)

BELGIAN REFUGEES

Another indication that war had come to Horley is shown in another postcard. As the German Forces rapidly swept through Belgium in the first weeks of the war, several families came to England as refugees; some came to Horley early in the war.

Belgian refugees who came to Horley. The board reads "Refugies Belges in Horley". It is not known where they stayed.
(Photo courtesy of Horley Local History Society.)

(In 2001 a young Belgian researcher encountered an elderly relative who had seen this photograph, and discovered that one of the children-in-arms was his father.)

INDUSTRIAL COMPANIES ON WAR WORK

In Honeycrock Lane, Salfords, a company called Lanston Monotype Corporation, set up a high precision engineering company in 1900, to design and produce new types of printing equipment. When war commenced, it became involved with the production of intricate mechanisms for machine guns for the duration of the war. Monotype, as it became known, provided employment for many local workers as well as others from further afield. Eventually the Company became so busy they felt able to ask the London Brighton and South Coast railway to construct a dedicated halt for their employees. This was opened on 8 Oct 1915 and eventually became Salfords Station although it was not opened to the public until 1932. Some idea of the work involved at Monotype can be gained by the autobiography of a young man who was unfit for the army. (This publication *Working Night Shift at the Monotype in WWI* published by Horley Local History Society 2012.)

Another well known company in Horley was G F Strawson, who specialised in building conservatories and greenhouses which were produced in his St Andrew's Works in Charlesfield Road. While he might have made other items to assist in the war effort, one that he was noted for was a revolving shelter for the open-air treatment of convalescing troops. It was reported that several shelters of this type were in use at Lady Henry Somerset's *"Industrial Farm Colony"* at Duxhurst, which was set up in 1894 for the reception and help of inebriate women. It consisted of a model village in some 180 acres off the A217 some 2 miles north of Horley and comprised several home-like cottages grouped around an open quadrangle with an adjacent chapel. It was taken over by the War Office as a Red Cross hospital for nursing wounded soldiers from 1915.

1915
By spring it had become clear that voluntary recruitment was

Strawson revolving shelter taken from an original Strawson advertisement.

not going to provide the numbers of men required for the continued prosecution of the expanding war. The Government passed the National Registration Act on 15 July as a step towards stimulating recruitment and to discover how many men between the ages of 15 and 65 were engaged in each trade. The results of this census became available by mid-September.

On 11 October, Lord Derby – who had played a major part in raising volunteers, especially for the King's Liverpool Regiment – was appointed Director-General of Recruiting. He brought forward a scheme five days later, often called the

Examples of Recruitment Posters

Derby Scheme although officially it was the Group Scheme, for raising the numbers. It was half-way to conscription.

During these early months of the war the army commandeered a vast number of horses throughout the whole country. They were needed to replace cavalry mounts and provide the horse power for pulling guns, ammunition wagons and supplies, and the effect of this measure was felt most severely in rural communities. In Horley, one of the elephants of Sangers circus, which was based in the south of the town, was photographed pulling a plough (see opposite page), though this was thought to have been a staged shot rather than a regular occurrence.

As the year progressed, Horley started to feel the impact of the war, not only through the steady loss of its men, but also because of what was starting to happen at home.

On 7 May a German U-Boat torpedoed the British passenger

One of Sangers Circus elephants pulling a plough

liner, *Lusitania*, off the Irish coast. This great ship sank in just 18 minutes, drowning 1,201 people including Benjamin Potter, a waiter, from Horley.

Alfred Gwynne Vanderbilt also died on the *Lusitania*. His name was known to many in Horley because his company once ran a regular stage coach service through the village. His coaches, Venture and Viking, were familiar sights at the Chequers Hotel, whilst en route from London to Brighton. However, the arrival of the railway eventually bought about its demise.

As the *Lusitania* went down, Vanderbilt reputedly gave his life jacket to a woman who could not swim, and as a result, he lost his life.

The sinking of the *Lusitania* outraged the public on both sides of the Atlantic and was a factor in the decision of America to eventually enter the war. President Woodrow Wilson subsequently sent four diplomatic protests to Germany about the sinking.

Throughout the year local casualties at the front continued to mount, many of them during the Battle of Loos.

More than 60,000 British casualties were sustained in this battle. 50,000 of them were in the main fighting area between Loos and Givenchy and the remainder in the subsidiary attacks. Of these, 7,766 men died. Many New Army units, rushed into a battle area for the first time only a matter of days after landing in France, were devastated. A significant proportion of the remaining pre-war regular troops were lost, and more than 2,000 officers were killed or wounded. This irreplaceable asset in experienced men and leaders was a most serious loss to the army. The New Army units that had taken part in a major action for the first time had suffered heavily – but had shown without doubt that they were worthy soldiers.

FILLING OF MUNITIONS IN HORLEY

In July, a Conference was held by the Ministry of Munitions to consider how to increase the production of shells to meet the growing demand of the Army. It decided to establish 15 National Filling Factories, one of which was the existing Royal Arsenal, Woolwich. Horley became one of its depots called *"Depot for completing foreign ammunition"*.

The exact reason why Horley was chosen is not known but it was probably selected because of its logistical connections. It was outside of London in a rural area and alongside a main railway line within easy reach of the port of Newhaven, which was used extensively to ship supplies to France. Horley had its own railway station to bring in workers from suburban areas and useful local amenities, like a fire station, police station and hospital.

The depot was thought to have been laid out in some 15 acres of Spier's farm land as shown below, late in 1915. From its letter heading it was always called "35 Munitions Store" but it is not known whether munitions were actually brought to the site for storage before the year was out. Nor was the size or quantity known.

Aerial photo of intended Horley Gardens Estate taken in 1935 showing the derelict site of 35 Munitions Store in WW1. Horley station is in the bottom right hand corner and the railway can be seen along the bottom of the photo.
(Photo courtesy of Michael Hall.)

In 2002 several footings and foundations were found within the "Stores" boundary sufficient to produce a map superimposed on today's residential estate. The central track of the railway siding could also be positioned showing its short distance from the main LB&SC railway and the short distance to walk from Horley station. Unfortunately no detailed map of the site layout has been located.

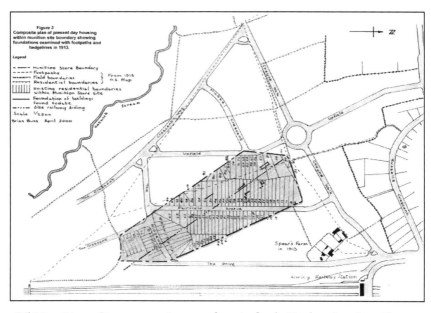

35 Munitions Store superimposed on today's Horley Gardens Estate showing position of footings, foundations, etc found.
(Courtesy of Brian Buss)
(A publication on this subject, "No 35 Munitions Store, Horley, Surrey, in WW1" by Brian Buss is available via Horley Local History Society, 3rd edition 2012.)

Horley Parish Council became very concerned about various aspects of the *"Store"*. For example, they worried about the lack of special precautions for protection against attack from enemy aircraft, and the noise and fumes emitted by the site.

Also, when there were rumours of an extension to the "*Store*", the Council were quick to suggest that it should be built on land towards Three Bridges and not in Horley. Nimbyism is not a new phenomenon.

Strike action in the munitions industry was made illegal by the Munitions Act of 1915.

On another postcard written during 1915, the writer states "*... four thousand soldiers billeted in Horley, nearly 200 in our road but I'm pleased I have none at present, love.....*" It is hard to believe that so many troops could be accommodated in the relatively small number of dwellings in Horley. It is not known why so many troops were billeted locally. Were they still guarding the railway, or perhaps building or guarding the Munitions Store?

1916

The Government were disappointed by the results achieved by Lord Derby's recruitment scheme and introduced the Military Service Act on 27 January. All voluntary enlistment was stopped. All British males were now deemed to have enlisted on 2 March 1916 – that is, they were "conscripted" – if they were aged between 19 and 41 and resided in Great Britain (excluding Ireland) and were unmarried or a widower on 2 November 1915. Conscripted men were no longer given a choice of which service, regiment or unit they joined, although if a man expressed a preference for the Royal Navy it had priority to take him. This act was extended to married men, and the lower age dropped to 18, on 25 May 1916.

A system of appeals tribunals was established, to hear cases of men who believed they were disqualified on the grounds of ill-health, occupation or conscientious objection. Some trades were deemed to be vital to the war economy and these were called *"starred"* occupations.

This Act was also unsuccessful in that only 43,000 of the men called up qualified for service in the army. At least 93,000 failed to answer their call-up and their appeals filled the courts. 748,587 men claimed some form of exemption and their cases filled the tribunals. In addition were the 1,433,827 classified as being in a *"starred"* occupation, or those who were ill or who had already been discharged on these grounds. The manpower of the army never caught up with its planned establishment.

At least 35 of the men named on our War Memorial died in 1916, many of them falling at the Battle of the Somme which lasted from July to November.

Its opening day, 1 July, was a tragic day for the British Army. There were some 60,000 casualties by the end of that day of which 20,000 were fatalities.

The names of the villages and woods on the Somme battlefields have become synonymous with the desperate fighting and tragic losses during the four and a half months of these battles: Gommecourt, Serre, Beaumont Hamel, Thiepval, Ovillers, La Boisselle, Courcelette, Fricourt, Contalmaison, Mametz, Montauban, Bazentin, Longueval, Delville Wood, Martinpuich, High Wood, Flers.

All of these locations have become fixed in the British psyche as places of gallantry, slaughter and suffering.

As the growing casualty lists appeared in local newspapers the feeling at home must have been unimaginable. Victory, if it was to come, seemed far away and the General Staff seemed to have few new ideas as to how it would ever be achieved. A growing feeling that our troops were "lions led by donkeys", was beginning to take hold and the regular demands for more men were starting to grate.

One of our greatest anti-war poets, Siegfried Sasoon (1886–1967), summed up this feeling amongst our troops when he wrote about a General.

'Good-morning; good-morning!' the General said
When we met him last week on our way to the line.
Now the soldiers he smiled at are most of 'em dead,
And we're cursing his staff for incompetent swine.
'He's a cheery old card,' grunted Harry to Jack
As they slogged up to Arras with rifle and pack.

But he did for them both by his plan of attack.

In 1916 the government introduced British Summer Time, allowing longer working days in factories during the summer months.

Horley's 35 Munitions Store became extremely active from 1916 into 1917. Its main activity was the filling of shrapnel shells for 18-pounder guns. Production figures for the factory show that 3,158,500 shells were filled in 1916 and 1,578,600 in 1917, giving a total of 4,737,100 shells over the two years whilst working continuous shifts over a seven day week.

The cast iron shell cases were made in Canada or the USA. Boxes for the filled shells were also constructed on site and this activity as well as the paint and inspection departments most probably employed well over 250 people, mainly women. Some were from within the Parish but most were believed to be from the south London area.

While annual reports of local casualties must have had a tremendous effect on families in Horley, this *"Store"*, its size, extent and complexity, along with the vast increase in the number of persons coming and going, must have made the war far more real to local people.

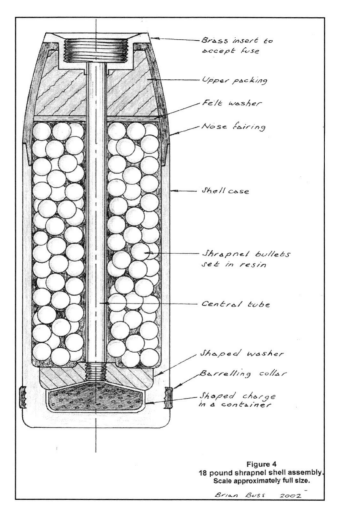

Brass insert to accept fuse

Upper packing

Felt washer

Nose fairing

Shell case

Shrapnel bullets set in resin

Central tube

Shaped washer

Barrelling collar

Shaped charge in a container

Figure 4
18 pound shrapnel shell assembly.
Scale approximately full size.

Brian Buss 2002

A filled 9 inch shell case typical of those undertaken in Horley.
(Courtesy of Brian Buss.)

The Women who filled the 9 inch shell cases. Photo taken beside one of the arches under the road leading to Horley station. (Courtesy of Peter Bennett.)

The Inspection Department. This photo was taken by a Horley photographer named Dore. (Courtesy of Sheila Hankin.)

The carpenters who made the transport boxes for the shell cases, known as the Box Factory. Note they are holding various tools. (Courtesy of Ray Warren.)

The Paint Department. (Courtesy of Ray Warren.)

Life in the Parish must have been hard to take at this period. Some food shortages were beginning to appear and there was a growing certainty that life would never be the same again.

1917

David Lloyd George became prime minister in December 1916 and immediately transformed the British war effort, taking firm control of both military and domestic policy.

On the 19 January 1917 the British intercepted a telegram sent by Alfred Zimmermann in the German Foreign Office to the German embassies in Washington DC and Mexico City. Its message outlined plans for an alliance between Germany and Mexico against the United States. According to the scheme, Germany would provide tactical support while Mexico would benefit by expanding into the American Southwest, retrieving territories that had once been part of Mexico. This document, the "Zimmermann Telegram" was passed by the British to the Americans and was then made public.

It caused an outcry from interventionists in the US and was another factor which would eventually pull America into the war.

By 1917 German U-boats were sinking British ships at a frightening rate and causing severe food shortages. This, with the need to release even more men from agriculture to serve at the front, led to the creation of the Women's Land Army. Their task was to maximise the output from the land to feed the nation and counteract the effect of the U-boats.

Some farmers resisted this measure and the Board of Trade had to send officers around the country to persuade farmers to accept women employees. The strategy was successful, and by the end of 1917 there were over 260,000 women working as farm labourers.

Another way of releasing men was found with the formation in 1917 of the Royal Defence Corps of soldiers too old for the front, who could guard ports, main roads and railway yards. In many ways, they were the forerunners of the Home Guard of 1940.

The financial situation in which the country found itself was dire by this time. Britain had been financing almost all of the Allies war effort and finally their reserves were exhausted. America took over the role of banker to the Allied cause and set Britain swingeing terms for the repayment of its loans when the war was won.

At least the fact that America was finally committed to fighting alongside our troops was some consolation, and the news of the success on the battlefield of the newly invented Tanks must have convinced many that the war could finally be won.

As the year drew to a close Horley families were mourning the loss of at least 30 more men.

1918

Following the October Revolution and the subsequent collapse of the Russian army many German troops were redeployed to the Western Front and as the effects were felt, British casualties mounted. Eventually, British troops recovered the situation and the arrival of American troops in March sealed the German fate.

Horley suffered another death in July 1918, however this time it was not at the front but at home. Miss Rosie Winifred Coomber who resided with her parents at 125 Albert Road, died of influenza that was sweeping through the country and Europe at that time. This young girl had been employed at the

Munitions Store as a painter. She was said to be universally popular with her comrades and that was confirmed when some sixty "munitionettes" assembled outside of her residence, all in their respective department coloured overalls, to escort the cortege to St Bartholomews Church, while many residents lined the streets.

Soldiers from all sides began to succumb to the same disease. Troop losses from the flu epidemic soon exceeded combat casualties, especially weakening the hard-pressed German Army. This became a worldwide epidemic and lasted for about a year killing an estimated 20 million people before vanishing as quickly and strangely as it had appeared.

As the war drew to a close in November, the people of Horley reflected on the four years of slaughter and the hundreds of young men who would never be the same again. Despite the Armistice, a number of local men were still to die. Some were hospitalised and suffering from wounds which were yet to prove fatal and others were still fighting in the middle east where isolated hostilities continued.

More of the 122 Men of Horley listed on our War Memorial died in 1918 than in any other year of the war.

The task of counting the dead men was about to begin.

ON WAR SERVICE BADGES

Any civilian engaged on war work was entitled to receive and wear either of the badges shown below. The large one was actually found in the garden of a house in Horley in the 1990s.

Two War Service badges, the smaller one is for evening wear.
(Courtesy of Brian Buss.)

A POST-WAR PHOTO

This unsourced photo was thought to be dated c1920.
It's caption read: "Gas Shells Dump in Surrey – Workmen removing
the mustard-gas shells from a dump near Gatwick Race Course
which has been causing annoyance to the villagers of Horley."
It is considered highly unlikely that these shells contained mustard
gas, but the number involved is noteworthy.

CHAPTER THREE

A TIMELINE OF HORLEY DEATHS

This timeline sets out the deaths of 120 of the 122 men listed on Horley War memorial against the main events and major battles of WWI.

Time	Event	Name/Date
1914		
28 June	Archduke Franz Ferdinand assassinated	
28 July	Austria declares war on Serbia	
1 August	Germany mobilises and declares war on Russia	
3	Germany declares war on France and invades Belgium	
4	Britain declares war on Germany.	
22	27,000 French troops die in abortive thrust towards German border.	
23	British troops in action at Mons.	
25	Retreat of BEF begins	
5–10 September	Battle of the Marne	
12-28	First battle of The Aisne.	
25	Race to the sea begins – trenches established.	
19–22 October	First Battle of Ypres	Arthur John Woods
1 November	Battle of Coronel (at sea)	George Flowers
		Norman Jonathan Borer
		George Terry
25 December	Unofficial Christmas truce	Thomas William Wilson
		William Hoare

TIME	EVENT	NAME/DATE

1915

TIME	EVENT	NAME/DATE
19 January	Zeppelin air raids on England begin	
24	Battle of Dogger Bank (at sea)	
		Joseph Albert Weller
4 February	Germany declares submarine blockade	
19	Royal Navy begins to bombard Dardenelles forts.	
10–13 March	Battle of Neuve Chappelle	Charles Coomber
22–25 May	Second Battle of Ypres.	
25	Allied landings begin Gallipoli	John Gordon Grahame
		Alec John Shoubridge
		Frederick George Marchant
7 May	'Lusitania' sunk.	
15–27	Battle of Festubert	
23	Italy declares war on Germany and Austria	
June		George William Barton
5 August	Germany captures Warsaw from Russians	
25 September–	Battle of Loos	Harry Thomas Buckell
14 October		Edgar Burden
		Harry Knowles
		William Maynard
		Percy Robert Pescud
September		James Edward Cornford
October		Charles Henry Bailey
		Alban Vincent Scollick
November		Frank Lennox Taylor

A TIMELINE OF HORLEY DEATHS

TIME	EVENT	NAME/DATE
7 December	Sir Douglas Haig becomes commander of BEF.	
19	Gallipoli evacuation begins	

1916

27 January	Conscription introduced in Britain.	Thomas Ledger
21 February–18 December	Battle of Verdun	Alec Joseph Pescud
9 April	Canadians take Vimy Ridge.	
29	Large British force surrenders at Kut in Mesopotamia	Thomas Bowen
		Edward John Lockyer
		Harry Edward Fish
31 May	Battle of Jutland	Sidney Killick
		George Alfred Morgan
		Ernest Cecil Peirson Smith
June		John Humphrey
		Richard Harmes
1 July	Battle of The Somme commences and lasts to 18th November	Charles Elson
		Thomas Brocklehurst
		Benjamin Harvey Killick
		Sidney Bourne
		Charlie Kenward
		Albert Charlwood
		Henry Webber
		Francis Stanley Mott
August		Ernest Cecil Leach
		Francis Hezekiah Cooper
15 September	Tanks first used near Flers.	William Budgen

45

Time	Event	Name/Date
September		James Albert Wiltshire
		Leslie Alfred Yardley
		Donald Russell
		William George Hansen
		Arthur Edwin Cheesman
October		George Cyril Freeman
October		John Sidney Henning
		Arthur Rowland Chessall
		James Thewless
		Thomas Arthur Swain
November		Kenneth George Perry
		Joseph Basil Reeves
		Douglas William Manners
7 December	David Lloyd-George becomes Prime Minister	Horace Frank Munn

1917

Time	Event	Name/Date
February		
15 March	Tsar Nicholas abdicates	
6 April	USA declares war on Germany.	
9–12	Battle of Arras and Vimy Ridge.	
16	French launch disastrous assault at Chemin-des-Dames. French troops mutiny.	
16–9 May	Second Battle of the Aisne	William Joshua Warner
	26th Battle of Gaza	Charles Sydney Bingham
		Archibald Remnant
May	18th: Draft bill passed in USA	Bertie Stringer
		Ernest Arthur Vallance
		William John Weller

A TIMELINE OF HORLEY DEATHS

Time	Event	Name/Date
May		Thomas George Holmes
		George William Peppiatt
		William Hugh Woollhead
7–14 June	Battle of Messines	Henry Walker Liles
		Edwin Payne
3 July	American troops land in France	
31–6 Nov	3rd Battle of Ypres – Passchendaele	Charles Robert Day
		Carl Frederick Hansen
August		Charles Tribe
		John James Martin
		Esme Brotherton
September		Arthur Edward Voice
		Henry Marchant
24 October	Battle of Caporetto – Italian army heavily defeated	Reginald John Boyes
		Henry George Richards
		Thomas Parsons
		Albert Edward Coutts
		Ronald John Saxton White
20 November	British tanks win major action at Cambrai	Charles White
		Charles Atkins
		Harry Robert Bugden
		Michael James Humphrey
5 December	Armistice signed between Germany and Russia	
9	British capture Jerusalem	Frank Comber
		Frank Roffey

TIME	EVENT	NAME/DATE

1918

January	Influenza begins to sweep Europe	Ralph Clifford Sotham Wilfred Sydney Hughes Geoffrey Saxton White William Walter Hards
21 March	Major German offensive begins and makes advances	
29	Marshall Foch appointed Allied Commander.	George McFarlane Brooker Thomas McKenzie Bradley Arthur Bert Turner George Garrett White Robert John Drewell George Alfred Etheridge Edward Albert Lambert
25 April	British and Australian troops halt the German advance near Amiens	Frederick Ernest Borer James Sidney Swinden Christopher Steer
25 May	Germans shell Paris	
31	German push towards Paris halted by American troops at Chateau Thierry	Alfred Geoffrey Luscombe
1–26 June	Battle of Belleau Wood	Ernest Alfred Peach George Walter Steer
15 July	Second Battle of The Marne starts	
	German army starts to collapse	Albert Daniel Strudwick Robert William Nixon

Time	Event	Name/Date
8 August	Allies advance on the Somme Front	Charles William Standing
		Albert James White
26 September–11 November	Meuse – Argonne offensive begins	
27	Allies break through Hindenburg Line	Edward George Lucas
		Herbert Stanley Todd
		Arthur Allen Burbridge
		Albert Frederick Stevenson
		William Alfred Still
		Alfred Roser
4 October	Germany request Armistice	Charlie Tomsett
28	German Navy mutinies	Richard Wilson
30	Turkey signs Armistice	William Charles Croxford
3 November	Austria makes peace	
9	Kaiser Wilhelm abdicates	Thomas Apps
11	Armistice signed	Sydney George Southgate

1919

Time	Event	Name/Date
4 January	Peace conference convenes at Versailles	Harry George Coburn
		George Banks
21 June	German Fleet scuttled at Scapa Flow	
28	Peace treaty signed	
19 July	Cenotaph unveiled in London	John Box

CHAPTER FOUR

MEN OF HORLEY 1914-1918

The details of each man listed on Horley War Memorial are given here as well as they can be put together from surviving records. Each man has been identified with the help of census records and military records held by Ancestry.com and the Commonwealth War Graves Commission.

When the townspeople gathered to dedicate the Horley War Memorial in February 1922, they probably never imagined that, 100 years on, the people of Horley would still honour their dead and gather at the War Memorial every November to remember their courage and sacrifice.

The crowds who gather each November read all too frequently that yet another young British soldier has died in some far away foreign field and wish to show solidarity with our present forces personnel. Remember, too, that this Memorial also honours the fallen of the Second World War and the horrors of this conflict are still clearly recalled by many elderly residents.

If errors of identification have occurred which have caused errors of fact to be incorrectly ascribed to individual men, the author offers an unreserved apology.

The Horley War Memorial in its original position outside The Thorns public house.
(Photo courtesy of Horley Local History Society.)

THOMAS APPS

Pte G/21577 10th Battalion, The Queens (Royal West Surrey) Regiment

Thomas Apps was born in 1895 and was the third son of George and Alice Apps of Ringly Oak Farm, Brighton Road, Horley. He worked as a carman or driver and had a younger brother and sister.

His service record is not traceable but we know that Thomas first served with the Sussex Yeomanry and that he enlisted at Brighton.

The 10th Queens (Service Battalion) was formed at Battersea on 3 June 1915 by the Mayor and Borough of Battersea and came under the command of the 124th Brigade, 41st Division. It fought in many of the major actions on the Western front including the 3rd battle of Ypres and various actions around the Menin Road in September 1917. In October, with a full strength of 962 all ranks, the Battalion moved to Italy and after a 120 mile march they arrived at Volpago.

In February 1918 they moved to Monte Grappa before returning to France in time to help counter the German 'Operation Michael' attacks wherein they sustained 350 casualties.

After a period in a quieter section of the line they were able to join in the final advance and by the time of the Armistice they had arrived at Tenbosch, Belgium.

Thomas's medal records show no trace of his ever being posted overseas.

No firm details of his cause of death are known but he may have been a victim of the influenza epidemic which swept through the country in 1918. He died in the Military Hospital at Shoreham on Armistice Day, 11 November 1918, aged 23, and is buried in the churchyard at St Bartholomews Church, Horley.

CHARLES ATKINS

Able Seaman Z/2660, Anson Battalion, Royal Naval Volunteer Reserve

Charles Atkins was born in 1892 at Witham, Sussex. In 1911 he lived with his parents, Charles and Alice Atkins at 2 Bridge Cottages, Salfords. He was employed as a milkman and was the eldest of six brothers and two sisters.

Charles enlisted in the RNVR in July 1915 and was trained as an infantryman joining the Anson Battalion at Mudros on the Greek island of Lemnos, in February 1916. In June 1916 he was sent home to England and hospitalised with a sceptic left foot.

This Naval force was formed from an idea by Winston Churchill and was to be used to seize and protect any ports or naval air stations abroad that the RN thought it needed to prosecute the war effectively. It was expanded to divisional size in 1914 with the addition of 8 battalions of naval infantry formed from Royal Navy reservists.

The formation was titled the 'Royal Naval Division' (RND) and fought at Antwerp in 1914 and then at Gallipoli in 1915. In 1916 it was re-deployed to France and came under the command of the War Office where it was re-named the 63rd (Royal Naval) Division.

On 26 October 1917 at 5.40 am, the Canadian divisions launched the attack for Passchendaele. The first battalion of marines and the Anson battalion of the 188th Brigade attacked at the same time. As during previous days, it was raining. A few hours later, Anson battalion took Varlet Farm, a reinforced German position midway between Poelkapelle and Passchendaele.

Less than 1 kilometre of territory was gained in the days that the Royal Naval Division fought at Passchendaele, at a cost of 2,000 casualties.

It was in this action that Charles received a shrapnel wound to the head and was evacuated to the 12th Casualty Clearing Station.

He died of his wounds, aged 23, on 7 November 1917 and is buried in Mendinghem Military Cemetery near Poperinge, Belgium.

CHARLES BAILEY

Guardsman 20816, 4th Battalion, Grenadier Guards

Charles Henry Bailey was born in 1895 in Sutton the eldest of the two sons of Henry and Ellen Bailey. He lived at 3 Brighton Terrace, Horley, near the Kings Head public house.

He enlisted at Guildford and served with 4th Battalion, Grenadier Guards which was formed at Marlow in 1915.

They proceeded to France on 14 July 1915 and joined 3rd Guards Brigade, Guards Division on 19 August.

In September 1915 the Battalion was at the Battle of Loos where the attack was preceded by a four day bombardment and would see the first use of poisoned gas by British troops.

The Chlorine gas was a great disappointment. It was released at 5.50 am, giving it forty minutes to do its work before the infantry attacked at 6.30. However, much of the gas either lingered in no mans land or drifted back over the British lines.

North of Loos the strong Hohenzollern Redoubt fell while further south the village of Loos was captured.

By the end of 25 September the British had advanced to within a thousand yards of the German second line to the north of Loos. The next afternoon the 21st and 24th Divisions launched an attack in ten columns across the open ground, taking horrific casualties all the time and were then forced to retreat. The battle had been so one sided that many Germans stopped firing during the British retreat.

When the fighting finally died down, the British front line stood close to the line reached at the end of the first day, although the Germans had recaptured the Hohenzollern Redoubt.

British losses at Loos were close to 50,000, with 16,000 dead and 25,000 wounded.

It seems likely that Charles was wounded during this action and was evacuated to hospital at Rouen. Charles Bailey died, aged 21, on 3 October 1915 and is buried at St Sever Cemetery, Rouen.

Guardsman Charles Bailey.
(Photo courtesy of Mrs P Woolford)

GEORGE BANKS

Gunner 276764, 34th Siege Battery, Royal Garrison Artillery

George Banks was born in 1881 at Ringmer in Sussex to William and Elizabeth Banks. In 1901 his family lived at Irons Bottom but by 1911 had moved to 3 Grove Cottages, Lee Street, Horley.

George enlisted in the Royal Garrison Artillery and the 34th Siege Battery moved to France in August 1915. It was in action continuously during the fighting in France and Flanders.

The whole of 34th Siege Battery, RGA went out to the Western Front in September 1915 and joined 26th Heavy Artillery Brigade, RGA. The Battery was continuously in action throughout the war and fought in many of the major strategic battles. On 15 November 1917 it joined 85th Heavy Artillery Group and remained with it for the remainder of the war.

Siege Batteries RGA were equipped with heavy howitzers, sending large calibre high explosive shells in high trajectory, plunging fire. The usual armaments were 6 inch, 8 inch and 9.2 inch howitzers, although some had huge railway- or road-mounted 12 inch howitzers.

As British artillery tactics developed, the Siege Batteries were most often employed in destroying or neutralising the enemy artillery, as well as putting destructive fire down on strongpoints, dumps, stores, roads and railways behind enemy lines.

The circumstances leading to his death are not recorded but George Banks died, aged 38, on 20 January 1919 and is buried at Belgrade Cemetery near Namur in Belgium. This was a large Casualty Clearing Station for some months after the Armistice and many men buried there died after the war ended.

GEORGE BARTON

Private 9339, 1st Battalion Royal Dublin Fusiliers

George William Barton was the eldest child born to George and Susannah Barton at Norwood near Croydon in 1887. The family later moved to Hadlow House, Parkhurst Road, Horley.

He was a Regular Army soldier having enlisted at Woolwich into the Royal Dublin Fusiliers before 1911.

He was serving in Madras in India before the outbreak of the First World War and his unit arrived back home on 21 December 1914.

They moved to billets in Torquay but early in 1915 came under orders of 86th Brigade in the 29th Division. On 16 March 1915 they sailed from Avonmouth for Gallipoli, going via Alexandria and Mudros, where they arrived on 9 April and finally landed at Cape Helles on 25 April 1915.

The landing at "V" Beach, in the early morning of 25 April, 1915, was to be made by boats containing three companies of the 1st Royal Dublin Fusiliers, followed by the collier "River Clyde" with the rest of the Dublins, the 1st Royal Munster Fusiliers, half the 2nd Hampshire Regiment, and other troops.

Out of the first 200 men down the gangway, 149 were killed outright and 30 were wounded. The packs the men were carrying weighed some 60lbs and it was because of this that many of the Irish were drowned when they jumped into the water to get ashore.

The place was very strongly fortified and during the 25th the landing was partially secured at the cost of many men dead or wounded.

Between 30 April and 19 May 1915, because of the high numbers of casualties sustained in both battalions, the 1st Dublins and 1st Royal Munster Fusiliers formed one composite unit, called the 'Dubsters'.

Throughout the next weeks the Battalion suffered dreadfully but, following reinforcements, mounted a major action at Gully Ravine on 28 June. During this action the Battalion lost another 236 officers and men including George.

George Barton was killed in action on 29 June 1915, aged 28, and is commemorated on the Helles memorial in Gallipoli.

CHARLES SYDNEY BINGHAM

Private 82606, 88th Company, Machine Gun Corps

Charles, known as Sydney, Bingham was born in Pelsall, near Worcester in 1881 to John and Lucy Bingham. He had a brother and two sisters.

The family later moved to Rotherfield in Sussex but by 1901 Sydney was working as an Ironmongers assistant and living in Lumley Road, Horley.

In 1906 he married Mary Hughes at Reigate and later moved into a house in Station Road, Horley with their daughter Theodora. Finally they moved to Oakdene, Church Road, Horley.

Sydney, by this time an Insurance Agent, enlisted on 18 October 1916 into the 14th Battalion, London Regiment (London Scottish) and sailed for France in March 1917.

Originally each infantry battalion maintained its own Machine Gun Section but these were later gathered together by Brigades to form Machine Gun Companies under a separate Corps. The 88th Machine-Gun Company was formed on 21 February 1916, attached to the 88th Brigade, 29th Division. In 1917 they were in action in the First and Second Battles of the Scarpe during the Arras Offensive.

The Vickers machine gun is fired from a tripod and is cooled by water held in a jacket around the barrel. The gun weighed 28.5lbs, the water another 10lbs and the tripod weighed 20lbs. Bullets were assembled into a canvas belt, which held 250 rounds and would last 30 seconds at the maximum rate of fire of 500 rounds per minute. No1, a Corporal, fired the gun, decided where to locate it and, when on the move, carried the tripod weighing 48 lbs. No.2 carried the gun and 4 litres of water for the cooling system. Nos.3 and 4 carried and fed the ammunition, No.5 was the scout spotting targets and No.6 was the range finder.

Sydney was wounded on 24 April, probably during the 2nd Battle of the Scarpe and he died of his wounds, aged 36, on 26 April 1917.

He is buried at Duisans British Cemetery, Etrun, near Arras, France.

A Vickers Machine Gun crew in action.

FREDERICK BORER

Private 130624, 16th Battalion, Machine Gun Corps (Infantry)

Frederick Ernest James Borer was born in 1899, the third of three sons and a daughter, to Jonathan and Kate Borer of Albert Road, Horley. The family later moved to Lingfield Cottage, Church Road, Horley.

Frederick enlisted at Redhill into The Queens (Royal West Surrey) Regiment but trained as a machine gunner and was later posted to The Machine Gun Corps. The 16th Company was formed in February 1916 and were in action in the Battles of the Somme, Morval and Le Transloy. In 1917 they fought at Hill 70 and Cambrai.

On 1 March 1918 they joined with other MG companies of the Division to become the 6th Machine Gun Battalion.

By March 1918 a large scale German attack towards Arras had been widely expected for some time. When under attack, the Battalion had a specific defensive role. Assuming it was at full strength (and the indications are that the 6th was not), then it would deploy all of its 64 heavy Vickers guns along the line held by the Division with their fields of fire carefully inter-locked. They would then pour fire into any advancing infantry. Used like this, machine guns were a devastating weapon, capable of firing off a belt of 250 bullets in 30 seconds.

The strength and ferocity of the German assault was greater than expected and the Allies were forced back over the next days towards the village of Vaux. A further, even stronger, attack was made by the Germans and this succeeded in forcing another British retreat.

It was several days after this action that Fred lost his life.

Frederick Borer was killed on 4 April 1918, aged 19. He has no known grave and is commemorated on the Pozieres Memorial. His brother, Norman, was killed in 1914.

NORMAN BORER

Ordinary Seaman J/21973, HMS "Bulwark"

Norman Jonathan Henry Borer was born in 1897, the second of three sons and a daughter, to Jonathan and Kate Borer of Albert Road, Horley. The family later moved to Lingfield Cottage, Church Road, Horley. His brother Fred also died.

At the outbreak of war Norman left his job as a Dairyman's assistant and joined the Royal Navy.

After his basic training he was posted to HMS *Bulwark*. HMS *Bulwark* belonged to a sub-class of the Formidable-class of pre-dreadnought battleships of the Royal Navy known as the London-class.

Entering service with the Royal Navy in 1902, *Bulwark* sailed with the Mediterranean Fleet until 1907. She then served with the Home Fleet, for a time under Captain Robert Falcon Scott. After a refit in 1912, she was assigned to the 5th Battle Squadron.

Following the outbreak of the First World War, *Bulwark*, along with the rest of the squadron was attached to the Channel Fleet, conducting patrols in the English Channel.

On 26 November 1914, while anchored near Sheerness, she was destroyed by a large internal explosion with the loss of 736 men. 14 men survived of whom 2 died later in hospital.

Witnesses on the battleship *Implacable*, the next ship in line at the mooring, reported that: "a huge pillar of black cloud belched upwards... From the depths of this writhing column flames appeared running down to sea level. The appearance of this dreadful phenomenon was followed by a thunderous roar. Then came a series of lesser detonations, and finally one vast explosion that shook the *Implacable* from mastheads to keel."

The destruction of *Bulwark* was also witnessed on board the battleship *Formidable*, where "when the dust and wreckage had finally settled a limp object was seen hanging from the wireless aerials upon which it had fallen. With difficulty the object was retrieved and found to be an officer's uniform jacket with three gold bands on the sleeves and between them the purple cloth of an engineer officer. The garment's former owner had been blasted into fragments."

The explosion was likely to have been caused by the overheating of cordite charges that had been placed adjacent to a boiler room bulkhead.

Norman Borer died in this disaster on 26 November 1914, aged 18. His body was never recovered for burial and he is commemorated on the Portsmouth Naval Memorial.

HMS Bulwark. *Norman Borer and George Terry were both killed in the explosion which sank her at Sheerness on 26 November 1914. Joseph Weller was on board* Formidable *nearby and may have witnessed the explosion.*

SIDNEY BOURNE

Private G/6308, 6th Battalion, The Queens (Royal West Surrey) Regiment

Sidney was born in 1895, one of five children born to George and Alice Bourne and he lived in Albert Road, Horley.

In 1911 he was a 'wash house' boy and living with relatives at Hope Cottage, Charlesfield Road, Horley. He worshiped at Horley Baptist Church and is commemorated on a plaque inside the church.

He enlisted into 6th Battalion The Queens Regiment at Guildford on 27 July 1915 and gave his address as Lonesome Lane and his sister Emily as next of kin. This was a 'New Army' unit formed in response to Kitcheners famous appeal. The 6th Battalion were in actions throughout 1915 and 1916 as part of 12th Division.

When the Battle of the Somme commenced on 1 July 1916 they were in the second wave and due to attack on the 2nd but this attack was cancelled. Forward assembly trenches had been dug to narrow the strip of no mans land that they would have to cross to 500 yards. They attacked the following day at 3.15am towards Ovillers-la-Boiselle but were met with heavy machine gun and rifle fire. Some men gained the enemy trench but supporting platoons were caught by heavy fire and impeded by the enemy wire which remained uncut by the artillery.

Having been beaten back, the Brigade was again ordered forward at 4.35am but they did not manage to gain any ground in the face of heavy machine gun fire and by 9.00am the Division reported total failure.

On this day alone, the Battalion lost 9 officers, dead or missing, 23 other ranks killed, 154 wounded and 117 missing.

Sidney Bourne died in this action on 3 July 1916, aged 20, and he has no known grave. He is commemorated on the Thiepval Memorial.

The Thiepval Memorial to the Missing of the Somme battlefield.

THOMAS BOWEN

Private 18798, 7th Battalion, Kings Shropshire Light Infantry

Thomas Bowen was born in 1882 at Coalport, Shropshire to Andrew and Susannah Bowen. He had four brothers and two sisters and by 1901 was working in the local mill.

In 1907 Thomas married Beatrice Bowles and they lived in Burgess Hill where Thomas worked as a bricklayer, probably with his father-in-law. They had two daughters and after Thomas died Beatrice married a man named Arthur Stoner at St Bartholomews Church in Horley (May 1921) and that is probably why Thomas appears on our Memorial.

He enlisted at Guildford into the Kings (SLI) Regiment which recruited heavily from Shropshire where he was born. His service record has been destroyed and his medal card gives no useful information so we do not know when he was posted overseas.

The 7th Battalion was a service battalion raised at Shrewsbury in September 1914.They landed at Boulogne on 28 September 1915 and became part of the 8th Brigade, 3rd Division.

They would have arrived too late for the disastrous battle of Loos and were directed to the Ypres sector where they took their turns in and out of the line.

In mid February 1916 Thomas would have fought in the fierce actions around The Bluff, close by the Ypres-Comines canal.

As spring approached the British decided that it was essential for an enemy salient near the village of St. Eloi to be eliminated.

A determined assault was made, beginning on 27 March, to clear the enemy from a series of craters close to the village.

Thomas Bowen was killed in this action. He died, aged 34, on 3 April 1916. He has no known grave and is commemorated on the Menin Gate memorial at Ypres.

The Menin Gate Memorial to the Missing who died in the battles around the Ypres Salient.

JOHN BOX

Private M/352155, Royal Army Service Corps

John Box was born in Cuckfield, Sussex in 1887. He was the son of James and Charity Box and was one of six children.

In 1908 he married Alice Partridge and they moved to Buxton Villas, Smallfield. They had a son, Arthur, in 1910 and John earned his living as a general Labourer. At the time of his death his address was listed as 5 Lumley Road, Horley.

John Box's service records are not available at present. He enlisted into the Army Service Corps which later became the Royal Army Service Corps.

The RASC was known amongst soldiers as Ally Slopers Cavalry.

Alexander "Ally" Sloper was a madcap fictional character who appeared in British serialized comics between 1867 and 1916. His name was derived from the term "alley sloper", which was Victorian vernacular referring to people who dodged the rent collector by sloping in the alley ("to slope off" was British slang for moving away slowly).

Despite this reputation the ASC were the unsung heroes of the British army in the Great War. Soldiers cannot fight without food, equipment and ammunition. In the Great War, the vast majority of this tonnage, supplying a vast army on many fronts, was supplied from Britain. Using horsed and motor vehicles, railways and waterways, the ASC performed prodigious feats of logistics and were one of the great strengths of organisation by which the war was won.

John was awaiting a posting or possibly his discharge at the Clearing Office at Blackheath at the time of his death, aged 32, on 28 July 1919. He may have been a victim of the influenza epidemic which swept Europe after the war.

On 11 August 1919 he was buried in St Bartholomews Churchyard, Horley.

REGINALD BOYES

Lance Corporal G/16616, 1st Battalion Queens Own

(Royal West Kent Regiment)

Reginald John Boyes was born in Redhill in 1889 to Alfred and Annie Boyes who also had seven daughters and three other sons. They lived at 1 Asylum Cottages, presumably on the Earlswood Hospital site but the family later moved to 3 Island Villas, Earlswood.

In 1910 he married Minnie West at Maidstone and they lodged at 97 Earlsbrook Road, Redhill where Reginald was employed as a domestic gardner.

Reginald enlisted on 3 June 1916 at the Maidstone Recruiting office of the Royal West Kents. He gave his address then as Springhead Cottages, West Street, East Malling, Kent and his enlistment documents show that he had a son, Cyril Reginald Boyes born in 1916 at East Malling.

He was posted to serve in France on 1 December 1916 and promoted to Lance Corporal in March 1917. Throughout October 1917 the 1st Battalion were involved in actions at Polygon Wood, Broodseinde and Passchendaele in the Ypres Salient.

3 October 1917 was a pleasant autumn day, though overcast, and the Battalion was preparing itself for an attack along the Menin Road the following day.

In the midst of their preparations they suddenly found themselves having to beat off a heavy German attack on their own positions.

Reginald Boyes was killed in this action. He died on 3 October 1917, aged 29, and is buried at Poelcapelle British Cemetery which is about half a mile east of the town of Poelcapelle, Belgium.

THOMAS BRADLEY

Gunner 74111, 110th Siege Battery, Royal Garrison Artillery

Thomas William McKenzie Bradley was born in 1897 at Meopham, Kent into a fairly affluent family. His father, William, is shown in the 1901 census as living on his own means and he and his wife Augusta also had a daughter, Mary born in 1895. William and Augusta later moved to South Norwood and later still, to Horley.

By 1911 Thomas was a pupil at Charterhouse School near Godalming.

He enlisted in Horley on 19 February 1916 and joined the RGA. He embarked for France at Dover in April 1916. It is recorded that he was given special leave in May – July1917 because of his father's illness and to attend to urgent family affairs.

Siege Batteries RGA were equipped with heavy howitzers, sending large calibre high explosive shells in high trajectory, plunging fire. The usual armaments were 6 inch, 8 inch and 9.2 inch howitzers, although some had huge railway – or road-mounted 12 inch howitzers. As British artillery tactics developed, the Siege Batteries were most often employed in destroying or neutralising the enemy artillery, as well as putting destructive fire down on strongpoints, dumps, stores, roads and railways behind enemy lines.

The 110th Siege Battery gave supporting fire during the attempts to halt the German advances in the early stages of their Spring offensive – Operation Michael – and Thomas was almost certainly killed during the exchanges of artillery fire in this action. He died, aged 21, on 21 March 1918. He has no known grave and is commemorated on the Arras Memorial together with 34,717 other officers and men of the Allied Armies.

TOM BROCKLEHURST

Captain, 2nd Battalion, The Queens (Royal West Surrey) Regiment

Thomas Pownall Brocklehurst was born in Horley in 1887, the son of Edward and Katharine Brocklehurst and lived at 48 Hans Mansions, Kinnersley Manor, Horley. He had two elder brothers and a sister.

Edward Brocklehurst was one of the principal landowners around Horley.

Before the war Thomas studied law. His military enlistment details are not accessible at present.

He appears to have enlisted quite early in the war as he was already a Captain with the 2nd Queens in September 1915 when he is recorded as having been wounded in action at Loos.

When the Battle of the Somme commenced on 1 July 1916 the 2nd Queens were part of 91st Brigade, 7th Division tasked with attacking the enemy trenches surrounding the German strongpoint of Mametz. They suffered heavy casualties amongst both officers and men.

The job of 91st Brigade was to advance across the German front line (Bulgar Trench), past the second line (Cemetery Trench), then capture the strongpoints in Mametz itself and push on past the deep Dantzig Alley communication trench and to take the third enemy line, Fritz Trench.

2nd Queen's were in close support behind the attacking battalions.

At 9.30am the support battalions were ordered up to reinforce – with little effect. The Germans tried to counter-attack from Mametz and Dantzig Alley but a heavy artillery bombardment by the British caused them to abandon their efforts.

Soon after 1pm 2nd Queens took Dantzig Alley (East) and their bombers then moved along Fritz Trench and into Bright Alley which was taken at about 6.30pm.

Tom Brocklehurst was killed in this action and died, aged 29, on 1 July 1916. He is buried in Dantzig Alley British Cemetery, Mametz.

GEORGE BROOKER

Private G/96186, 18th Battalion, Duke of Cambridge's Own
(Middlesex Regiment).

George Macfarlane Brooker was born in 1892, the son of George and Ann Brooker of Rectory Lane, Charlwood. He had five brothers and a sister.

He followed his father's occupation and became a carpenter.

Georges service record is not available but we know he enlisted at Redhill and joined The Queens (Royal West Surrey) Regiment.

He was later transferred to the 18th Battalion Middlesex Regiment which was a New Army Service (Pioneer) Battalion.

The 18th (1st Public Works) Battalion, Middlesex Regiment (Duke of Cambridge's Own) was raised in London on the 19 January 1915 by Lt-Col. John Ward MP. Initially they trained at Alexandra Palace but moved to Rayleigh in May. They joined 33rd Division as a Pioneer Battalion at Clipstone Camp in July and moved to Salisbury Plain for final training in August. They proceeded to France on 15 November, landing at Le Havre.

33rd Division concentrated near Morbecque, being strengthened by the exchange of 98th Brigade for the experienced 19th Brigade from 2nd Division.

In 1916 they were in action in the Battle of the Somme. In 1917 they took part in the Arras Offensive, the actions on the Hindenburg Line, the operations on the Flanders coast and the Third Battles of Ypres.

In March 1918 they were preparing for the Battle of the Lys and it was during this period that George died.

George Brooker was killed in action, aged 26, on 8 March 1918 and is buried at Potijze Chateau Cemetery which is a short distance north east of Ypres.

ESME BROTHERTON MM

Sergeant 203576, 1st Battalion, The London Regiment

(Royal Fusiliers)

Esme Brotherton was born in 1890 in Guildford to Francis and Hannah Brotherton. He was the fourth child of eleven and had six brothers and four sisters. The family owned the Bowling Green Restaurant in Castle Square, Guildford.

Before the war Esme was employed as a clerk for the Inland Revenue and in 1915 he married Lilian Holdforth at St Bartholomews Church and probably moved in with her at 112 Lumley Road, Horley.

He enlisted at Fulham as 2540 Pte Brotherton in the 25th Cyclists Battalion (The London Regiment) and later transferred to 1st Battalion The London Regiment (Royal Fusiliers), part of 1st London Division.

In August 1914 they were fully mobilised and posted to guard the London–Newhaven railway but in mid-September they sailed for Malta where they stayed until February 1915.

By March they had landed at Le Havre and joined the 25th Brigade in 8th Division. 25th Brigade were in action throughout 1915 and fought at Neuve Chapelle, Aubers, and at Bois Grenier which was a diversionary attack coinciding with the Battle of Loos.

In February 1916 the battalion was transferred to 167th Brigade in 56th (London) Division and were in action throughout the Somme campaign.

Esme was promoted to the rank of Sergeant and at some point in his service he was awarded the Military Medal for bravery but it is not known when this occurred.

In mid-summer of 1917 the British Army embarked on the 3rd Battle of Ypres. Heavy rain soon made the ground impassable and it was not until 16 August that the attack could be renewed.

The village of Langemarck was attacked on that day and it seems likely that Esme died near there.

He was killed in action, aged 27, on 6 August 1917, and has no known grave. He is commemorated on the Menin Gate Memorial at Ypres.

HARRY BUCKELL

Acting Bombardier 75981, 130th Battery, Royal Field Artillery.

Harry Thomas Buckell was born in Redhill in 1897 and lived at Somerset Road, Reigate, the second of five sons and a daughter, to William and Charlotte Buckell.

By 1911 the family had moved to 30 Clarence Walk, Meadvale, Redhill and Harry was employed as a stable lad. William and Charlotte later moved to 86 Cornfield Road, Reigate.

Harry enlisted into the Royal Field Artillery at Guildford fairly early in the war. 130th Battery was a heavy howitzer battery and was part of 3rd Division.

9.2 inch Heavy howitzers, sent large calibre high explosive shells in a high trajectory, plunging fire. As British artillery tactics developed, the heavy Batteries were most often employed in destroying or neutralising the enemy artillery, as well as putting destructive fire down on strong points, dumps, stores, roads and railways behind enemy lines.

In early 1915 the division fought in the Ypres salient and were in action at Messines Ridge, St Eloi, and the Bluff.

They later moved up to the Menin Road sector at Hooge and Bellewarde.

On 21 February 1915 the Germans exploded the first mine beneath the trenches at Hooge and the British responded in a similar manner.

On 19 July they exploded one and a half tons of ammonal beneath the German positions and consolidated the huge crater torn in the German lines. A few weeks later the Germans used flamethrowers to recapture the crater only to lose it again to determined attacks from the British in August.

Harry Buckell was killed in action in this area, aged 19, on the 1 September 1915 and is buried at Birr Crossroads Cemetery just west of Hooge.

WILLIAM BUDGEN

Private 2515, 9th Battalion, East Surrey Regiment

William Budgen was born in Horley in 1890, the son of William and Mary Budgen. He had two sisters and lived at Rose Cottage on the Balcombe Road near Fernhill.

Before the war William was employed on the railways as a platelayer and lodged at Dulwich.

William was a Territorial Army soldier and he was among the first men to enlist at Redhill in September 1914. He was enrolled into the 9th (Service) Battalion of the East Surreys.

The Battalion embarked for France on 31 August 1915 and fought at the battle of Loos with heavy losses.

In 1916 they suffered in the German gas attack at Wulverghem when a mixture of chlorine and phosgene was used causing 338 casualties.

They took part in The Somme offensive which started on 1 July and were heavily involved in actions in and around Delville Wood throughout August.

Saturday 2 September was a dry, warm summers day and the 9th East Surreys were preparing for an attack south of Guillemont. The British artillery opened the barrage to soften up the enemy for the main attack on 3 September.

German artillery responded to this fire and a number of casualties were sustained.

William Bugden was killed in this action, aged 27, on 2 September 1916. He has no known grave and is commemorated on the Thiepval Memorial.

HARRY BUGDEN

Gunner 146317. A Battery, 86th Brigade, Royal Field Artillery

Harry Robert Bugden was born in 1898 near Frimley, one of three sons, to Thomas and Emily Bugden and lived at Whitewood Lane, Horne. His father Thomas was a Police Constable.

In 1911 the family lived at Warwick Wold, Merstham but later moved to 25 Queens Road, Horley.

Harry enlisted at Guildford into the Royal Field Artillery. His service record is not available.

86th Brigade was originally attached to the 19th Division and entered active service in France in July 1915. They were in action at the battle of Loos which, compared with the small-scale British efforts of spring 1915 was a mighty offensive indeed – so much so that it was referred to at the time as 'The Big Push'. Taking place on ground not of their choosing and before stocks of ammunition and heavy artillery were sufficient, the opening of the battle was noteworthy for the first use of poison gas by the British Army.

The Brigade also took part in the battle of the Somme in July 1916.

This battle was one of the largest of World War I, in which more than 1,000,000 men were wounded or killed, making it one of histories bloodiest battles.

Early in 1917 the Brigade was detached from 19th Division and was used as a mobile force to be sent wherever it was most needed.

During the autumn of 1917 the Second battle of Passchendaele was fought and it is possible that Harry was wounded during this action.

He died of his wounds, aged 20, on 8 November 1917 and is buried at Vlamertinghe New Military Cemetery which is just west of Ypres.

ARTHUR BURBRIDGE

Private TF/320195, 16th Battalion, Royal Sussex Regiment (Sussex Yeomanry)

Arthur Allen Burbridge was born in Horley in 1898 and was the third son of George and Mary Burbridge of Victoria Road, Horley. He had two older brothers and by 1911 they were all employed in the family bakery business. Arthur was a cheerful and popular boy with a wide circle of friends.

Arthur's formal service records are not available but we know he enlisted when aged only 16.

He served in the Balkan Theatre (Gallipoli) and he would have embarked at Liverpool and sailed on the *Olympic*, landing on 8 October 1915.

In December 1915 they were withdrawn from Gallipoli and between February and July 1916, were in Egypt on the Suez Canal defences.

In July 1916 the Brigade moved to join the Western Frontier Force and early in 1917 they came under the command of 230th Brigade (74th Yeomanry Division).

In May 1918 the 16th Sussex Yeomanry landed at Marseille and spent the remainder of the war on the Western Front.

As the war drew to a close the 16th Sussex was part of the attacking force at Epehy on 18 September 1918.

1,488 guns opened fire at 05.20am and supported the infantry with a creeping barrage. 300 machine guns were also made available. The objective consisted of a fortified zone roughly 3 miles (4.8 km) deep and 20 miles (32 km) long, supported by subsidiary trenches and strongpoints.

The promised French assistance did not arrive, resulting in limited success on that flank. On the left flank troops also found difficulty when attacking the fortifications erected at "the Knoll", Quennemont and Guillemont farms, which were held determinedly by German troops.

Arthur Burbridge was killed in action by shellfire, aged 20, on the following day, 19 September 1918 within two months of the Armistice.

He has no known grave and is commemorated on the Vis-en-Artois Memorial which is about midway between Arras and Cambrai.

EDGAR BURDEN

Private 10335, 5th Battalion, Oxford and Bucks Light Infantry

Edgar Burden was born at Tenterden, Kent in 1896 to Edward and Sophia Burden. He had three brothers and two sisters.

By 1911 the family had moved to a house opposite Myrtle Cottages in Charlesfield Road, Horley and Edgar was employed as a chemist's errand boy.

Already serving as a Territorial Army soldier, Edgar enlisted at Redhill in September 1914 into the 5th Ox and Bucks which was raised as part of Kitcheners First New Army and were part of 42nd Brigade, 14th (Light) Division.

Edgar arrived in France in June 1915 and the battalion took part in the Battle of Hooge in July which was the first occasion that the Germans used flamethrowers against our troops.

British troops lost ground in this action though some ground, up to the stables of Hooge Chateau, was regained in August.

The Division was in action again at the second battle of Bellewaarde, just east of Ypres, which commenced on the 25 September.

This attack, while subsidiary to the Loos offensive, was designed with limited goals; to recover the remainder of the lost ground, as well as to provide a diversion from the main attack and tie up German reserves.

The attacking troops assembled in a steady downpour on the night of the 24th and spent a miserable few hours waiting for their barrage to start at 03.50am. Zero hour was fixed for 04.20am.

Though not for want of bravery and effort, neither objective was achieved. German losses were comparatively light.

Edgar was killed, aged 19 on this day, 25 September 1915.

He has no known grave and is commemorated on the Menin Gate Memorial at Ypres.

BERTIE CHARLWOOD

Lance Corporal G/2016, 7th Battalion, The Queens
(Royal West Surrey) Regiment

Albert (Bertie) Charlwood was born in Redhill in 1892 to Robert and Sarah Charlwood. He had five brothers and a sister and the family lived at 58 Broadfield Villas, Lower St Johns Road, Earlswood.

In 1913 Bertie married Harriett Earle and was earning his living as a general labourer. Harriett later moved to live at Horne near Horley. Bertie was a typical 'Kitchener Volunteer' and enlisted at Redhill early in the war.

The 7th (Service) Battalion Queens was sent to France and Bertie landed there on 27 July 1915. They became part of the 55th Brigade of the 18th (Eastern) Division.

Through the autumn of 1915 the Battalion was engaged on several fronts and carried out the usual activities of trench warfare. At the Battle of The Somme the Division was placed on the extreme right of the British attack. On 1 July 1916 they were to assault the trenches south and west of the village of Montauban and this became the first village to be captured on the first day of the Somme campaign.

The pre attack barrage lasted almost a week and during the final hours before the infantry attack was due to start, the troops, packed together in the forward trenches, sat through a deafening roar of British and French guns.

At 7.30 a.m. the 7th Queens assaulted the German trenches on a front of about 400 yards.

After 12 hours of fighting the final objective west of Montauban was reached and consolidated on a front of about 260 yards.

The Battalion sustained dreadful casualties during this attack losing 174 other ranks killed, 284 wounded and 56 missing.

The British Army suffered 60,000 casualties on this day.

It was almost certainly here that Bertie suffered the wounds that caused his death, aged 25, on 16 July 1916. He is buried at La Neuville British Cemetery which is west of Corbie.

ARTHUR CHEESMAN

Captain 1st/5th Battalion, The Buffs (East Kent Regiment)

Arthur Edwin Cheesman was born in 1877 in Newbridge, Co Kildare, Ireland, to Captain Edwin Cheesman (RAVC) and Mrs. Anna Cheeseman of Sissinghurst Castle, Cranbrook, Kent.

Sometime before 1911 Anna, now widowed, came to live at Victoria Lodge, Victoria Road, Horley with another son, the Rev Reginald Cheesman who was the assistant Curate of Horley and, later, vicar of Salfords Church.

Arthur was a witness when Reginald married at St Bartholomews, Horley in July 1915. The 1911 census shows Arthur describing himself as a Farmer so he probably joined the army soon after the outbreak of war. 1/5th was a Territorial Battalion and it is possible that he was a TA soldier when the war started.

Known as the 'Weald of Kent' battalion, the 1/5th was at Ashford in August 1914 as part of the Home Counties Division but were soon despatched to India. Their stay was only to last about a year because by November 1915 they moved to Mesopotamia (now known to us as Iraq) and landed at Basra as part of 35th Indian Brigade.

The enemy here was the Turkish army which was frequently led by German officers. The British forces suffered a huge setback at Kut-al-Amara when, after a siege lasting 147 days, 11,800 British and Indian troops inside the garrison town finally surrendered on 29 April 1916. Throughout the remainder of 1916 the British Army struggled to recover from this disaster.

1/5th Buffs suffered a steady stream of casualties during the early part of 1916 and so formed a composite battalion with 1/4th Hampshires until May when they were sent to 14th Indian Division.

Arthur Cheesman was killed on 26 September 1916, aged 39. He is buried in Amara War Cemetery which is a little east of the town between the left bank of the river Tigris and the Chahaila Canal.

Although his middle name is inscribed as Edward rather than Edwin on both Horley War Memorial and Salfords Church it is possible that this is an error caused by use of the abbreviation Edw. for either name. It is thought likely that, despite Arthur's tenuous connection with either village, the Rev Reginald Cheesman was instrumental in having his brother commemorated at both Horley and Salfords.

ARTHUR CHESSALL

Private 6568, 15th County of London Battalion

(Civil Service Rifles)

Arthur Roland Holmes Chessall was born in 1878, the second of three sons to William (MD, MRCS) and Adelaide Chessall. William was a doctor and they lived in Station Road, Horley between Albert Villas and Horley Brewery.

By 1911 William had died and Arthur was living with his mother at 64 Home Park Road, Wimbledon. He was a clerk in the civil service.

He enlisted at Kensington and may have been with the Battalion when they landed at Le Havre on 18 March 1915. They fought in many actions throughout 1915 including the battle of Loos and in 1916 resisted the German attack at Vimy Ridge. In 1916 they were at the Somme and took part in the capture of High Wood.

On 1 October the Battalion was part of the 44th Division attack on a line between Eaucourt and Le Sars (on the Albert-Bapaume road) on a front of 3,000 yards. This became known as the Battle for the Transloy Ridges lasting for three weeks and it included the capture of the Butte de Warlencourt, a heavily defended German strongpoint. This hillock looks little more than a pimple today but in 1916 it was somewhat higher and connected to the German lines by part of the Gird Trench system.

The 7 October was a fine warm autumnal day. The 8th Londons led the attack but were beaten back by machine gun fire. The 15th Londons, with the 7th in support, met a similar fate and all that was achieved was the capture of some enemy positions near the road to Le Barque.

Arthur Chessall was killed in this attack on 7 October 1916, aged 38 and has no known grave.

He is commemorated on the Thiepval Memorial.

HARRY COBURN

L/Cpl G/9952, 26th (Pioneer) Battalion, Middlesex Regiment

It has proved difficult to identify Harry George Coburn. It is known that he was a lance corporal in the Middlesex Regiment because it is noted on the 1922 Roll of Honour and the soldier above is the only one listed by the CWGC that fits.

This soldier made a will leaving over £1000 and the probate announcement gives his address as 98 Albert Road, Horley. We know little more about him except that his medal card suggests that he was posted to France in August 1915.

A soldier of this name served with the Royal Artillery from 1909 until he bought himself out at Gibralter in 1914. He re-joined the army in mid 1915 and this may be the same man. If so, he came from Penge in south east London, as did the man to whom he bequeathed his money. Harry Coburn almost certainly served in a different unit before being transferred to 26th Middlesex.

The 26th Middlesex was a Pioneer (service) battalion. They worked behind the front line troops making and repairing roads and railways, digging trenches and making corduroy roads from logs to haul guns out of mud. Following the armistice with the Ottoman Empire, Britain sent troops from Macedonia to secure Constantinople (Istanbul) and the Straits. In addition, troops were sent eastwards to Turkish ports on the Black Sea and into Caucasus region of Russia to influence the outcome of the struggle against the Bolsheviks.

Many of these soldiers died from disease and hardship within a few weeks of their arrival.

Harry Coburn died of pneumonia on 7 January 1919 aged 30. He was buried in Batoum British Cemetery but the grave has since been lost.

He is commemorated on the Haidar Pasha Memorial which stands within the war graves plot of Haidar Pasha Cemetery near Istanbul. It commemorates more than 30 Commonwealth servicemen of the First World War who died fighting in South Russia, Georgia and Azerbaijan, and in post Armistice operations in Russia and Transcaucasia, whose graves have been lost. An Addenda panel was later added to commemorate over 170 Commonwealth casualties who are buried in cemeteries in South Russia and Transcaucasia whose graves can longer be maintained.

FRANK COMBER

Private 206734, 2nd/4th Battalion, The Queen's
(Royal West Surrey) Regiment

The inscription on the War Memorial to Frank Coomber is thought to refer to the soldier named above, Frank Comber. The name is given as Comber on the plaque in St Bartholomews church. A Frank Coomber lived in Church Road and served in the RAMC but, despite being gassed, he survived the war. Frank was born at Horley in 1892 to William and Mary Comber and was one of seven children. The family lived in Charlesfield Road before moving to 65 Lumley Road, Horley.

Frank enlisted at Reigate and his medal record card suggests that he may have joined up in about 1915 or 1916.

2nd/4th Battalion, The Queens was formed at Croydon in August 1914 and in April 1915 became part of 160th Brigade, 53rd Division.

The Division was in action at Gallipoli and the effects of fighting, few reinforcements and the dreadful blizzard of November 1915, reduced it to just 162 officers and 2428 men – about 15% of full strength.

The Queens were then sent with the rest of 53rd Division to fight in Palestine. They were heavily engaged at the Battles for Gaza (where the Division suffered 600 casualties) and Beersheeba and the capture of Tell Khuweilfe.

The British launched their assault on Jerusalem early in December 1917 and Turkish resistance was much less stubborn than expected. The last Turkish troops left Jerusalem early on the morning of 9 December and on 11 December General Allenby made his formal entry into the city.

On the morning of 27 December the enemy launched heavy attacks preceded by accurate artillery bombardments against the defenders. Although they inflicted heavy casualties on the Turkish forces the 2/4th Queens also suffered and were withdrawn from the line at about midday.

Frank Comber was killed in this action as well as 34 other soldiers. He died on 27 December 1917, aged 25 and is buried in the Jerusalem Military Cemetery which is just north of the walled city near the Mount of Olives.

CHARLES COOMBER

CSM 5608, 2nd Battalion, East Surrey Regiment

Charles Coomber was born in Horley in 1882, the youngest child of George and Esther Coomber who lived at Ironsbottom, near Horley. He had four brothers and two sisters.

Charles enlisted into the Regular Army at Kingston and by 1901 was a Lance Corporal. He may well have caught the tail end of the Boer War, certainly saw service in India and returned to England in 1914 when the East Surreys became part of 85th Brigade, 28th Division.

The Battalion landed at Le Havre on 19 January 1915 and, with the rest of the Division, concentrated in the area between Bailleul and Hazebrouk. By this time Charles was acting Company Sergeant Major (WO2) and so had made a significant military career for himself.

The rate of attrition suffered by the 2nd East Surreys is typical of an infantry battalion in an active area of the trenches and is clearly illustrated by entries in their war diary. In March they received replacements as follows: 4 March – 46 men arrived mainly sick and wounded returning from base, 10 March – 125 men arrived, 16 March – 117 men arrived, 20 March – 50 men arrived.

Death was a constant companion to those serving in the line, even when no raid or attack was launched or defended against. In busy sectors the constant shellfire directed by the enemy brought random death, whether the victims were standing to in a trench or resting in a dugout.

It has been estimated that up to one third of Allied casualties on the Western Front were actually sustained in the trenches. Aside from enemy injuries, disease also wrought a heavy toll.

The circumstances of Charles's death are not known but the Battalion war diary records that the battalion was in trenches east of St Eloi on 28 March 1915.

Only one casualty is recorded on this day and it appears to have been Charles Coomber.

He is recorded as having been killed in action, aged 33, on 28 March 1915 and is buried at Voormezeele Cemetery Enclosure No 3 which is a few miles south west of Ypres.

FRANCIS COOPER

Private 24419, 1st Battalion, Northamptonshire Regiment

Francis Hezekiah Cooper was born in 1885 at Battersea to Edward and Elizabeth Cooper the eldest of two sons and three daughters.

By 1901 they had moved to Yattenden Road, Horley and Francis was employed as a Telegraph Messenger boy.

The 1911 census shows that the family had moved again to 3 Kings Terrace, Balcombe Road, Horley and Francis was a house painter.

He worshiped at Horley Baptist Church and is commemorated on a plaque inside the church and also at Horley Infant School.

It is not known exactly when Francis enlisted but, for some reason, it was at Harlesden, Middlesex.

It is likely that he was in a reinforcement draft to replace men killed in the 1914–1915 battles but he may have taken part when the Battalion fought at the Battles of Aubers and Loos in 1915.

In early August 1916, during the Battle of the Somme 1st Northamptons were in reserve at Helencourt Wood behind the lines in the Albert Sector. They were part of 2nd Brigade, 1st Division, Fourth Army.

On the 13 August 1916, the battalion began its move up to the front line at Bazentin-le-Petit where the southern slope of the ridge was capped by the German fortress in High Wood. This was an extremely active area of the Somme offensive and both Bazentin and High Wood appear among the 16 battle honours on the Thiepval Memorial to the Missing.

The various companies of the battalion were involved in operations in and around High Wood and the Elgin Trench system suffering, according to the War Diary of the 1st Battalion, more than 140 casualties, mainly killed, in only one action inside High Wood.

Wednesday 16 August 1916 was a warm day but with a steady drizzle. Francis Cooper died this day, aged 31, and his body was never identified for burial.

He is commemorated on the Thiepval Memorial.

FRANK COOPER

This man has proved impossible to identify.

The name appears on the 1918 'Appeal' list immediately above that of Francis Hezekhia Cooper and both names appear on the 'Parsons plaque' in St Bartholomews Church for which these names were collected.

The names to be inscribed on Horley War Memorial were fixed in August 1921 and, again, both names are included. However when the Dedication Roll of Honour was prepared in February 1922 the name of Frank Cooper was left off. This maybe because Regiments were included on the Roll of Honour and, for the first time, someone realised that a duplication had occurred. In the event that this conclusion is incorrect there were several other Frank Coopers who were killed though only two local men are real possibilities.

Frank Cooper, born 1871, was a gardener at Earlswood and he had a son, also Frank, born in 1900. Neither of these men, if they served, can be identified militarily and neither is listed at either Salfords Church or St Johns, Redhill. They appear on the 1911 census.

It seems most probable that Frank Cooper and Francis Cooper are one and the same and that the duplication arose because Francis was known as Frank to some people.

The Loos Memorial to the Missing at Dud Corner Cemetery.

JOHN CORNFORD

Private G/4074, 2nd Battalion The Queens
(Royal West Surrey) Regiment

The name John Edward Cornford appears on Horley War Memorial but on the 1922 Roll of Honour the name is given as James.

James Edward Cornford (who had an older brother named John) is listed by the Commonwealth War Graves Commission and this inscription is presumed to apply to him.

James was born at Salfords in 1891, the second son of Edmund and Hannah Cornford and they lived at Rose Cottage, Masons Bridge, Salfords.

Before the war James was employed at Horse Hills, near Horley as a gardener.

He enlisted at Guildford fairly early in the war and joined the 2nd Battalion, Queens. This unit had suffered severe casualties in 1914 and James was amongst the first batch of reinforcements. The battalion became part of the 7th Division and were amongst the first troops to entrench in front of Ypres. They were in action at Neuve Chapelle, Aubers, Festubert and Givenchy.

At Loos on 24 September 1915 the battalion arrived at Verquigneul and dumped their surplus gear before marching until 03.30am when they reached the reserve lines. At 05.50am on the 25th the artillery barrage opened up and continued for nearly an hour. The battalion was at full strength – 29 officers and 995 men.

They attacked in extended order by companies with the machine gun company in an advanced position to harass the German defenders. Having taken their first objectives part of the battalion was directed to occupy the Quarries and also the Cite St Elie area. At around 11.15pm a determined German counter attack was resisted but the battalion pulled back to the original German support trenches.

Ten officers and 271 other ranks became casualties in this attack and James was one of them.

James Cornford died, aged 24, on 25 September 1915 and has no known grave. He is commemorated on the Loos Memorial.

ALBERT COUTTS

Private G/16630, 1st Battalion Queens Own
(Royal West Kent) Regiment

Albert Edward Coutts was born in Horley in 1891, to Alexander and Frances Coutts, the younger of their two sons and lived at Poplar Terrace, Massetts Road, Horley. Alexander and Frances later moved to Roseberry Cottage, Church Road, Horley.

Albert attended Horley Infant school and later became a clothiers assistant and lived at Anerley near Crystal Palace. In 1915 he married Elsie Spashett in West Ham and they had a son, Albert Francis Barnett Coutts in March 1916. They later moved to Slade Green, Kent.

Albert appears to have been a rather sickly man and had a deformed chest. He enlisted into the Royal West Kents on 19 July 1916 at Maidstone and, when medically inspected at Bromley, was passed fit only for Home Base duty. Nevertheless, he was posted to France in February 1917 and by May was in hospital at Rouen.

Elsie wrote to the Army to enquire whether he could be sent home and assigned to lighter duties and even offered her own services in place of his as she was "young, strong and in far better health" than Albert. This appeal was rejected and Albert recovered sufficiently to rejoin the 1st Battalion on 11 August 1917.

He returned just in time to take part in the Second Battle of Passchendaele.

On 26 October 1917, 1st Queens as part of 13th Brigade, 5th Division attacked at 5.40am. Together with the 15th Royal Warwicks and the 14th Warwicks in line they attacked down the Scherriabeek and found it an impassible morass. They attempted to push on under heavy fire from Gheluvelt. Although the Warwicks managed to occupy the Polderhoek Chateau for a short while they were forced to pull back and the Germans reoccupied it.

Albert Coutts was posted as missing presumed killed, aged 26, on 26 October 1917.

He has no known grave and is commemorated on the Tyne Cot Memorial, near Zonnebeek, just north east of Ypres.

Tyne Cot Cemetery contains nearly 12000 graves and the Memorial to the Missing commemorates another 35,000 men.

WILLIAM CROXFORD MM

Private 47472, 9th Battalion, Welsh Regiment

William Charles Croxford was born in 1885 at Hanworth, Middlesex to John and Mary Croxford. He was one of fourteen children.

William became a Seedsman, perhaps one step up from an agricultural labourer, and in 1907 married Mary McArdle. They remained living in Middlesex but his parents moved to Gatwick Cottages, Horley.

Williams' service record no longer exists but we know he enlisted at Hounslow and first served in the Royal Welsh Fusiliers, though his exact unit cannot be ascertained.

He is known to have won the Military Medal for bravery and this was probably during his time with the Welsh Regiment

The 9th Battalion, Welsh Regiment was formed at Cardiff in September 1914 as part Kitcheners New Army. They came under orders of 58th Brigade in 19th (Western) Division. In mid July 1915 they were despatched to France.

The exact date of Williams arrival in France is not known but the notice of his death in St Bartholomews parish magazine suggests that he had been there for about eighteen months before his death so he may have been in a draft of replacements in early 1917.

In 1917 9th WR were in action in The Battle of Messines and the Third Battles of Ypres where they fought through the horrors of Passchendaele.

In May 1918 they fought in the Battle of the Aisne when the German army threatened to drive a deep wedge into the allied lines and were in action through the old Somme battlefields during the Battles of St Quentin and Bapaume.

Williams life came to an end in October as the battalion prepared to join the British advance across Picardy at the battle of the Selle.

William Croxford died in action on 15 October 1918, aged 33. He is buried in Hermies Hill British Cemetery which is in the village of Hermies about 8 miles east of Bapaume.

CHARLES DAY

Corporal 76245 'C' Battery, 189th Brigade, Royal Field Artillery

Charles Robert Day was born in Horley in 1894 to John and Alice Day. He had two older brothers and a younger sister and they lived at 94 Albert Road, Horley. He attended Horley Infant School.

Before the outbreak of the war Charles was a baker's assistant in Horley. No service record survives for Charles but we know he enlisted at Guildford giving his place of birth as Redhill and joined the Royal Field Artillery.

Many RFA brigades started the war with 15 pounder field guns, ironically a development of an original Krupps design from Germany. In 1916, batteries started being issued with the improved 18 pounder field gun. A field gun fired its shells on a low trajectory – generally the target was in sight. Shells were usually high explosive or shrapnel as required. By 1916, an artillery brigade consisted of four batteries each of six guns. The first three, A B and C, were field guns and the fourth, D battery, had 4.5" howitzers at their disposal. The howitzer lobbed its shell high into the air so that it dropped more directly down onto its target. This meant that the target could be behind obstacles, perhaps a wood or a hill.

189th Brigade was a siege artillery unit and, as part of 41st Division, they were engaged through the Somme battles of 1916 and also at the Battles of Menin Road and Pilkem Ridge (3rd Battle of Ypres) through the summer of 1917.

It is thought that Charles was killed just before the 3rd Battle of Ypres began and he died, aged 23, on 22 July 1917. He is buried in Chester Farm Cemetery which is about 3 miles south of Ypres.

ROBERT DREWELL

Sapper 134792, 97th Field Company, Royal Engineers.

Robert John Drewell was born in 1895 at Harlesden, London, the eldest of two sons, to Robert and Margaret Drewell. By 1911 the family lived in Newbury, Berkshire and Robert was apprenticed to a carpenter. Robert and Margaret later moved to West Villa, Brighton Road, Horley.

Robert's service records are not available so we know no details of his enlistment or service dates.

The Royal Engineers carried out a number of different roles for the army both in the battlefield and along the lines of communication. They were organised into different types of units, none of which was bigger than a Company in size. These units were attached to Divisions, or to larger formations at Corps, Army or even GHQ. The main ones, of which there were many, were the Field Companies and the Signals Companies. As they were attached to the fighting portions of the Divisions, these Companies often saw action and took part in the fighting.

97th Field Company RE arrived in France in September 1915 and suffered heavy casualties at the Battle of Loos.

In 1916 they were in action during the Somme offensive and in 1917 they were at the Hindenburg Line, the Arras offensive and 3rd Ypres. In 1918 they were again in the Somme area at what became known as the Battle of St Quentin which straddled a line between Arras and Chauny and it was in this action that Robert was killed.

On 21 March 1918 the Germans launched a ferocious assault on the British lines. At 4.40am a terrific German bombardment began. British communications were shattered and many of our guns were neutralised or destroyed over the next few hours of shelling.

The Germans made substantial advances over the next few days and Robert was killed during this battle.

He died on 23 March 1918, aged 23, and has no known grave.

He is commemorated on the Pozieres Memorial which lies on the north side of the Albert–Pozieres road just south west of Pozieres.

CHARLES ELSON

Sergeant S/721, 7th Battalion, The Queens, (Royal West Surrey) Regiment

Charles Elson was born at Cobham, Surrey, in 1877 and was one of 12 children born to Charles and Sarah Elson.

By 1911 Charles had left his labouring job and enlisted into the West Surreys as a Regular Army Soldier. He joined up at Redhill and gave an address in Horley.

Charles' service record is not available but we know that he was serving before 1911 so it is likely that he was transferred into the 7th Battalion.

The 7th (Service) Battalion Queens were sent to France and landed there on 27 July 1915. They became part of the 55th Brigade of the 18th (Eastern) Division.

On 1 July 1916 the Battle of the Somme commenced and at 7.30 a.m. the Battalion assaulted the German trenches on a front of about 400 yards.

Under a cloudless blue sky which gave full promise of the hot mid-summer day which was ahead, wave after wave of British infantry rose and, with bayonets glistening, moved forward into a blanket of smoke and mist as the barrage lifted from the enemy's front trench. Almost simultaneously the German gunners ceased their counter-battery work and concentrated their fire upon the assault.

After 12 hours fighting the final objective west of Montauban was reached and consolidated on a front of about 260 yards. Casualties in this action were 'Other ranks' killed 174, wounded 284 and 'missing' 56.

One of the dead was Charles Elson. He died on 1 July 1916, aged 39, and is buried in Dantzig Alley Cemetery which is just east of Mametz and about a mile from Montauban where he was killed.

GEORGE ETHERIDGE

Private 103463, 8th Battalion, The Machine Gun Corps (Infantry)

George Alfred Etheridge was born in Horley in 1896 to George and Sarah Etheridge. He had five brothers and three sisters and the family lived at 113 Albert Road, Horley.

By 1911 George was employed by Crawfords in Station Road as a chemist's errand boy and later worked for George Burbridge, the baker.

His service record is not available but we know he enlisted at Guildford into the Army Service Corps fairly early in the war.

George's medal card makes neither mention of the ASC nor the award of a 1914–1915 Star which suggests that he did not serve overseas before 1916.

In 1917 he transferred (or was posted) into the Machine Gun Corps and joined its 8th Battalion on its formation in January 1918 after which it became part of the 8th Division, 5th Army.

On 21 March 1918 the Germans launched Operation Michael. Around 10,000 guns fired over a million shells in five hours against Lieutenant General Byng's Third and General Gough's Fifth Armies before 47 German divisions attacked.

Using infiltration tactics the German storm troopers by-passed pockets of resistance and broke through the British trench system, leaving the following waves of troops to 'mop up' any resistance.

Lacking reserves, Gough's line soon gave way and by the evening of 23 March the Germans had advanced 12 miles.

The British line was forced to withdraw in the face of the German advance. Bapaume (or what remained of it) was abandoned and it was in this action that George Etheridge was killed.

He died on 25 March 1918, aged 22, and has no known grave.

He is commemorated on the Pozieres Memorial which lies on the north side of the Albert – Pozieres road just south west of Pozieres.

George Alfred Etheridge (Photo courtesy of Mr K Etheridge)

HARRY FISH

Stoker 1st Class K/14099, Royal Navy, HMS Russell

Harry Edward Fish was born in 1894 to Harry and Jane Fish. He had a younger brother and five sisters and the family lived at 13 Charlesfield Road, Horley. Harry attended Horley Infant School.

Before the war Harry worked as a gardener and it is not known when he enlisted into the Navy, nor what other ships he served on but at some point, following his basic training he was posted to the battleship HMS *Russell*. It is worth noting that any man, who, on call-up, expressed a preference for the Royal Navy, could not be drafted into any other service.

HMS *Russell* joined the Channel Fleet in November 1914 when at Portland and after bombarding the coast of Belgium was sent to the Dardanelles. She stayed at Mudros as support alongside HMS *Hibernia* in November 1915 and eventually took part in the evacuation on 7 January 1916.

HMS *Russell* arrived in Malta on the night of 26 April 1916. As Grand Harbour was closed due to the boom defence, she had to wait until morning before entering. While manoeuvring outside the harbour, she struck a mine and became one of the first victims of the German mine laying submarines, one of which, U-73, had voyaged from Kiel to Malta under the command of Captain Gustav Siess. On the 23 April U-73 laid several mines at about 50m in front of Grand Harbour before proceeding to Cattaro.

HMS *Russell* was mined on 27 April 1916 just over 4 miles off the coast of Malta. She floated for 20 minutes before capsizing, her huge hull showing above the water before being engulfed by waves. 126 sailors died but 625 were saved including the Captain.

Harry Fish was killed in this disaster aged 21. His body was not recovered and he is commemorated on the Chatham Naval Memorial. The Memorial overlooks the town of Chatham and is approached by a steep path from the Town Hall Gardens.

HMS Russell, *sunk by a mine off Malta 27 April 1916.*

GEORGE FLOWERS

Joiner 341781, HMS Good Hope, *Royal Navy*

George Flowers was born in 1873 at Sutton St Edmunds, Lincolnshire. His parents were John and Ann Flowers and he had a younger brother and three sisters.

He cannot be traced on the census's of 1891 but a RN entry in 1901 could be George on a ship at Sheerness. George married Sarah Taylor at Horley in 1901 and they moved to Portsmouth but it is probable that Sarah came back to Horley following his death. They had two children, a boy and a girl. He joined the Navy as a carpenter well before the outbreak of war and probably as early as the 1890s.

HMS *Good Hope* was launched on 21 February 1901, with her heaviest gun being of 9.2 inch (234mm) calibre. She became the flagship of the 1st Cruiser Squadron, Atlantic Fleet, in 1906, and in 1908 became the flagship of the 2nd Cruiser Squadron. She went into the Reserve Fleet in 1913, but just before the outbreak of the war she joined the 6th Cruiser Squadron.

The Admiralty thought it likely that German liners in New York and other ports on the United States Atlantic seaboard could convert themselves to armed merchant cruisers by installing guns which the Admiralty believed they carried in their holds. HMS *Good Hope* left Portsmouth on 2 August 1914 under the command of Captain Philip Franklin to guard against such vessels.

After a few days in the Falkland Islands she left Port Stanley on 22 October and embarked on the search for the German East Asiatic Squadron.

When they met in the late afternoon of 1 November 1914, the Germans, with their newer, lighter ships, took quick advantage. They opened fire at 7 pm and HMS *Good Hope* was hit before its crew could return fire; it sank within half an hour.

She was sunk by the German armoured cruisers *Scharnhorst* and *Gneisanau* with the loss of her entire crew of 900 hands, in what became known as the Battle of Coronel off the Chilean coast.

George Flowers died in this action on 1 November 1914, aged 40, and is commemorated on the Portsmouth Naval Memorial.

Some of the crew of HMS Good Hope

HMS Good Hope *sunk on 1 November 1914.*

GEORGE FREEMAN

Captain, 6th Battalion, Royal Berkshire Regiment

George Cyril Freeman was born in 1890 at West Norwood to George and Charlotte Freeman – he was one of seven children.

In 1895 George Freeman bought Picketts Farm and had "Picketts" in Picketts Lane, Horley built nearby. This is still a substantial family home and reflects the fact that George senior was a stock broker. The family were wealthy enough to employ a kitchen maid, housemaid, cook and footman.

George's service record does not survive but by comparing death dates and Probate records we can identify him as serving in the 6th Berks and his medal index card shows that he may have been in the Army soon after the Battalion was formed in September 1914.

As part of the 53rd Brigade in 18th (Eastern) Division they landed in France on 26 July 1915. They took part in several actions in 1915 and in 1916 were engaged in various parts of the Somme campaign.

In the autumn of 1916 the 6th Berks were part of an attacking force attempting to gain possession of The Ancre Heights. This would deprive the German army of observation towards Albert which lay to the south-west and allow the British to observe the German positions around Beaumont Hamel, Serre and Beaucourt.

Towards the end of September the 53rd Brigade were tasked with an assault on a heavily defended German strongpoint called the Schwaben Redoubt.

During this period from 26 September till 5 October the 18th Division sustained 3,344 casualties.

At 5.30am on 1 October 1916 the Germans launched a major counter attack to dislodge the British troops from the ground they had gained over the previous few days and it was on this day that George Freeman was killed, aged 25.

George is buried in Blighty Valley Cemetery which is near Authuille a short way north east of Albert.

JOHN GRAHAME

Lance Corporal 1894, Honourable Artillery Company

John Gordon Grahame was born in Glasgow in 1885 to Thomas and Margaret Grahame. His father was the Canadian Government Agent for Scotland and John was one of 13 children born to this couple.

John attended Glasgow High School and Dulwich College and by 1911 was living in Thurleigh Road, Balham and working as a shipping clerk. Sometime after 1911 his mother, Margaret, moved to Cumberland House, Horley.

John volunteered immediately war broke out and enlisted in the HAC in September 1914 at Finsbury and was sent to France on 23 January 1915.

The Honourable Artillery Company was one of the oldest units in the British Army and despite its title also maintained an Infantry Battalion. John served as an infantryman.

In early 1915 the 1st HAC were in action as part of the 3rd Division in the area of St Eloi, south of Ypres.

Late in March the British exploded six huge mines in an effort to drive German troops from a commanding position on Wytschaete Ridge. The explosions made huge craters and these together with the effects of shellfire turned the whole area into a quagmire.

In their attempts to secure the craters the British made a series of assaults and it was almost certainly whilst attacking these positions that John died.

John Grahame was killed in action on 24 April 1915, aged 29 and was buried behind the trenches near St Eloi in the grounds of the Chateau of Elsinvelles.

In 1920 his body was exhumed and reburied at Voormezeele Cemetery which is a short distance south west of Ypres.

His commanding officer wrote that: "he was much loved and respected by all his platoon and he, as well as others, would miss him, both as a friend and a soldier."

John Gordon Grahame (De Ruvignys Roll of Honour)

CARL HANSEN

Lieutenant 165th Coy Machine Gun Corps
(attached 9th Bn, The Kings Liverpool Regiment)

Carl Frederick Hansen (not Hanson as on our Memorial) was born at Liverpool in 1893 to Charles Lauritz and Mary Hansen. He had a younger brother, William, who also died. The family lived in north west London. It is not known how the family are connected to Horley. Charles and Mary later lived at Hansen's Farm, Cholsey, Berks.

Details of Carl's military career are difficult to ascertain. He appears to have been posted to France in 1916, probably with 9th Kings. The Machine Gun Corps was formed at the end of 1915 and a specialist Company was allocated to each infantry brigade taking its number.

The 9th Kings were in the 165th Brigade of the 55th Division and in February 1916 were in action south of Arras before moving south where they were in and out of the line throughout the Battle of the Somme until October 1916 (during which time William Hansen was killed) when they were moved north again to the Ypres Salient.

The first half of 1917 was a comparatively quiet time, if being surrounded by enemy on three sides and under constant artillery fire could be described as quiet.

By June 1917 machine gunners were employing creeping barrages, with fire falling ahead of the artillery barrage to catch enemy troops moving to the rear. They would concentrate fire on specific targets, or sweep the enemy ground behind his front and support positions. Machine guns for these tasks were generally placed about 1000 yards behind the advancing infantry and were moved up as soon as the enemy positions were captured.

When the Battle of Passchendaele commenced on 31 July the Division attacked near Wieltje and in the course of the next few days, no fewer than 168 officers and 3384 men were killed, or missing.

Carl Hansen was killed in this action on 31 July 1917, aged 24. He is buried in Potijze Chateau Lawn Cemetery which is about a mile north east of Ypres.

WILLIAM HANSEN

2nd Lieutenant, 9th Battalion, The Kings Liverpool Regiment

William George Hansen (not Hanson as on the memorial) was born at Didsbury, near Chester, in 1894 to Charles Lauritz and Mary Hansen. Known as George, he had an older brother, Carl, who also died in the war. The family lived in north west London. It is not known how the family are connected to Horley. Charles and Mary later lived at Hansen's Farm, Cholsey, Berks.

William was educated at Steyning School and then went to Denmark for two years to learn farming. When he returned he entered Harper Adams Agricultural College in Shropshire.

He joined the Inns of Court officer training corps in 1915 and was gazetted 2nd Lieutenant in January 1916. William was sent to France in June and joined the Battalion as they were preparing to move to The Somme.

On 5 August, they were in the front line close to the German-held village of Guillemont. The fighting that followed is often referred to as some of the hardest of the whole battle – for both sides. In less than 24 hours the battalion suffered over 100 casualties, a terrible toll when they weren't even attacking. They attacked the village on 12 August and made no ground at a cost of over 200 men. The battle went on and a month later, they found themselves in the line once more, a short distance away near to the village of Longueval.

25 September 1916 was a warm autumnal day with temperature into the 70's as the battle of Morval got under way.

The 9th King's attacked with the rest of 165th Brigade and by 1.00pm had had captured Gird Trench and cleared Grove Alley to leave the way clear through to Gueudecourt having achieved all of their objectives.

William was killed in this action on 25 September 1916, aged 22.

His commanding Officer said, "He was loved by everyone in the Company."

He was buried locally but the grave was subsequently lost and he is commemorated on the Thiepval Memorial.

William George Hansen (De Ruvignys Roll of Honour)

WILLIAM HARDS

Leading Stoker K/11357, HM Submarine E50, Royal Navy

William Walter Jordan Hards was born in 1892 at Redhill to John Jordan and Mary Hards but appears to have been raised by his mother's parents, John and Emily Hards, at Poplar Terrace, Horley and later in Church Road, Horley.

By 1911 the census shows that he was a tool grinder and worked at Monotype in Salfords.

In 1915 William married Florence Mary Smith at Reigate.

No service record survives for William but it is likely that he enlisted in the Royal Navy in 1916. At some point following his basic training he volunteered for service in Submarines and was ultimately posted to E50.

The E class were the backbone of the submarine fleet during WWI and bore the brunt of its contribution to the war effort. Various experiments were carried out with the 'E' class including trials to see if they were suitable for the carrying of seaplanes.

The 8th and 9th submarine flotillas of the Royal Navy were based at Parkeston Quay, including all of the E-Class submarines.

E50 was 181 feet long and displaced 807 tons submerged. She was capable of about 14.5 knots on the surface, 9.5 knots submerged and carried 10 torpedoes.

E50 entered service late in January 1917 and William may well have been included in the first crew which was 30 strong.

A few weeks later E50 was damaged in a collision while submerged on 19 March 1917 off the North Hinder Light Vessel.

Whilst submerged at about 30ft below the north sea and heading towards Germany E50 was suddenly subjected to a violent shock. At first the crew thought they were under attack from a Zeppelin but after finally rising to periscope depth the captain saw the enemy submarine, UC-62, that they had hit. E50 was badly damaged and limped home.

William Hards survived this collision but finally lost his life, aged 25, when E50 was mined off the South Dogger Light Vessel on 31 January 1918.

All of the crew were lost and William is commemorated on the Chatham Naval Memorial.

RICHARD HARMES

Gunner 94395, 127th Battery, Royal Field Artillery

Richard Harmes was born in Horley in 1897 and was the third child of Edward and Sarah Harmes. He had two older sisters and they lived in Poplar Terrace, Horley. He attended Horley Infant School.

In 1911 Richard was still at school and the family had moved to 26 Lumley Road, Horley.

Richard enlisted at Guildford and after his basic training was sent to France on the 29 July 1915.

Richard's service record is not available but at about the time of his arrival, the 4th Division, of which 127th Battery were part, moved down from the Ypres sector to the Somme area.

This was a very much quieter sector compared to the Salient, and the division stayed here until just prior to the Battle of the Somme when it took up positions on the Redan Ridge.

The horse drawn Royal Field Artillery was the most numerous arm of the artillery being responsible for the medium calibre guns and howitzers deployed close to the front line and was reasonably mobile. It was organised into brigades.

Richard may well have crewed an 18 Pounder gun. These fired 3.3inch (84mm) calibre shells each weighing 18.5lb (8.4kg) each. A well trained crew could fire 30 rounds a minute, to a range of up to 3 miles or more. 4 types of shell were fired; High explosive, Shrapnel (375 lead balls with an explosive charge), Smoke and Gas. About 176 rounds would be held at each battery position. 1000 rounds would be available for each gunpit and held in various locations.

In the event of a retreat field guns could not be abandoned to the enemy since they were the equivalent of an Infantry Regiments 'Colours'. Regimental Colours, of course, were no longer carried into battle. If possible, guns would almost always be destroyed by removing the gun sights or exploding a charge in the barrel or breech.

Richard was killed during the opening artillery exchanges for the Battle of The Somme on 23 June 1916, aged 19, and he is buried at the Sucrerie Military Cemetery which lies in open countryside midway between Colincamps and Beaumont Hamel.

JOHN HENNING

Private 110234, 5th Battalion, Canadian Mounted Rifles

John Sidney (not Sydney as on our memorial) Henning was born in 1893 at Norwood to Arthur and Lucy Henning. He was one of eight children and sometime between 1901 and 1911 the family moved to The Brambles in Massetts Road, Horley.

On 22 April 1909, three days before his 16th birthday and giving his occupation as 'Farmer', John sailed from Liverpool on board the White Star Liner 'Canada' bound for Ontario and Montreal.

He appears to have settled in Sweetsbury, a small town near Cowansville on the edge of Lac Davignon some 45miles south east of Montreal, and it was here that he volunteered for service with the Canadian Army six years later on 16 March 1915.

The regiment embarked at Quebec on 18 July 1915 aboard *Hesperian*, disembarking in England on 27 July 1915. Its strength was 35 officers and 601 other ranks. They arrived in France on 24 October 1915, becoming part of the 2ndBrigade, Canadian Mounted Rifles.

John would certainly have been present at the Battle of Mount Sorrel which took place on 2 June 1916 between Zwarteleen and Hooge.

Between 2 June and 14 June 1916, the Canadian Corps lost a total of 73 officers and 1053 other ranks killed; 257 officers and 5010 other ranks wounded; 57 officers and 1980 other ranks missing, a total of 8430.

When the Battle of The Somme began in July 1916 the Canadian Divisions were soon engaged.

In late September the 5th CMR were in action to the east of Thiepval and a few days later, on 1 October, were tasked with the capture of Regina Trench beyond the village of Courcelette.

They carried out a sustained attack through heavily wired defences and, despite heavy enemy machine gun fire, finally achieved their objectives.

John was killed in this action. He is listed as being killed on 2 October 1916, aged 23. He has no known grave and is commemorated on the Vimy Memorial on Vimy Ridge.

WILLIAM HOARE

Private 12881, 1st Battalion, Lincolnshire Regiment

It is thought that William was born in Maesteg, Wales in about 1882 but his family is not traceable with any certainty nor can he be identified on the 1911 census or an earlier one.

William joined up in London probably as soon as war was declared in August 1914 along with 51,646 others.

He landed in France on 12 November 1914 and would have been a welcome replacement for the many casualties taken by 1st Lincs since their arrival on 14 August.

The 1st Battalion had been in the thick of the fighting and seen action at Mons, the rearguard action at Solesmes, the Battle of Le Cateau, the Battle of the Marne, the Battle of the Aisne, at La Bassee and Messines and William arrived towards the end of the First Battle of Ypres.

He must have been wounded almost as soon as he arrived at the front. He was moved, probably by wagon and train, to The Duchess of Westminister's Hospital (No.1 B.R.C.S) at Le Touquet.

The Base Hospital was part of the casualty evacuation chain, further back from the front line than the Casualty Clearing Stations. They were manned by troops of the Royal Army Medical Corps, with attached Royal Engineers and men of the Army Service Corps. In France and Flanders, the British hospitals were generally located near the coast. They needed to be close to a railway line, in order for casualties to arrive by train (although some also came by canal barge); they also needed to be near a port where men could be evacuated for longer-term treatment in Britain.

William Hoare died from his wounds on 28 December 1914. He is buried in Le Touquet Paris-Plage Communal Cemetery which is on the Avenue du 18 Juin, Le Touquet.

THOMAS HOLMES

Lieutenant, 100 Squadron, Royal Flying Corps

Thomas George Holmes was born in Whetstone in 1893 and lived with his parents Thomas and Mary Holmes. By 1911 he had two younger brothers and the family had moved to 'The Croft', 18 Hadlow Road, Tonbridge near The Manor House school which Thomas attended. His parents later moved to Petridge Wood at the southern tip of Earlswood Common.

It is not known when Thomas joined the RFC but given the life expectancy of pilots at this time it is likely to have been sometime in 1916.

100 Squadron was a bomber squadron flying FE2b's and went into action for the first time on 5/6 April 1917 when they attacked the German airfield at Douai, the base of the famous Richthofen circus.

Thomas took part in this attack which was a great success. Indeed, Manfred von Richthofen himself wrote a report which praised the individual bravery of the British pilots.

The FE2b was a pusher aeroplane, with the gunner seated in front of the pilot, far forward in the nacelle. The FE2 was one of the first aircraft to fly with a machine gun, on 24 July 1912. From 1917 onwards it was used as a bomber. Around 1000 were built.

F.E. stands for 'Farman Experimental', 'Farman' being used as a generic name for pusher biplanes as they looked vaguely like those designed by the Farman brothers. The advantages of this arrangement were primarily in the lack of a propeller to fire through and a gunner to take a lot of work off of the pilot, as in the related FE8. While the engine protected the pilot somewhat from bullets fired from behind, it was easier to destroy the engine. Also, in the event of a nose-down crash, the engine and fuel tended to land on top of the crew, usually killing them.

Thomas flew on several more bombing raids over the next few weeks but on the night of 5/6 May 1917 he was killed, aged 23, whilst attacking the aerodrome at Dorignees. His observer, Air Mechanic Ekins, was also killed. He is buried in Douai British Cemetery near Cuincy a short distance north west of Douai.

An FE2b as flown by Thomas Holmes.

WILFRED HUGHES

Leading Telegraphist J/4083, HMS Racoon, *Royal Navy.*

Wilfred Sydney Hughes was born in Islington in 1893 to John and Annie Hughes. He was one of eleven children of which five brothers and four sisters survived.

Wilfred joined the Royal Navy prior to 1911 but his service record is not available.

In late 1916 whilst serving in HMS *Campania* he married Constance Wood at St Bartholomews Church and after the war she gave her address as The Fire Station, Horley.

It is not known what other ships he served in during the war but he was serving in HMS *Racoon* at the time of his death.

HMS *Racoon* was a Beagle class, three funnelled coal burning destroyer displacing some 950 tons and was built and launched from the Cammell Laird shipyard in 1910. Her official crew compliment was 96 but at the time of her loss she was carrying 91 seamen under the command of Lt. George Napier.

During the early hours of 9 January 1918 she was en route from Liverpool to Lough Swilly to take up anti-submarine and convoy duties in the Northern Approaches.

In heavy seas and poor visibility, including snow blizzards, she struck rocks at the Garvan Isles off Malin Head on the northwest coast of Ireland and sank with the loss of all hands.

Wilfred died in this disaster on 9 January 1918, aged 25, and his body was never recovered.

He is commemorated on the Chatham Naval Memorial.

HMS Racoon *sunk off Malin Head, 9 January 1918.*

JOHN HUMPHREY
Private 1450, 22nd Battalion, Royal Fusiliers

John Humphrey was born at Felbridge in 1896 to William and Clara Humphrey. He was the sixth of seven children. William was a blacksmith and seems to have moved around a lot, possibly following any available work, but in 1901 was settled at 2 Clara Villas, Tismans Common, Rudgwick, Sussex.

After William died Clara moved to Crawley and later to Horley.

By 1911 John was employed as a shop assistant to an upholsterer and lived with his widowed mother, Clara at 13 High Street, Crawley.

John's service record is not available so it is not known when he enlisted though it was certainly at Shepherds Bush where he gave his place of residence as Hove, Sussex.

22nd Battalion (The Kensingtons) were raised by the Mayor and Borough of Kensington in 1914. After training they landed at Boulogne in November 1915 as part of 99th Brigade, 3rd Division.

Early in 1916 they saw action south of Ypres around the St Eloi craters and later at the battle for Vimy Ridge.

Early in May 1916 the Germans began to intensify their artillery and mortar activity from Vimy Ridge. Having observed intense Allied troop movements around Arras, in preparation for the Somme assault their offensive began on 21 May with a powerful bombardment lasting several hours. In relative terms, the bombardment was one of the heaviest of the Great War with 70,000 shells fired in four hours. The Germans exploded a mine and then sent in their infantry which easily took the British front line, capturing numerous soldiers in their shelters and "turning" the trenches in on their makers.

A British counter-attack on 23 May was nipped in the bud by German shelling and machine gun fire.

It is likely that John was wounded in this action and removed to 6th Casualty Clearing Station at Barlin.

It was here that he died on 1 June 1916 aged 20. The graves surrounding the hospital were eventually gathered together and became the Barlin Communal Cemetery which lies about 10 miles north west of Vimy and 5 miles south of Bethune.

His older brother, Michael, also died in France on 30 November 1917.

MICHAEL HUMPHREY

Rifleman 553742, 16th Battalion, The London Regiment
(Queens Westminster Rifles)

Michael James Humphrey was born in Horley in 1892 to William and Clara Humphrey. He was the third of seven children. William was a blacksmith and seems to have moved around a lot, possibly following any available work, but in 1901 was settled at 2 Clara Villas, Tismans Common, Rudgwick, Sussex.

After William died Clara moved to Crawley and later to Horley.

By 1911 Michael was employed as a footman, one of seven servants, by the Pawle family at Wray Common, Reigate.

He married Emily Easton in 1914 in Kensington. After Michael's death Emily remarried and, as Emily Underdown, lived at 34 Redstone Road, Redhill.

Michael's service record is not available but we know he enlisted, probably in 1916 or 1917, at Piccadilly into 16th Battalion, The London Regiment which became part of 169th Brigade of the 56th London Division.

In July 1917 the division moved to Ypres, and fought in the Battle of Langemarck at Inverness Copse and Glencourse Wood on 16/17 August. Following these operations the division withdrew from the line, and moved south to the Cambrai area, taking over trenches at Lagnicourt in early September.

On the opening day of the Battle of Cambrai, 20 November 1917, the division was involved in diversionary operations opposite Moeuvres, and two days later attacked and captured Tadpole Copse and the Hindenburg Line near Moeuvres itself. During the German counter-attack on 30 November, the positions held near Tadpole Copse were overrun and the division forced back towards the old British front line.

It was on this day, 30 November 1917, that Michael was killed in action, aged 26. He is buried in Moeuvres Cemetery which is about 8 miles west of Cambrai.

His younger brother, John, also died in France on 1 June 1916.

CHARLES KENWARD

Corporal G1843, 7th Battalion The Queens
(Royal West Surrey) Regiment

Charles Kenward (his birth was registered as Charlie) was born in Horley in 1896, one of six children, to Stephen and Harriett Kenward. The family lived in Albert Road, Horley and later moved to 72 Lumley Road, Horley.

Before the war Charlie was a general labourer but he soon answered Kitchener's call and enlisted at Redhill.

The 7th (Service) Battalion Queens were sent to France and Charlie landed there on 27 July 1915. They became part of the 55th Brigade of the 18th (Eastern) Division.

This Division was placed on the extreme right of the British attack on the first day of the Battle of The Somme.

On 1 July they were to assault the trenches south and west of the village of Montauban. This became the first village to be captured on that day when the British Army suffered some 60,000 casualties.

On 12 July 55th Brigade was once again moved into the front line near Trônes Wood, and were detailed to capture the wood on the night of the 13th. Having had their numbers reduced from 300 strong to 280 in the afternoon by German shelling, the Queen's were ordered to attack Trônes Wood at 7pm. Their attack was repulsed by heavy machine gun fire and fire from unsuppressed German 150 and 105mm howitzers and 77mm guns. The battalion could not close within 100 yards of the wood, and withdrew under the cover of darkness.

Charlie was missing, presumed killed, during this attack on the night of 13/14 July 1916 aged 19. His body was never recovered and he is commemorated on the Thiepval Memorial.

HARVEY KILLICK

Private G/1960, 7th Battalion The Queens
(Royal West Surrey) Regiment

Benjamin Harvey Killick (always known as Harvey) was born in Horley in 1896, one of eight children, to Albert and Esther Killick. The family first lived in Vicarage Road then in Charlesfield Road, Horley but in 1911 were living at The Duxhurst Home for Lady Inebriates, where Albert was a driver. Albert and Esther later moved to Victoria Road, Horley.

Harvey enlisted at Reigate in answer to Kitcheners call for volunteers and joined 7th Queens.

The 7th (Service) Battalion of The Queens were sent to France and Harvey landed there on 27 July 1915. They became part of the 55th Brigade of the 18th (Eastern) Division.

Through the autumn of 1915 the Battalion was engaged on several fronts and carried out all the usual activities of trench warfare.

At the Battle of The Somme on 1 July 1916 this Division was placed on the extreme right of the British attack.

At 7.30 a.m. the 7th Queens assaulted the German trenches on a front of about 400 yards and after 12 hours fighting the final objective west of Montauban was reached and consolidated on a front of about 260 yards.

The Battalion sustained dreadful casualties during this attack losing 174 other ranks killed, 284 wounded and 56 missing.

Montauban became the first village to be captured on this day during which the British Army suffered 60,000 casualties.

It was in this assault that Harvey died, aged 19, on 1 July 1916.

He is buried in Dantzig Alley Cemetery which is a short distance north east of Mametz.

Harvey's older brother, Sidney, was killed exactly two months earlier.

SIDNEY KILLICK

Private G/2875, 8th Battalion The Queens (Royal West Surrey) Regiment

Formerly of the East Kent Regiment

Sidney Killick was born in Horley in 1889, one of eight children, to Albert and Esther Killick. The family lived first in Vicarage Road, Horley and later in Charlesfield Road. In 1911 they were living at The Duxhurst Home for Lady Inebriates, where Albert was a driver. Albert and Esther later moved to Victoria Road, Horley.

Sidney's service record is not available but we know that 8th Battalion, The Queen's was raised at Guildford in September 1914 as part of Kitchener's Third New Army and joined 72nd Brigade, 24th Division.

They proceeded to France at the end of August 1915. The Division was in reserve for the main British assault at Loos, going into action on the 26 September and suffering heavy losses.

On the night of the 29/30 April 1916 8th Queens were in the line near Wulverghem when the enemy carried out a gas attack on a front of 3,500 yards held by the 3rd and 24th Divisions. The operation was opened by heavy rifle and machine-gun fire under cover of which the gas was released.

Immediately afterwards, a heavy 'barrage', or curtain of artillery fire, was placed on this area, and eight infantry attacks were launched. Of these attacks, only two penetrated the British trenches; one was immediately repelled, while the other was driven out by a counter-attack after about 40 minutes occupation.

It was in this action that Sidney was wounded and he died on 1 May 1916, aged 27, and is buried at Bailleul Communal Cemetery which is just on the eastern edge of the town of Bailleul.

His younger brother, Harvey, was killed exactly two months later.

HARRY KNOWLES

Private L/7316, 2nd Battalion, Royal Sussex Regiment

Harry Knowles was born in Billingshurst in 1884 to Alfred and Mary Knowles and lived at 2 West Park, Ifield, near Crawley. He had two brothers and three sisters.

In 1907 Harry married Elsie May Baldwin and they had two children, Frederick and Florence. He worked as a general labourer and they lived at 131 Albert Road, Horley.

Harry's service record is not available but it is known that he enlisted at East Grinstead into the East Kents but was later transferred to 2nd Royal Sussex. He was posted abroad on 31 August 1914. This means that he probably enlisted as a regular soldier and may have joined up before 1914.

2nd Royal Sussex were part of the 2nd Brigade, 1st Division and were involved in the Battle of Mons and the subsequent retreat, the Battle of the Marne, the Battle of the Aisne, the First Battle of Ypres and the Winter Operations of 1914–15. In 1915 they were in action during the Battle of Aubers.

At the Battle of Loos on 25 September 1915 the Division attacked along both banks of the La Bassee canal but met with no success at all. It was discovered that the enemy wire was undamaged, having been out of direct observation over a crest line, and two German machine guns and heavy rifle fire played across the lines of advancing troops as desperate efforts were made to cut the wire. Further attacks by 2nd Brigade were met with the same devastating fire as the first, and were held up, with a large number of men lying out in the open, close under the German wire.

2nd Royal Sussex lost 481 men on this day and Harry was one of them.

He was killed on 29 September 1915, aged 29. His body was never found and he is commemorated on the Loos Memorial which is part of Dud Corner Cemetery just north west of Lens.

EDWARD LAMBERT

Private 26688, 1st/4th Battalion, Duke of Wellington's
(West Riding Regiment)

Edward Albert Lambert, one of nine children, was born in 1886 to Edward and Maria Lambert and the family lived at Little Lake Farm, Horley.

Edward, (sometimes known as Albert), was a cowman on the farm before enlisting into The Royal Fusiliers on 7 February 1916.

Despite his outdoor occupation the doctor who examined him described his physical condition as 'poor' and in May 1917 he was transferred to 102 Labour Company and a few months later transferred again into the 1/4th Battalion, West Riding Regiment.

Late in 1917 the Battalion took part in the 3rd Battle of Ypres and remained in and around the Salient for the next few months.

This battle was, in effect, a series of limited and costly offensives, often undertaken in the most difficult of waterlogged conditions which were a consequence of frequent periods of rain and the destruction of the Flanders' lowlands drainage systems by intense artillery bombardments.

The cost to both sides in human casualties was immense at between 200,000 and 400,000, although exact figures will never be known. The greatest tragedy is that the few miles of shell churned mud from Ypres to the Passchendaele Ridge was recaptured by the German Army during its April offensive in 1918.

Edward was lucky to survive this period in the Ypres Salient but his luck did not last much longer.

Sometime in March 1918 Edward was wounded in action and died of his wounds whilst in the care of the West Riding Field Ambulance Unit, aged 32, on 30 March 1918.

He is buried in the Menin Road South Military Cemetery which is on the eastern edge of Ypres.

ERNEST LEACH

Lance Corporal F/428, 17th Battalion, The Middlesex Regiment

Ernest Cecil Leach was born in 1891, one of four sons and two daughters, to Frank and Olive Leach. He was born in Chelsea, but grew up in Dorset, not far from Yeovil.

By 1911 his family were farming near Alton in Hampshire and later moved to farm at Burgess Hill. By the time Ernest enlisted in 1915 they had moved to Meath Green Farm, Meath Green Lane, Horley, where he worked on the farm.

Ernest joined up at Kingsway, London, together with his brother, Wilfred. They had both played football for Crystal Palace and were accepted into the 17th Middlesex (Footballers) Battalion, so called because of the large number of well-known footballers in their ranks. He had already seen some service as a Territorial soldier with the Dorset Yeomanry.

The 17th was raised in London on 12 December 1914 by W. Joynson Hicks MP. They proceeded to France on the 18 November 1915 landing at Boulogne and on the 8 December transferred to 6th Brigade, 2nd Division.

Although not in action during the opening stage of the Battle of the Somme 17th Middlesex were bought into the line in mid July 1916 and were part of the attacking force at Delville Wood which was a dominating feature enabling the holders to direct artillery fire onto the other side. It was on the right flank of the British advance and proved to be one of the bloodiest confrontations of the Somme Battles.

During this assault on 8 August 1916, Ernest was known to have been wounded. His brother, Wilfred, searched for his body without success and he survived the war.

Ernest was posted as missing and later confirmed as dead, aged 25. He was buried close to where he fell but in 1920 his body was recovered and reburied at Delville Wood Cemetery, Longueval.

THOMAS LEDGER

Private T/4245, 3rd/4th Battalion, The Queens
(Royal West Surrey) Regiment

Thomas Ledger was one of four children and was born in 1882 to Benjamin and Eliza Ledger, at Clayton, near Pycombe in Sussex.

By 1901 the family were living in Queens Road, Horley just a few doors from Alec and Percy Pescud who were also to die in the war. Thomas was working as a house boy for a family in Hookwood.

By 1911 Benjamin and Eliza had moved to Plaistow Cottage, Lee Street, Horley, but Thomas is not traceable.

His service record is not available but he enlisted at Guildford in 1915 into the 3rd/4th Battalion of The Queens which was a territorial unit raised in answer to Kitcheners' appeal.

It was formed at Windsor in June 1915 and initially attached to 200th Brigade, 67th (2nd Home Counties) Division.

It remained at home throughout the war. Along with other 'second line' Divisions it suffered greatly from lack of equipment of all sorts, and training was inevitably affected. Some units of infantry received Japanese rifles, quite different to the Lee-Enfields that equipped the British armies in the fields, and most only received modern rifles and ammunition in late November 1915. The artillery were initially given some French guns and some 15-pounders for which there was no ammunition, and the gunners were not fully equipped until well into 1916.

Thomas must have been taken ill during late 1915 and he was moved to the 1st Eastern General Hospital in Cambridge which had 1,173 beds and was located in the Leys School and Trinity College.

Thomas Ledger died from natural causes on 30 January 1916, aged 34, in Cambridge, without seeing active service.

He is buried in Cambridge City Cemetery.

HENRY LILES

Private 35046, 23rd Battalion, Northumberland Fusiliers

(4th Tyneside Scottish Battalion)

Henry Walker Liles was born in Paddington, London, in 1882 to Frederick and Caroline Liles. He had two younger sisters and grew up in a succession of Public Houses as his father was a publican.

By 1911 Henry had married Lilian and was a licensed victualler, a publican like his father, and they lived at 62 Akerman Street, Brixton.

Later on, Caroline, now widowed, and Lilian lived at The Nags Head, near Earlswood Common and this was probably Henry's last address.

Henry enlisted at Acton and it is not known how he came to join a northern based Regiment. The 4th Tyneside Scottish came under orders of 102nd Brigade, 34th Division and landed in France in January 1916.

The Tyneside Scottish first saw action in the Battle of the Somme when, on 1 July 1916, they lost 629 men (19 officers and 610 other ranks), the third worst battalion loss of the day.

It is unlikely that Henry had joined the battalion by this time and he was probably in the draft that supplied replacements for men killed in this action.

In April and May 1917 the battalion was in action at the Battle of Arras where they sustained 275 casualties and it seems certain that Henry received the wounds from which he died in this battle.

In the thirty-nine days that the battle lasted the average casualty rate was far higher than at either the Somme or Passchendaele.

He was taken to the 8th Casualty Clearing Station where he died from his wounds on 11 June 1917, aged 35.

Henry Liles is buried at Duisans British Cemetery near Etrun about 2 miles north west of Arras.

EDWARD LOCKYER

Private G/766, 6th Battalion, The Queens

(Royal West Surrey) Regiment

Edward John Lockyer was born at Sutton in 1894 to John and Emily Lockyer. The family moved to Shirley Cottage, 17 Chestnut Road, Horley, sometime before 1901 and by 1911 Edward was apprenticed to a local barber.

He enlisted at Guildford fairly soon after the outbreak of war and was with 6th Queens when they embarked for France on the 1st[t] June 1915. They were part of 37th Brigade, 12th (Eastern) Division.

On 23 June 1915 the Division took over a sector of the front line for the first time, at Ploegsteert Wood. By 15 July the Divisional front had extended south to reach east of Armentieres. In July alone the Division suffered the loss of 7 officers and 64 men killed, 18 officers and 413 men wounded.

They were in action in September at The Battle of Loos and relieved outgoing units in the Gun Trench – Hulluch Quarries sector on the night of 30 September – 1 October whereupon the Division began to consolidate the position under heavy artillery fire. The officer commanding, Major-General Frederick Wing CB, was killed in action on 2 October 1915 and his ADC, Lieutenant Christopher Tower DSO, was killed by the same shell. The Division succeeded in capturing Gun Trench and the south western face of the Hulluch Quarries but during this period at Loos, 117 officers and 3237 men were killed or wounded.

This whole area had become one where underground mine warfare was very active. Following the detonation of 4 mines on 2 March the craters were captured and British troops gained important observation positions over enemy lines.

The 6th Queens enjoyed a relatively quiet period for the next few weeks but on 19 April 1916 the enemy sent over a few trench mortars and rifle grenades, killing 5 men and wounding 10.

Edward Lockyer was one of the men killed on the 19 April 1916, aged 21. He has no known grave and is commemorated on the Loos Memorial.

EDWARD LUCAS

Rifleman R/16533 13th Battalion, Kings Royal Rifle Corps

Edward George Lucas (always known as George) was born at Worth in 1895 and was the son of Edmund and Annie Lucas. He had four sisters and the family lived at Keepers Cottage, Fen Place, Worth.

By 1911 George was working as a farm labourer and living with his married sister, Lilian, and his widowed mother at Fir Tree Cottage, Langshott, Horley.

He enlisted into the Kings Royal Rifle Corps in November 1915 and his attestation papers were certified correct by Henry Webber, a local JP, who was, himself, to die in the war.

He was posted to France in March 1916 and almost immediately contracted a bacterial skin disease as a result of the awful conditions there. He appears to have had either scabies or impetigo and was hospitalised for a good deal of time but was finally back with his unit in May and took part in several actions throughout 1917.

At some point George was wounded badly enough to be bought home for hospitalisation in Manchester but he recovered sufficiently to rejoin his unit again.

He was home on leave for a few short days in August 1918 and when he returned 13th KRRC were again bought into action just north of Bapaume.

George was wounded again in this assault and evacuated via a casualty clearing station to a main hospital near Rouen where he died from his wounds, aged 23, on 17 September 1918.

He is buried near the base hospital at St Sever Cemetery, which lies south of the River Seine in Rouen.

GEOFFREY LUSCOMBE

Lieutenant Commander HMS Blackmorevale *Royal Navy*

Geoffrey Alfred Luscombe (his birth was registered as Alfred Geoffrey) was born at Norwood, South London, in 1885 to Alfred and Kate Luscombe. He had three brothers and a sister and his parents were wealthy enough to employ several servants.

By 1901 Geoffrey was serving as a Naval Cadet at HMS *Brittania*, Dartford and, following his training became a Midshipman in 1902.

Early in 1905 he was promoted to Sub Lieutenant and by 1908 was a full Lieutenant serving on the cruiser HMS *Juno* in the channel fleet.

At the outbreak of the war Geoffrey was serving in the battleship HMS *Dominion* in the 3rd Cruiser Squadron and in June 1915 he was promoted to Lieutenant Commander.

Dominion served in the Grand Fleet until April 1916, serving temporarily as flagship of the Vice Admiral, 3rd Battle Squadron. During sweeps by the fleet, she and her sister ships often steamed at the heads of divisions of the far more valuable dreadnoughts, where they could protect the dreadnoughts by watching for mines or by being the first to strike them.

On 29 April 1916, the 3rd Battle Squadron was rebased at Sheerness, and on 3 May 1916 it was separated from the Grand Fleet, being transferred to the Nore Command.

When *Dominion* was refitted in early 1918 Geoffrey was posted to HMS *Blackmorevale*, a Hunt class minesweeper.

On the 1 May she struck a mine off Tod Head, Aberdeenshire and sunk with the loss of 26 of her 74 crew.

Geoffrey was killed in this incident and died on the 1 May 1918, aged 33. He is commemorated on the Plymouth Naval Memorial which overlooks Plymouth Hoe.

His connection with Horley is not known.

*Geoffrey Luscombe who died 1 May 1918 on
HMS* Blackmorevale.

DOUGLAS MANNERS

Private G/6319 2nd Battalion, Royal Sussex Regiment

Douglas William Manners Manners was born in Lincolnshire in 1896, one of four boys and four girls to Frederick and Gertrude Manners.

The family later moved to Victoria Terrace, Hove but by 1911 were living in Victoria Road, Horley. In October 1912 Douglas was a witness at his sister's wedding when she married at St Bartholomews Church, Horley.

Although his service record is not available it is known that Douglas enlisted at Hove, probably in 1916.

In the spring of 1916 the 2nd Royal Sussex moved, with the rest of the 1st Division, from the Loos sector, south to the Somme.

The battle of the Somme was a large-scale offensive launched on 1 July against the German Front Line on both sides of the Somme River; the British Army attacked north of the river and the French Army attacked south of the river.

The 2nd Royal Sussex was engaged in many of the decisive actions, from the attacks around Albert, including the capture of Montauban, Mametz, Fricourt, Contalmaison and La Boisselle in early July to the capture of Combles, Lesboeufs and Gueudecourt in September.

The battle lasted for a gruelling four months and was carried out in several phases with many thousands of casualties on both sides.

The 2nd Royal Sussex lost 1723 men during the war, the highest losses of any of the Regiments battalions.

The first battle of the Somme officially ended on 18 November and at some point in the immediate aftermath Douglas was killed.

He died, aged 20, on 27 November 1916. He has no known grave and is commemorated on the Thiepval Memorial.

FREDERICK MARCHANT

Sergeant 6159 2nd Battalion, Seaforth Highlanders

Frederick George Marchant was born in 1877 at Shipley, Sussex, to Thomas and Ann Marchant. He had three older sisters and three brothers. By 1911 Thomas and Ann had moved to Station Road, Horley and later they moved again to 37 Lumley Road.

Frederick's service record is not available but his Medal entitlement card shows that he was sent to France on 23 August 1914. This was the day that the British Army was first in action near Mons and his early arrival proves that Fred was a regular soldier before the war and one of the 'Old Contemptibles', so called because the German Kaiser referred to them as "that contemptible little army".

As part of 4th Division, 2nd Seaforths were assembled in France by 23 August and moved quickly up to the front to take part in the Battle of Le Cateau on 26 August where the Division lost some 3,000 men. Following service on the Aisne in September, they moved to Flanders, north-east of Armentières.

Some units of the Division took part in the Christmas Truce and they stayed in this area until the Spring of 1915.

On 23 April 1915 the 2nd Seaforths were moved to Dranoutre and placed on readiness for the start of the 2nd Battle of Ypres, which was to run on into May and would claim 70,000 Allied and 35,000 German casualties. It was also to see the first deployment of poison gas on the Western Front.

Two days later they came under heavy fire whilst preparing for the assault near Wieltje and attacked in heavy rain at 5.30am.

Although successful, this action cost the lives of 20 Officers and 61 Other Ranks as well as 239 wounded and 16 men missing.

This fighting all but wiped out the division, and many of those who had survived the battles of 1914 were killed or wounded here.

Frederick Marchant was killed in this action on 25 April 1915, aged 38. He is buried in Seaforth Cemetery, Cheddar Villa, just north east of Ypres.

HENRY MARCHANT

Gunner 200202 6th Reserve Brigade, Royal Field Artillery

There are at least five Henry or H Marchants on the Commonwealth War Graves list of soldiers who died in the 1914–18 war.

The name Marchant is quite uncommon and to have two unrelated soldiers from one town the size of Horley is most unlikely. Thus it is thought that the Henry Marchant named on Horley's War memorial is likely to be the younger brother of Frederick Marchant detailed on the previous page.

Henry was born in 1882 at Horsham, Sussex, to Thomas and Ann Marchant. He had 3 older sisters and three brothers. By 1911 Thomas and Ann had moved to Station Road, Horley and later they moved again to 37 Lumley Road.

In 1910 Henry married Ethel Rose and moved to Southend on Sea and the 1911 census shows his occupation as Dairy Manager.

His service record is not available and his Medal entitlement card gives no useful information.

We cannot be sure of exactly when and where Henry received the wounds that lead to his death but we do know that the 6th Reserve Brigade were in action in the summer of 1917 at the 3rd Battle of Ypres when the British Army launched a series of attacks towards Passchendaele. The Battle commenced in late July and was hampered by the heaviest rainfall in the area for thirty years. By mid August the fighting had progressed to the village of Langemarck with heavy casualties on both sides.

It is probable that Henry Marchant received the wounds that lead to his death in this action.

He was evacuated to a base hospital at Rouen and died, aged 35, on 10 September 1917. He is buried in St Sever Cemetery Extension which is south of the River Seine in that town.

JOHN MARTIN

Lance Corporal 5304, 54th Company, Machine Gun Corps (Infantry)

John James Martin was born in 1897 at Falmer, Sussex, one of three children, to Simon and Ann Martin.

On the 1911 census the family is shown as living in Horsham and John's occupation is given as a farm labourer.

By the time he enlisted into The Queens (Royal West Surrey) Regiment at Guildford, John was living in Horley but his exact address is not known.

No service record survives for John but it is likely that he joined up as soon as he was 18. It is probable that John was part of the machine gun unit of the Queens' and transferred into the new Corps soon after its formation.

The Machine Gun Corps was created on 22 October 1915. The companies formed in each brigade would transfer to the new Corps. The 54th Machine Gun Company joined 18th (Eastern) Division on 13 February 1916.

They were in action on the Somme in the Battle of Albert, capturing their objectives near Montauban and also at Bazentin Ridge, Delville Wood, Thiepval Ridge and the Ancre Heights where they played a part in the capture of the Schwaben Redoubt and Regina Trench.

In 1917 they took part in the operations on the Ancre including Miraumont and the capture of Irles. They fought during the German retreat to the Hindenburg Line and in the Third Battle of the Scarpe before moving to Flanders.

When the 54th Brigade opposed the German advance near Glencourse Wood on 11 August, the 54th Machine Gun Company had two guns with each assaulting battalion, four to go forward to the strong points, and four in reserve. These guns did splendid work, especially those garrisoning the strong points, and there is no doubt that more of the enemy were killed this day by rifle and machine – gun fire than in any previous action by the Brigade.

John James Martin was killed in this defensive action at Sanctuary Wood on 11 August 1917, aged 20. He has no known grave and is commemorated on the Menin Gate at Ypres.

WILLIAM MAYNARD

Private G/4189 1st Battalion, The Queens (Royal West Surrey) Regiment

William Maynard was born in Reigate in 1887 to William and Elizabeth Maynard. The family lived in Lower Road and William was later joined by a younger brother and sister. He also had a half-sister born after his father married again in 1903.

By 1911 William was employed as a carpenter and joiner and living with his family at 1 Lavender Cottages, Shocks Green, near Earlswood.

William enlisted at Guildford into The Queens, the county Regiment of Surrey and this was probably quite early in the war. Curiously the only medal roll card in his name shows a service number of G/4190 and does not give a date for his arrival in France.

On the 24 September 1915, 1st Queens, reinforced by a draft of 40 men, returned to a familiar part of the front line at Givenchy, near Loos. They were tasked for an attack early the next day.

At 6.00am on the 25 September the battalion advanced on a narrow front and moved slowly to keep behind the smokescreen put down by our artillery.

They met little opposition and reached the German third Line with few casualties. The Support Company moved forward to join the advancing line but at about 8.30am the Germans mounted a fierce counter attack with bombers on both flanks.

By 9.45am the Queens were driven back to their start lines under heavy machine gun fire.

Nineteen men were killed in this action, as well as 21 missing believed killed and 180 wounded. William Maynard was one of the dead men. He died, aged 28, on 25 September 1915. William has no known grave and is commemorated on the Loos Memorial.

FRANK MILLS

This man has proved impossible to identify.

The only local man with this name would appear to be the Frank Mills who was born in 1881 at York Town, Camberley. By 1911 he was married and employed as head gardener at Earlswood Mount, a large house near the Earlswood hospital. This man would have been about 33 at the outbreak of war and would not have been called up. He may have volunteered, as many men of that age did, but he cannot be identified militarily.

Although not on the original 'appeal' list in 1918 when the 'Parsons plaque' was being prepared for St Bartholomews Church the name of Frank Mills appears on the plaque near that of Frank Miller with whom he may have easily been confused.

Ultimately, Frank Miller, although living in Church Road, was commemorated on Charlwood War Memorial because he was born there.

The name of Frank Mills is not mentioned on the Salfords Church plaque or at St Johns Church, Earlswood.

GEORGE MORGAN

Bombardier 50986, 'D' Battery, 80th Brigade, Royal Field Artillery

George Albert Morgan is difficult to positively identify. The entry on the CWGC list of war dead shows him as G.A.Morgan born in 1896 and confirms that he was the son of William and Ray Morgan of 'St Andrews', Massetts Road, Horley.

The official list of soldiers killed in the war shows the same soldier as George Alfred Morgan and adds the information that he was born in Glasgow.

Both show the same regimental number and unit. Our Memorial shows him as George Albert Morgan. No firm trace can be found of this family in England or Scotland census records.

His service record is not available but his medal entitlement card survives and shows that he landed in France on the 15 July 1915. 80th Brigade was part of the 17th (Northern) Division and after its arrival in France the Brigade spent its first few months on trench familiarisation and then holding the front lines in the southern area of the Ypres salient.

In the spring of 1916 the Division was involved in fighting at the Bluff (south east of Ypres on the Comines canal), part of a number of engagements officially known as the Actions of Spring 1916.

None of these actions were regarded as 'major' by Sir Douglas Haig but he wrote that: "The maintenance and repair of our defences alone, especially in winter, entails constant heavy work. Bad weather and the enemy combine to flood and destroy trenches, dug-outs and communications; all such damages must be repaired promptly, under fire, and almost entirely by night.

Artillery and snipers are practically never silent, patrols are out in front of the lines every night, and heavy bombardments by the artillery of one or both sides take place daily in various parts of the line".

It was during this period of 'relative' inactivity that George Morgan died, aged 20, on 17 May 1916.

He is buried in Cite Bonjean Military Cemetery which is just south west of Armentieres.

FRANCIS MOTT

2nd Lieutenant, 24th Battalion, Royal Fusiliers

Francis Stanley Mott was born in 1896 at Brixton, South London, to Francis and Alice Mott and in 1901 they lived at Streatham. He had one younger sister and at some time before 1911 the family moved to Vulcan Lodge in Massetts Road, Horley.

Francis enlisted in 1914 and was sent to France on 29 August.

He served as a Private soldier attached to the Australian Voluntary Hospital which later became the 32nd Stationary Hospital based at Wimereux.

The military unit with which Francis served at this time is not known.

The 24th (Sportsmans Battalion) Royal Fusiliers was not raised until the autumn of 1914.

The 23rd and 24th RF were raised in autumn 1914 by a Mrs Cunliffe-Owen and were specially selected from upper class men who were physically fit and proficient in shooting and riding and who 'walked well'. After full training they arrived in France in November 1915.

The character of Francis Mott seems to indicate that he would have taken an early opportunity to transfer to a fighting unit and after he did so he clearly made a speedy advance through the ranks.

When the news of Francis's death reached Horley he received a fulsome tribute in the Parish Magazine:

"He enlisted... and by ability and force of character he soon gained his Commission... he carried about him the white flower of a stainless life, and it was this that made his personality so loveable and his influence so strong. There lay the secret, all knew this and all loved him in consequence."

Francis was wounded during the summer of 1916 as the 24th were preparing to move south for action at the Battle of The Somme.

Francis Mott died of his wounds on 23 July 1916, aged 20, and is buried at Lapugnoy Military Cemetery which is about 5 miles west of Bethune.

An authority was given for the award of the 1914 star in response to a request by his father in January 1918 and was sent in via the 32nd Stationary Hospital.

HORACE MUNN

Acting Corporal G/37010, 1st Battalion, The Queen's
(Royal West Surrey) Regiment

Horace Frank Munn was born at Guildford in 1894 to Horace and Ruth Munn and he had two sisters. By 1911 the family had moved to live at 50 Albert Road, Horley, and Horace was working as a tailor/improver. He worshiped at Horley Baptist Church and is commemorated on a plaque inside the church.

No service record survives for Horace and his medal card shows no useful information. He is recorded as having enlisted at Horley and as the 1st Queens were a regular army unit he may have enlisted before the war began.

The 1st Queens arrived in France in November 1915 as part of 100 Brigade, 33rd Division. It spent the first six months on the La Bassee front, a period of mining, counter-mining and trench raids.

Sir Douglas Haig's report of May 1916 mentions 1st Queens (amongst others) "as having been specially brought to my notice for good work in carrying out or repelling local attacks and raids."

In mid-summer 1916 1st Queens were moved down to the Somme where, as part of 100th Brigade, they were engaged in heavy fighting on Bazentin Ridge, at High Wood and Delville Wood.

In November 1916 1st Queens were tasked as part of a Brigade assault on Boritska Trench near Lesboufs and pressed home their attack successfully.

Some weeks later the Battalion were in the line north east of Bouchesnes. It had been snowing but a thaw had started and the trenches were in a very poor condition. Most of 21 December was spent on trench maintenance and during this relatively quiet spell in the line Horace Munn was killed.

He died on 21 December 1916, aged 22, and is buried in Sailley-Sailliesel British Cemetery which is midway between Bapaume and Perrone near the village of Rancourt.

ROBERT NIXON

Private 200960, 3rd Battalion, South Lancs Regiment

(later 359223 Labour Corps)

Robert William Nixon was born in Preston, Lancashire in 1866 to John and Elizabeth Nixon. He had a sister and two brothers. He became a cotton weaver when he started work.

Robert's marriage to Anna E South was his second marriage when it was registered at Reigate in 1915. In 1921, three years after his death she married a Frank Parker and lived at 2, Brockley Cottages, Charlesfield Road, Horley.

The Commonwealth War Graves website shows that he enlisted at Warrington and served in the South Lancs Regiment but does not state which Battalion. He was later transferred to the Labour Corps.

The 1st Battalion of the South Lancs spent the war on garrison duty in Quetta, Baluchistan, on the North-West Frontier. The 2nd Battalion spent the entire war on the Western Front. The 3rd (Reserve) Battalion was a depot and training battalion stationed in Lancashire throughout the war.

It seems possible that, because of his age, Robert may have been in the 3rd Battalion and stayed in the UK.

We do not know the circumstances of his transfer to a Labour Corps unit. Military labour units were the poor relations of the Army. In November 1918 there were 325 Labour Corps Companies in Britain – almost 173,000 men. None of the companies kept War Diaries and there are almost no other references to them in other Army records. Although the Labour Corps kept its own records these were destroyed by German bombing in 1940.

Robert died in Birmingham on 14 July 1918, aged about 52 and is buried at Birmingham (Lodge Hill) Cemetery.

The cause of his death is not known but it is possible that he was a victim of the influenza epidemic which spread across the world in 1918, though this was mainly a 'young person's disease'.

Glasgow was the first British city to be affected, in May and within weeks the illness had spread south, reaching London by June. During the next few months, 228,000 people died in Britain.

THOMAS PARSONS

Private M/225647 Army Service Corps Attached 258th Siege Battery,
Ammunition Column Royal Garrison Artillery

Thomas Parsons was born in about 1885 near Storrington in Sussex. The 1891 census shows him as a boarder with Mark and Martha Harden at West Chiltington so his birth family cannot be traced though it is likely that Martha Harden was his aunt.

In 1901 he was still living at the same address and was employed as a market garden labourer.

Thomas married Ethel Wright in 1909 and two years later was working as a carman for a laundry. They had at least one child, a daughter named Gladys, and lived at 70 St Mary's Road, Reigate.

By the time he enlisted at Guildford, Thomas and Ethel were living at 'Buleigh', Lee Street, Horley.

No service record survives for Thomas and his medal index card contains no useful information.

Siege Batteries RGA were equipped with heavy howitzers, sending large calibre high explosive shells in high trajectory fire. As British artillery tactics developed, the Siege Batteries were most often employed in destroying or neutralising the enemy artillery, as well as putting destructive fire down on strongpoints, dumps, stores, and roads and railways behind enemy lines.

258th Siege Battery were part of the 64th Heavy Artillery Group (First Army) and supported the 2nd Canadian Division at the battle for Vimy Ridge in April 1917.

As a member of the Army Service Corps, Thomas would have been involved in the movement of ammunition and supplies for the 258th Siege Battery.

The circumstances of Thomas' death cannot be ascertained but it may be that he was wounded and evacuated, as he died, probably in a base hospital, on 25 October 1917, aged 32, and is buried at Etaples Military Cemetery.

EDWIN PAYNE

Private 727325, 4th Canadian Mounted Rifles

Edwin Payne was born at Arundel, Sussex, in 1895. He was one of six children born to Thomas and Alice Payne and grew up in Copthorne. By 1911 the family lived at 5 Kitsbridge Cottages, Copthorne but may have moved to Horley later.

In March 1914 Edwin sailed for Canada, possibly with the intention of emigrating permanently. He lived with his uncle, John Illman, in Ontario, where he worked as a farm labourer and learned to be a fireman.

Attesting into the 110th Battalion on 29 December 1915, in Stratford, Ontario, Edwin later found himself transferred into the 4th CMR on 22 April 1917.

On 13 May 1917 the 4th CMR were at Villers-au-Bois, north west of Arras, as Divisional Reserve, spending the time through to the 20th on training in extended order and physical and arms drill, interspersed with concerts and sports. Later they moved to Toronto Camp where they were harassed by hostile aircraft and had to mount Lewis guns for defence.

It was during a baseball game on 26 May 1917 that one of the soldiers, Private McCabe, sought to clear some military debris from their makeshift diamond. He picked up a "blind" (dud) shell, which subsequently went off killing him instantly as well as 8 other men and wounding 10 more.

Edwin Payne, aged 22, who was initially wounded, died later on 18 June 1917, in hospital in Etaples.

Edwin is buried in Etaples Military Cemetery, and is one of 14 men of the 4th CMR known to lie at rest there.

ERNEST PEACH

Gunner 68779, 'A' Battery, 158th Brigade, Royal Field Artillery

Ernest Alfred Peach was born in Catsfield, Sussex in 1888, one of five children, to William and Mercy Peach. William was a gamekeeper and by 1901 had moved with the family to Keepers Cottage, Langshott, Horley. By the end of the war they had moved again to 'Oakdene', Church Road, Horley.

On the 1911 census Ernest is shown as having followed his father's profession and he had become a gamekeeper at Faygate, near Horsham.

Ernest enlisted at Chichester, probably in answer to Lord Kitchener's famous appeal and joined the Royal Field Artillery.

His service record is not available but his medal card states that he was sent to France on 28 August 1915.

158th Brigade, Royal Field Artillery served as Divisional Artillery with 14th (Light) Division which was formed as part of Kitchener's First New Army. They fought in the Action of Hooge, being the first division to be attacked by flamethrowers and were also in action at the second attack on Bellewaarde.

In 1916 they were on the Somme seeing action in the Battle of Delville Wood and the Battle of Flers-Courcelette. They left 14th Division on 7 January 1917.

A Battery then became part of 158th Army Field Artillery Brigade where it became C Battery.

In early summer 1918 the battery was in action north of Bethune and by early June had moved to Givenchy where their time in action was interspersed with rest at Houchin.

Ernest was killed in that area on 12 June 1918, aged 30, and is buried at Houchin British Cemetery which is about 3.5 miles south of Bethune.

GEORGE PEPPIATT

Rifleman 372621, 8th (City of London) Battalion, London Regiment,
(Post Office Rifles)

George William Peppiatt was born in Horley in 1891 to George and Elizabeth Peppiatt.

The 1901 census shows George (described as nephew) living with his grandfather, John Peppiatt and his married aunt, Hannah, at 121 Cromwell Road, Redhill. Two more of John's daughters lived next door.

By 1911 he was employed as a monumental mason and still living in the same household though they had moved along the road to number 174.

In 1916 he married Clara Lewis and lived with her at 34 High Street, Redhill, which was the address given for Clara after the war.

No service record survives for George but it seems likely that he enlisted at Redhill late in 1916, though it may have been sooner.

The 8th Battalion, London Regiment, were sent to France in March 1915 as part of the 140th Brigade, 47th Division. The Brigade was in action throughout the Battle of the Somme in 1916, notably at High Wood, the Transloy Ridges and the Butte de Warlencourt.

In 1917 the Division was part of the British assault at Arras. The Canadians captured Vimy Ridge and the British forces made significant gains astride the Scarpe river. Following these initial successes, British forces engaged in a series of small-scale operations to consolidate the newly won positions. Although these battles were generally successful in achieving limited aims, they were gained at the price of a large number of casualties.

It seems that George was wounded near the village of Bullecourt during this series of actions.

He died of his wounds on 19 May 1917, aged 26, and is buried at Achiet-le-Grand Communal Cemetery Extension which is about 10 miles south of Arras.

The original grave marker for G W Peppiatt at Achiet-le-Grand. This gives his unit as 2nd Battalion Post Office Rifles though his CWGC details state that he was in the 8th Battalion.
(Courtesy of Mr P Schultze.)

KENNETH PERRY

2nd Lieutenant, 11th Battalion, Royal Sussex Regiment

Kenneth George Perry was born in Croydon in 1883 to Charles and Caroline Perry and attended Whitgift School. By 1901 the family had moved to Chipstead and Kenneth was training to be a Railway Surveyor. Charles and Caroline later moved to 'Hazleglen', Russells Crescent, Horley.

The 1911 census shows Kenneth as a visitor with the Bruckshaw family at Exning, near Newmarket, and he married Dorothy Bruckshaw there in 1914. Dorothy returned there after his death.

No service record exists for Kenneth but his medal card shows that he enlisted as a Private in The London Regiment. It is possible that he rose through the ranks as NCO's were killed and was posted to the Royal Sussex when he was commissioned.

The 11th Royal Sussex was part of 116th Brigade, 39th Division and arrived in France in March 1916. On 30 June 1916 they were engaged in an attack to divert attention from the battle of the Somme due to start the next day. Over a period of less than five hours, three Battalions of The Royal Sussex lost 17 officers and 349 men killed. A further 1000 men were wounded or taken prisoner. In the regimental history this is known as 'The Day Sussex Died'.

Following reinforcements, the Brigade fought in the Somme campaign, notably at Thiepval Ridge and this lead into the Battle of the Ancre which began early in October and lasted for six weeks.

One of the strongest German positions was the Schwaben Redoubt which was attacked on 9 October. On 16 October the 116th Brigade took over the Redoubt, which was heavily shelled.

It was in this period that Kenneth was wounded and evacuated to a Casualty Clearing Station.

He died of his wounds on 1 November 1916, aged 33, and is buried at Puchevillers Cemetery which is about 12 miles north east of Amiens.

ALEC PESCUD

Private 1455, 22nd Battalion, Royal Fusiliers

Alec Joseph Pescud (his birth was registered as Joseph Alec) was born in 1895 in Croydon, one of six children, to Joseph and Amelia Pescud.

By 1901 the family were living in Queens Road, Horley and Alec and his brothers attended Horley Infant School.

Alec and his older brother, Percy (who was also to die), were, by 1911, employed at the Monotype works in Salfords where Alec operated a drilling machine, and the family had moved to 10 St Johns Terrace Road, Earlswood.

Alec enlisted at Shepherds Bush in 1915 and after his basic training, was sent to France, landing at Boulogne on 16 November 1915.

22nd Royal Fusiliers were part of 99th Brigade, 2nd Division. This was an all Fusilier Brigade made up of the 17th, 22nd, 23rd and 24th Battalions.

Alec arrived too late to see action in the Battle of Loos but in the early part of 1916 the 22nd Royal Fusiliers were in and out of the line in that general area, to the east and south of Bethune.

In February they were in the line at this location and it seems likely that Alec was killed here during a relatively quiet period.

He was killed in action on 11 February 1916, aged 20, and is buried in Veille-Chappelle New Military Cemetery which is about five miles north east of Bethune.

This cemetery contains graves from several other cemeteries that were gathered together after the Armistice and it is possible that Alec was originally interred elsewhere.

PERCY PESCUD

Private 1779, 9th Battalion, East Surrey Regiment

Percy Robert Pescud was born in Croydon in 1893, one of six children to Joseph and Amelia Pescud.

By 1901 the family were living in Queens Road, Horley.

Percy and his younger brother, Alec (who was also to die), were, by 1911, employed at the Monotype works in Salfords where Percy operated a milling machine. By this time the family had moved to 10 St Johns Terrace Road, Earlswood.

Percy enlisted at Redhill in 1915 and after his basic training was posted to France... just in time to take his place in the front line at The Battle of Loos.

9th Battalion, The East Surrey Regiment was part of 72nd Brigade in 24th Division. They proceeded to France and landed at Boulogne on 1 September 1915. The Division concentrated in the area between Etaples and St Pol on 4 September and a few days later marched across France for the British assault at Loos, going into action on 26 September. Together with the 8th Royal West Kents they formed part of the firing line of 72nd Brigade.

The attack was launched at 11 a.m. and was carried right up to the enemy trenches. Because the artillery bombardment had failed to cut the enemy barbed wire, it was impossible to get through the enemy lines, although several fruitless attempts were made.

The casualties were very heavy at this point chiefly owing to some machine guns which formed a heavy cross fire on our men.

The Germans continued to shell very heavily until about 5 pm in the afternoon and many of the slightly wounded were wounded again or killed.

The battalion casualties numbered 14 Officers and 438 other ranks.

Percy was killed in this action on 26 September 1915, aged 22. He has no known grave and is commemorated on the Loos Memorial that forms part of Dud Corner Cemetery, which is 3 miles north west of Lens.

JOSEPH REEVES

Private G/24608 'B' Coy, 17th Battalion, Royal Fusiliers

Joseph Basil Reeves was born in Weybridge in 1892 to Joseph and Alice Reeves. A few years later Joseph senior died and Alice remarried. She became Alice Martin and later came to live at 'Oakhurst', Lee Street, Horley.

By 1911 Joseph was a salesman in a grocery business in Islington.

When he enlisted at Ealing, probably in 1915, Joseph gave a west Ealing address and joined the Royal Fusiliers.

No service record exists for Joseph and his medal card gives no useful information, though it does not mention the award of a 1915 star. This suggests that he did not arrive in France until 1916.

17th Royal Fusiliers were part of the 5th Brigade, 2nd Division and were in action at Delville Wood in the Battle of the Somme, where they sustained heavy casualties. The British attempts to capture this vital feature began about the middle of July and continued until early September.

On 13 November 1916, as part of 5th Army, the 17th Royal Fusiliers were in actiion during a renewed attack on the slopes either side of the River Ancre. In wet and foggy weather, the 2nd Division advanced along Redan Ridge. The 5th Brigade on the right formed up in no man's land and two battalions reached Beaumont Trench on schedule. By 7:30 a.m. the 5th Brigade was ready to advance on the second objective but reached Frankfurt Trench so depleted, that the troops fell back to Munich Trench, Wagon Road then Crater Lane in the German front line.

The 17th Royal Fusiliers lost 187 men in this attack.

It was in this action that Joseph Reeves was killed. He died on 13 November 1916, aged 24, and he is buried in Munich Trench British Cemetery, Beaumont Hamel which is just north east of the village.

Along with Arthur Turner, Joseph has the distinction of being named on both Horley and Charlwood War Memorials.

ARCHIBALD REMNANT

Driver 20808 9th Field Company, Royal Engineers

Archibald Remnant was born in 1893 at Petworth, Sussex to Charles and Sarah Remnant. He grew up at Piltdown Lodge, Fletching, near Uckfield, with an older brother and two older sisters.

Archibald's service record, although badly burned during the London Blitz, shows us that he enlisted as a reservist at Guildford on 26 November 1910. It confirms that he was a stableman at the Prince Albert Inn, Salfords (now a McDonalds burger bar) and that his family home was at 4 Dunraven Avenue, Salfords.

When his service expired, he immediately re-enlisted and was amongst the first troops to arrive in France with the BEF on 23 August 1914.

9th Field Company were amongst the Divisional Troops of the 4th Division and arrived in France in time to play a major role in the Battle of Le Cateau during the retreat from Mons.

They supported the front line troops during many of the major actions throughout the whole of the war, including at Messines, Ypres, the Somme and the Scarpe.

The Scarpe action began early in April 1917 and the Field Companies of the Royal Engineers were involved with tunnelling, entrenching and the preparation of defensive positions.

As a driver, Archie would have been tasked with the delivery of materials for all these activities.

It would seem that Archibald was seriously wounded at this time and evacuated to 42nd Casualty Clearing Station.

He died of his wounds on 30 April 1917, aged 23, and is buried at Aubigny Communal Cemetery which is about 8 miles north west of Arras.

HENRY RICHARDS

Private 71932, 29th Battalion, The Middlesex Regiment.

Henry George Richards was born in 1875 but neither his birthplace nor his early family details can be ascertained.

He married Sarah Mitchell in 1898 and they lived at 127 Albert Road, Horley, with their three children, Albert, Ethel and Martha.

Although he was employed as a bricklayer, which implies a reasonable level of fitness, Henry was classified medically as B1, and had 'a slight cough' when he joined up on 3 November 1916.

The 29th Middlesex were raised in June 1916 as a 'Works' Battalion and Henry may have been posted to this unit because of his age or generally poor fitness.

In April 1917 the 29th Middlesex were transferred to The Labour Corps as the 5th Labour Battalion.

The Corps always suffered from its treatment as something of a second class organisation: for example, the men who died are commemorated under their original regiment, with Labour Corps being secondary. Researching men of the Corps is made extra difficult by this, as is the fact that few records remain of the daily activities and locations of Corps units.

Henry was hospitalised in the City of London Hospital at Victoria Park and was discharged from the army at Hounslow on 9 June 1917 as being unfit for further military duties. He appears to have returned to Horley. His discharge papers show him to have been of good character but suffering from tuberculosis.

He died on 6 October 1917, aged 42, and is buried in St Bartholomews Churchyard, Horley.

His wife applied for an army pension and, early in 1918, was asked if he could attend for a medical. She replied that he was already dead and buried. A small pension was awarded for his children but was only payable from the date of his discharge until his death.

FRANK ROFFEY

Private T/206700, 2nd/4th Battalion, The Queens
(Royal West Surrey) Regiment

Frank Roffey was born in Redhill in 1895. He was the eldest of four children born to Albert and Fanny Roffey and lived at 51, St Johns Road, Earlswood.

On the 1911 census Frank is recorded as having been employed as an errand boy.

He enlisted at Reigate as a Territorial (T prefix on number) though it is not known when. No service record survives for Frank and his medal card has little useful information. It does not, however, record the award of a 1914 or 1915 Star and this suggests that he did not see active service until at least 1916.

2nd/4th Queens were part of General Allenby's Army fighting the Turkish Army in what was then Palestine. In 1917, as part of 160th Brigade, 53rd Division, they took part in actions against the Turkish forces through the areas of Gaza, Beersheeba and Tell Khuweilfe and the capture of Jerusalem.

Following the capture of Jerusalem early in December, 2nd/4th Queens were heavily engaged in preventing the Turks from regaining the city and fought continuous defensive actions around it's boundary for the next few weeks.

On the morning of 27 December, the enemy launched heavy attacks preceded by accurate artillery bombardments, against the defenders. Although they inflicted heavy casualties on the Turkish forces, the 2nd/4th Queens also suffered badly and were withdrawn from the line at about midday.

Frank was killed in this action as well as 34 other soldiers. He died on 27 December 1917, aged 22 and is buried in the Jerusalem Military Cemetery which is just north of the walled city near the Mount of Olives.

ALFRED ROSER

Private 99735, 7th Battalion, The Kings (Liverpool) Regiment

Alfred Roser, born at Ewhurst in 1882, was the younger of the two sons of George and Ellen Roser. He married Emma Jane King in 1904 and early 1911 they were living at New Road, Ewhurst with their two children and Alfred earned his living as a Hay Trusser.

The family may have moved to Horley before the war began, as this is where he enlisted, initially into the Royal Fusiliers, but later being transferred to 7th Kings.

No service record survives for Alfred but it seems likely that he did not see service overseas before 1916.

7th Kings were part of 165th Brigade, 55th Division and spent the early part of 1917 in the Ypres Salient where they took huge casualties. At the battle for Pilkem Ridge at the end of July the Division sustained around 3500 casualties and, after being reinforced, at the Menin Road another 2700 men became casualties.

Following a disastrous performance in the line in November 1917, the Division was withdrawn from the area for intensive reinforcement and training.

By February 1918 they were back in action at Festubert and Givenchy. In early April the defence of Givenchy was to become the single most famous action that the Division fought. Afterwards, it was publicly stated by an officer of the German General Staff that the stand made by the Division on 9 April and the days which followed marked the final ruination of the supreme German effort of 1918.

By the end of September 1918 the Division were preparing to join in the final Allied advance and it was during this period that Alfred was killed.

He died on 27 September 1918, aged 36, and is buried at Queant Communal Cemetery Extension which is in the village of that name about 8 miles north east of Bapaume.

DONALD RUSSELL

Guardsman 23700, 3rd Battalion, Grenadier Guards

Donald Russell was born in Horley in 1892 to John and Alice Russell. He was one of three children and the family lived at 32 Lumley Road, Horley.

By 1911 the family were still at the same address and Donald had followed his father's occupation and was working as a shoeing blacksmith.

Donald enlisted at Kingston probably in 1915. His medal card shows that he did not serve overseas in 1914 or 1915.

3rd Grenadier Guards arrived in France in mid 1915 and came under the command of 2nd Guards Brigade, Guards Division.

The Battle of the Somme commenced on the 1 July 1916 but the Grenadiers did not arrive until the middle of August and Donald would certainly have been with 3rd Grenadier Guards at this time. At the beginning of September, they undertook a period of training at Morlancourt with the rest of the Brigade and marched to Happy Valley camp on 9 September. Three days later, the Brigade marched to Carnoy before moving into the reserve front line positions ready to make an assault towards the village of Flers.

On the night of the 13 September all surplus kit – packs, greatcoats etc – were sent to the divisional stores at Meaulte and bombs, sandbags, flares and tools were issued to the men for the coming attack. Movement began towards the assembly area, which was the best available, though it had the disadvantage of causing the troops to line up at the wrong angle relative to their proposed line of advance.

It was on this day, 14 September 1916, whilst preparing for this attack, that Donald was killed, aged 23. He is buried in Guards Cemetery, Lesboeufs, which is about half a mile south west of this village, and is about 4 miles dead south of Bapaume.

The Guards Cemetery, Lesboufs, where Donald Russell is buried.

ALBAN SCOLLICK

Driver T/2348, 1st/3rd Kent Field Company, Royal Engineers

Alban Vincent Scollick was born at Denmark Hill, London in 1889 to Joseph and Florence Scollick and was one of seven children.

Joseph was a railway signalman and the family moved regularly. By 1901 they were living in Railway Cottages, Warnham Station, near Horsham and in 1911 lived at Railway Cottages, Brook Road, Earlswood, by which time Alban was a boot repairer. Sometime later, the family moved again to 102 Earlsbrook Road, Redhill.

No information is available regarding Alban's enlistment but he was certainly a Territorial Army soldier.

The 1st/3rd Kent Field Company were founded by Sir David Lionel Salomons (1851–1925) of Tunbridge Wells, Kent. He was the Honorary Colonel of the Kent Royal Engineers.

Royal Engineers were required in the Dardanelles to fill vacancies, no doubt caused by the appalling losses there.

The company had a farewell dinner on 11 October 1915 and were cheered by crowds, including their relatives, as they left for Devonport dockyard.

They sailed to the Dardanelles via Malta where they were allocated two ships, HMS *Redbreast* and HMS *Hythe,* for the final leg of their journey. The 1/3rd were allocated to HMS *Hythe.* On 28 October 1915 the *Hythe* left Mudros at 4pm and had 50 miles to go to Cape Helles.

The ship was travelling in a darkened state to avoid enemy bombardment. At about 8pm there was a warning that another ship was bearing down on them. This other ship was HMS *Sarnia.* She was much larger than *Hythe* and struck her almost head on. HMS *Hythe* sank into a cold sea in just 10 minutes.

129 members of 1st/3rd Company were lost in this disaster and Alban was amongst them.

Alban Scollick died on 28 October 1915, aged 27, and is commemorated on the Helles Memorial, Cape Helles, Gallipoli.

ALEC SHOUBRIDGE

Private D/5909 4th Dragoon Guards (Royal Irish)

Alec John Shoubridge was born at Horsham in 1894, one of five children, to William and Hannah Shoubridge. The family lived at Slaugham for some years but by 1911, were at 1 Andrews Cottages, Southwater, near Horsham. Alec was employed as a butcher's boy. He gave an unknown Horley address on enlistment.

Alec joined the army as a regular soldier because his medal card shows him as being sent to France on 16 August 1914, and he may well have been present when, at dawn on Saturday 22 August 1914, C Squadron of the 4th Royal Irish Dragoon Guards, pushed out two patrols north from Mons towards Soignies and met the Germans for the first time. C Squadron commenced a reconnaissance along the road heading out from Maisières. Four enemy cavalrymen of the 2nd Kuirassiers emerged from the direction of Casteau. They were spotted by the British and turned around, whereupon they were pursued and engaged.

There were other cavalry encounters with the enemy in the areas of La Louvière and Binche, and the 4th were also engaged at the Battle of Le Cateau and subsequent rearguard actions.

4th Dragoon Guards were part of the 1st Cavalry Division and although trained as mounted troops, were frequently used as infantry. They were used in both roles and were engaged in trench warfare at the first Battle of Ypres and through the winter of 1914/15.

This was a relatively quiet period between the First and Second Battles of Ypres. The German Army mounted several determined assaults in early March and their artillery continued to bombard the allied lines and the city of Ypres.

It was during this period that Alec sustained the wounds that led to his death on 24 April 1915, aged 21, and he is buried in Duhallow Cemetery, which is on the site of an Advanced Dressing Station on the Diksmuidseweg in Ypres.

ERNEST SMITH

Midshipman, HMS Queen Mary, *Royal Navy*

Ernest Cecil Peirson Smith was born at Wandsworth in 1897 to Ernest and Maud Smith. They lived at 31 Spencer Park, Wandsworth.

By 1911 Ernest was a student at HMS *Worcester* preparing for entry into the Royal Navy and was commissioned as a midshipman on 7 August 1913.

He was posted to HMS *Queen Mary,* a newly built battle-cruiser, and part of the 1st Battle Cruiser Squadron. Ernest would have been present at the Battles of Heligoland Bight and Dogger Bank.

Off Jutland, Denmark, on 31 May 1916, Admiral Beatty's battlecruisers, supported by battleships of the 5th Battle Squadron, encountered Admiral Hipper's German Fleet at 2:28pm. At 4.10pm Beatty's flagship, HMS *Lion* came under fire from extreme range. At the same time, HMS *Queen Mary* came under heavy fire from at least two German cruisers. For about five minutes she withstood it gallantly. Twice she had been straddled by shells from the *Derfflinger,* when at 4.26pm a plunging salvo crashed upon her forward deck. In a moment there was a dazzling flash of red flame where the salvo fell, and then a much heavier explosion rent her amidships. Her bows plunged down and she disappeared. There was nothing of her left but a vast, dark pillar of smoke.

Beatty famously turned to his flag captain, saying, "Chatfield, there seems to be something wrong with our bloody ships today."

Both the Germans and the British claimed victory in this Battle. The Germans claimed to have won because they sank more ships, (14–11), and the British because the German High Seas Fleet would never again venture from their ports for the rest of the war.

British losses were 6,784 men in this action including 57 Officers and 1209 men of Queen Mary's crew, Ernest being amongst them.

Ernest Cecil Peirson Smith died on 31 May 1916, aged 20. He is commemorated on the Portsmouth Naval Memorial.

The destruction of HMS Queen Mary *on 31 May 1916 in which Ernest Smith was killed*

RALPH SOTHAM

Lieutenant, 1 Squadron RFC and 5th Battalion Queens Own
(Royal West Kent) Regiment

Ralph Clifford Sotham was born at Horley in 1895 to George and Amelia Sotham. He was one of six children and the family lived at Hatchgates, Massetts Road, Horley.

By 1911 he was a boarder at Tonbridge Grammar School.

No service record is available for Ralph and his medal card gives no useful information. The 1st/5th Battalion of the Queens Own were in India throughout the war and it is more likely that Ralph was in the 2nd/5th Battalion which was in reserve in Kent for much of the first half of the war.

The reason for, or the date of, Ralphs transfer to the RFC is not known but the glamour of the new service must have been attractive to young officers and far more appealing than a short life in the trenches on the Western Front.

1 Squadron crossed to France in March 1915, equipped with a mixture of Avro 504s and Royal Aircraft Factory B.E.8s and were based at Baillieul. It operated mainly in the reconnaissance role, with a few single seat fighters for escort purposes. By the time of the Battle of Arras in 1917, the squadron had amassed a total of 200 enemy aircraft claimed as destroyed.

An Avro 504 as flown by Ralph Sotham.

By the beginning of 1918 aeroplanes had become a little more robust than those of 1914. Nevertheless, they were still held together by little more than wire and strong glue. Accidents were frequent, especially on take-off and landing. Anti-aircraft fire (known as Ack-Ack or Archie to the pilots) was a constant threat once they were airborne.

The exact circumstances of Ralph Sothams death are not known. He died on 9 January 1918, aged 23, and is commemorated on the Arras Flying Services Memorial. This can be found in the Faubourg-d'Amiens Cemetery on the Boulevard du General de Gaulle in the western part of the town of Arras.

A memorial tablet is displayed in St Bartholomews Church, Horley and states that he was killed in action in Flanders.

The Arras Flying Services memorial where Ralph Sotham is commemorated.

SYDNEY SOUTHGATE

Private 59929, 3rd Battalion, Northamptonshire Regiment

Sydney George Southgate was born in 1900 at Chesham, Buckinghamshire. By 1901 his parents, Alfred and Ellen Southgate, were living at Grange Lodge, a property which was a coachman's accommodation and part of The Oaks in Bonehurst Road, Horley.

On the 1911 census, the family are shown at Brookside, Copthorne and Sydney, who was still at school had a younger brother and sister. Later, they moved again to Allingham Farm, Copthorne and this is the address given by Sydney when he enlisted.

Sydney joined the Northamptonshire Regiment at Brighton in July 1918. He had completed his basic training and been posted to E Company, 3rd Battalion at Scrapsgate, Sheppey, where they were part of the Thames and Medway Garrison.

Whilst providing a military presence close to the vital Naval dockyard at Sheerness, the garrison here also acted as an assembly point and training establishment for men who were being prepared for shipment to France. When the battalions had sufficient men to make up a draft to replace men killed at the front, they shipped them out and started to train up the next intake.

Sydney may have been awaiting a posting to a front line battalion when he was struck down by the influenza epidemic which swept the world in 1918/19.

He was taken to Broadway Military Hospital at Sheerness and died there eight days later.

Sydney died of pneumonia caused by influenza on 22 November 1918, aged 18.

He is buried in St Bartholomews Churchyard, Horley.

CHARLES STANDING

Private 204443, 12th Battalion, East Surrey Regiment

Charles William Standing was born in 1899, one of three children, to Jesse and Emily Standing and lived at South Villa, Balcombe Road, Horley. He worshiped at Horley Baptist Church and is commemorated on a plaque inside the church.

Charles enlisted into the 5th Reserve East Surrey Regiment at Redhill in June 1917 and states that he was employed as a grocer's assistant.

After his basic training at Tonbridge, Charles was posted to the 12th Battalion and joined them in France on 7 April 1918.

12th East Surreys had recently returned to the Western Front after a period of action in Italy and, as part of 122nd Brigade, 31st Division, were in the line around Ypres when Charles joined them.

Although this was a generally quiet period, it was punctuated by ferocious trench raids by both sides and continuous heavy artillery exchanges.

It appears that Charles was wounded on 29 June. He was admitted to a Field Ambulance unit and then to 36 Casualty Clearing Station. He was not fit to return to his unit until 27 July.

The 12th Battalion were in the line at La Clytte and their war diary states for the 16 August 1918:

"Situation normal during the day – active at night. During the night our front system of posts was attacked by raiding party but they were successfully driven off by machine gun fire and bombs. The attack was launched under heavy bombardment".

It was on this day, 16 August 1918 that Charles Standing died, aged 19. His body was never identified so it is likely that he was killed by an artillery explosion. He is commemorated on the Tyne Cot Memorial which is five miles north east of Ypres.

He is one of 35,000 unidentified soldiers commemorated on this memorial.

CHRISTOPHER STEER

Private 42056, 2nd Battalion, Worcester Regiment

Christopher Steer was born at Lower Beeding, Sussex, in 1891 to Albert and Edith Steer. He had five sisters and two brothers and they grew up on several farms where his father was a labourer.

Later the family moved to Jobs Cottage in New House Lane, Horley.

Christopher enlisted at Guildford, probably on the outbreak of war, and was originally drafted into the Army Service Corps as a driver. He was posted to France in February 1915. The mere fact that he survived until 1918 suggests that he may have spent most of his service in the ASC. He was later transferred to 2nd Worcesters.

The 2nd Worcesters were part of 100th Brigade, 33rd Division and fought in several major actions throughout 1917, including the Battles of Menin Road and Polygon Wood.

On 10 April 1918, the German Fourth Army attacked north of Armentières with four divisions and broke through to capture Messines. By 11 April, the British situation was desperate. It was on this day that Field Marshall Haig issued his famous "Backs to the wall" order forbidding further retreat.

As fighting moved towards Hazebrouck, the British 5th and 33rd Divisions were brought in to strengthen the line, but by 15 April the Germans had taken Bailleul despite increased British resistance.

It seems likely that Christopher was wounded during these engagements. He was evacuated to a Casualty Clearing Station near Mendinghem. The next CCS was at Bandaghem and another was not far away at Dozinghem, so these aid posts became known to soldiers as Dosing'em, Bandaging'em and Mending'em.

Christopher Steer died of his wounds on 18 April 1918, aged 26.

He is buried in Mendinghem Military Cemetery which is about four and a half miles north west of Poperinghe.

GEORGE STEER

Private 2523, 1st Battalion, East Surrey Regiment

George Walter Steer was born in 1898 at Merstham to Walter and Elizabeth Steer. His father re married after Elizabeth died, and, with his second wife, Gertrude and George's two younger sisters, was living at 2 Masons Bridge Road, Salfords by the time of the 1911 census.

At some later date the family moved to 71 Earlswood Road, Redhill. George enlisted at Redhill, probably in early 1915 and was in a draft to France on 31 August. Although 1st East Surreys was a regular battalion, many of the pre-war regulars had gone and the regular battalions themselves were often largely composed of new recruits.

They were part of 95th Brigade, 5th Division and early in 1916 were in several actions around Vimy Ridge and Arras.

The Battalion saw action on the Somme at High Wood, Guillemont and the Transloy Ridges and were finally moved into a quieter position near Festubert in October.

In 1917 the Division was engaged throughout the Battles of Arras and the Third Battle of Ypres.

Early in 1918 the 5th Division were moved to Italy in an effort to stiffen Italian resistance but were hurriedly recalled to France in April, in time to take part in the Battles of the Lys.

There followed a period of 'relatively quiet' trench warfare with the 1st East Surreys in the general area of Tannay, south west of Hazebrouck.

On 28 June 1918 1st East Surreys were tasked with an assault on enemy lines near Tannay, which was carried out with no casualties except for two men killed whilst carrying ammunition for the 95th Trench Mortar Battery.

One of these men was George Steer. He was killed on 28 June 1918, aged 20. He has no known grave and is commemorated on the Ploegsteert Memorial which is situated about seven miles south of Ypres.

ALBERT STEVENSON

Able Seaman J/43488(PO), HMS Pembroke, *Royal Navy*

Albert Frederick Stevenson was born at Redhill in 1900 to Frederick and Emily Stevenson. The family lived at Lingfield for some years and later on moved to 20 Chestnut Road, Horley where they were living when Albert enlisted.

The date of Albert's enlistment is not known and details of his service are not available, although burial transcripts at St Bartholomews Church state that he served in HMS *Chester* alongside Boy Jack Cornwell V.C. at the Battle of Jutland in 1916.

The *Chester* was nearest to the enemy, and at 5.27 her commander, Captain R. N. Lawson, hearing the sound of guns to the south-westward, turned in that direction to investigate. Soon, he could see a three-funnelled cruiser with some destroyers crossing ahead of him. In a minute or two, the *Chester* was smothered in bursting shells. Within five minutes she had three of her guns disabled and the majority of the gun crews were lying dead or wounded. With only her after-gun in action, she turned away north-eastward at utmost speed, dodging the salvoes like a snipe. During this action, although mortally wounded, John Cornwell, aged 16, remained standing alone at a most exposed post, quietly awaiting orders, until the end of the action, with the gun's crew dead and wounded around him. He was awarded the Victoria Cross.

At the time of his death Albert was attached to HMS *Pembroke* which was the main Royal Naval Barracks at Chatham and it is possible that he was awaiting a posting when he died.

One source says that Albert's death was caused by something "other than disease, accident or enemy action" but the list of Royal Navy WWI casualties states that he was drowned. If this is the case, it was almost certainly an accident, though influenza is also a possibility.

The circumstances of his death are thus unclear.

What is certain, is that he died on 20 September 1918, aged 19, and is buried in St Bartholomews Churchyard, Horley.

WILLIAM STILL

Private103413, 10th Battalion, Sherwood Foresters

(Notts and Derby Regiment)

William Alfred Still was born in Bristol in 1899 to Edward and Minnie Still.

He enlisted at Redhill in April 1917, giving his occupation as a stable lad and his address as 82 Albert Road, Horley, but he was not called up until October.

His basic training saw him pass through training camps at Clipstone and Brocton, and he was posted to France in April 1918.

10th Sherwoods were part of 51st Brigade of the 17th (Northern) Division. They were heavily involved in many of the major actions throughout the spring and summer of 1918.

At about 2.15am on 15 August the enemy started a very heavy gas bombardment on the whole area occupied by the 17th Division; mustard gas predominated. The casualties from the gas poisoning steadily mounted up, and long strings of men with their eyes bandaged, each holding the man in front, trailed slowly backwards down to the dressing station. The battalion sustained losses of 18 officers and 510 other ranks; a total which for the moment made it almost cease to exist as a fighting unit but the large majority of these casualties subsequently recovered.

William was almost certainly amongst them.

The battalion recovered in time to mount an attack on Flers and Gueudecourt at the end of August.

By the 19 September the Division had advanced further eastwards and on this day William received shrapnel wounds to his back and abdomen. He was evacuated by 53rd Field Ambulance unit to No 3 Casualty Clearing Station but he died three days later.

William Still died of his wounds on 22 September 1918, aged 19, and is buried at Thilloy Road Cemetery, Beaulencourt which is about one and a half miles south of Bapaume.

ALBERT STRINGER

Private G/13250, 7th Battalion, The Buffs (East Kent Regiment)

Bert Stringer was born as Bertie Hawk in 1892. His mother, Emma Hawk became the housekeeper to William Stringer at 3 Balcombe Road, Horley, and Bert, and his four sisters, took his name. It appears that William and Emma were later married.

Bert enlisted at Kenley into the 12th Lancers on 27 November 1915 and was mobilised in February 1916. His attestation papers give his occupation as a Gardener. He was posted to the Cavalry Reserve but in November 1916 was transferred into The Buffs joining 7th Battalion on 2 December.

The battalion alternated between being in the trenches at Fransu, St Pierre Divion, and Acheux, and being in billets at the rear for training. When practice grenades were not available for training, they used turnips, with nails stuck into them to represent the pin.

Early in 1917 the Battalion found itself back in the old Somme battle area and Bert would have fought in the actions at Miraumont in February and been involved in the capture of Irles.

The British captured Irles on the morning of 10 March 1917. Previous to the attack, their howitzers had deluged the place with shells. In a sunken ravine the British found a small garrison of old men with machine guns. Here, thirty prisoners were taken and the rest killed. The British swept on over the German trenches, meeting with very little opposition.

Towards the end of April British troops engaged upon the Third Battle of the Scarpe and Bert was killed during attempts to capture the village of Fresnoy.

Bert Stringer was posted as missing, presumed killed, on 3 May 1917, aged 26. His body was never recovered for burial and he is commemorated on the Arras Memorial, which is in the Faubourg-d'Amiens Cemetery in the Boulevard du General de Gaulle in the western part of the town of Arras.

ALBERT STRUDWICK

Lance Corporal 6672, 8th Battalion, The Queens
(Royal West Surrey) Regiment

Albert Daniel Strudwick was born at Redhill in 1894 to Henry and Jane Strudwick and was one of ten children. The family lived at 2 Prince Albert Cottages, Earlswood.

Albert left his employment as a farm labourer and enlisted at Guildford just at the outbreak of the war. After a spell of training and home duty he arrived in France in October 1915 in a draft to replace men lost at the Battle of Loos.

At the start of 1916, the 24th Division, including the 8th Queens, moved north toward the Ypres area.

On the night of 29 April 1916 the 8th Queens were subjected to an intense German gas attack supported by infantry, at Wulverghem.

Soon after the Battle of the Somme began in July 1916 they were moved south again.

By 1 September the 8th were in positions consolidating possession of Delville Wood, the scene of bitter fighting from 15 July until its final capture on 25 August. They suffered 143 casualties before they were finally withdrawn from the line on the night of 5/6 September 1916.

Early in 1917 Albert enjoyed two weeks home leave but was hospitalised with tonsillitis soon after he returned. In June he received a shrapnel wound to his right hand and returned to the 8th Queens while they were engaged in the 3rd Battle of Ypres.

In May 1918 Albert was promoted to Lance Corporal.

On 4 July 1918 the 8th Queens were in a relatively quiet sector of the line just west of the old Loos battlefield. Shortly before midnight, the enemy artillery bombarded their front positions with 4.2cms and 7.7cms shells, as well as mortar fire. C Company was in the left front sector and it was here that one man was killed and another injured.

It seems that Albert Strudwick was the man killed and his death is recorded as occurring on 5 July 1918, aged 23.

He is buried at Bully-Grenay Communal Cemetery which is about five miles west of Lens.

THOMAS SWAIN

Private 10112, 2nd Battalion, Seaforth Highlanders

Thomas Arthur Swain was born in 1890 at Plumstead in south east London. His parents were Thomas and Jane Swain and he had five brothers and two sisters. His father was a policeman and the family appears to have moved quite often. In 1911 they were living in Elmers End Road, Beckenham and Thomas worked as a greengrocer's assistant.

The family moved to Horley after 1911 and Thomas's sister, Ethel, married here in 1916.

No service record survives for Thomas but his medal card shows that he arrived in France on 9 December 1915 suggesting that he joined up earlier that year.

He originally joined the Royal Field Artillery and whether he was simply posted to, or applied for a transfer to the Seaforths is not known.

2nd Seaforths arrived in France in August 1914, so by the time Thomas joined them at the end of 1915, few of the 'old soldiers' remained.

In the early part of 1916 they were in and out of the line south west of Arras but in the summer, they were at the Somme as part of the 10th Brigade in the 4th Division.

They attacked near Serre on 1 July and sustained around 350 casualties. Despite this, they were kept in action until reinforced sufficiently to attack again early in October at the Battle for the Transloy Ridges.

Following this engagement, the 2nd Seaforths stayed in the field near Le Transloy. The trenches were in a very bad state with no cover of any kind for officers or men and had been very badly blown in. On 20 October it was bitterly cold. A large working party went out to fill in old trenches just east of Guillemont. The party had 14 casualties owing to some live rounds or a dud shell being struck by a pic or shovel.

Thomas was killed a few days later. He died on the 23 October 1916, aged 26, and is buried in the Guards Cemetery at Lesboeufs which is about half a mile south west of the town.

JAMES SWINDEN

Private 315439, 2nd Battalion, Cheshire Regiment.

James Sidney Swinden (not James Sydney Swindon as on the War Memorial) was born at Charlwood in 1896 to Francis and Fanny Swinden. He had four brothers and a sister and the family lived at 3 Derby Cottages, Lee Street, Horley.

On enlistment at Camberwell, James gave an address at Sydenham but no further information on his service is available.

2nd Cheshires were part of 84th Brigade, 28th Division and were engaged in many of the major actions through 1915 including the second Battle of Ypres and the Battle of Loos.

In October 1915 they were ordered to prepare to move to the Balkan theatre and after travelling via Egypt, arrived in Salonika early in January 1916.

The British Forces dug-in until the summer of 1916, by which time the international force had been reinforced and joined by Serbian, Russian and Italian units. The attempted invasion of Greece by the Bulgarian army in July was repulsed near Lake Doiran.

At the beginning of October 1916, the British, in co-operation with her allies on other parts of the front, began operations on the River Struma towards Serres. The campaign was successful, with the capture of the Rupell Pass and advances to within a few miles of Serres.

During 1917, there was comparatively little activity on the British part of the front in Macedonia, except around Lake Doiran until, eventually, a stable front was established, running from the Albanian Adriatic coast to the Struma River.

From October 1915 to the end of November 1918, the British Salonika Force suffered some 2,800 deaths in action, 1,400 from wounds and 4,200 from sickness.

The exact circumstances of James Swinden's death are not known but he died on 15 April 1918, aged 22. He has no known grave and is commemorated on the Doiran Memorial which is on the south east edge of Lake Doiran in northern Greece.

FRANK TAYLOR

Sergeant L/9064, 2nd Battalion The Queens (Royal West Surrey) Regiment

Frank Lennox Taylor was born in 1889 at Redhill to Robert and Emma Taylor and, with his three brothers and two sisters, lived at 10 Common Road, Earlswood. Before 1901 the family had moved to 52 Earlsbrook Road. By a strange coincidence 10 Common Road was later to become the home of another casualty, William Warner.

Frank enlisted at Guildford as a regular soldier before the war, probably before 1911, and would have been with 2nd Queens in South Africa when war broke out. The Battalion was rushed home and shipped out to the BEF, arriving at Zeebrugge on 6 October 1914.

They were part of 22nd Brigade, 7th Division and ordered to assist in the defence of Antwerp. However, by the time they arrived, the city was already falling and the 7th was instead ordered to hold certain important bridges and other places that would help the westward evacuation of the Belgian army. Once the Belgians were through, the Division was moved westwards, where they entrenched in front of Ypres, the first British troops to occupy that fateful place.

The Division fought the advancing German army to a standstill at Ypres. All units suffered grievous losses, and it was not until the following January/February that it was once more in a complete enough condition to be considered at full fighting strength.

Throughout 1915 the Division was in action at many of the major engagements including, Neuve Chappelle, Aubers, Festubert and the Battle of Loos.

On 24 November 1915 2nd Queens were out of the line and marched to rest billets at Le Hamel near Bethune. It was a relatively 'quiet' day and they provided 200 men for a working party to reinforce trenches near Festubert.

Frank was killed on this day, 24 November 1915, aged 26. He was probably killed by an artillery shell and has no known grave. He is commemorated on the Loos Memorial.

GEORGE TERRY

Stoker 1st Class, SS/103854, HMS Bulwark, *Royal Navy*

George Terry was born at Earlswood in 1882 to Henry and Anne Terry and was one of eight children. In 1901 they lived at 4 Asylum Cottages, probably close to the old Royal Earlswood Hospital.

Later the family moved to 6 Irrigation Road, Earlswood (now Maple Road).

George joined the Royal Navy before 1911 as he is to be found on the census as 'Sailor – home on leave'.

No details of his service before the war are available but by the time war broke out, he was serving on HMS *Bulwark* attached to the Channel Fleet patrolling the English Channel.

HMS *Bulwark* belonged to a sub-class of the Formidable-class of pre-dreadnought battleships of the Royal Navy, known as the London-class.

On 26 November 1914, while anchored near Sheerness, she was destroyed by a large internal explosion with the loss of 736 men.

Other crew were ashore at the time of the explosion.

Two of the 14 survivors later died in hospital. The explosion was likely to have been caused by the overheating of cordite charges that had been placed adjacent to a boiler room bulkhead.

An inquiry investigated various theories, including the overheating of older cordite cartridges or their mishandling. Survivors reported some charges were out of the magazine and were being stored in a passageway that morning, under Royal Marine guard.

The explosion occurred around breakfast time when smoking was normally allowed.

As a stoker, it is likely that George was in the boiler room when this explosion occurred.

George Terry died on 26 November 1914, aged 32. His body was never recovered for burial and he is commemorated on the Portsmouth Naval Memorial.

Norman Borer also died in this explosion.

JAMES THEWLESS

Private L/10980, 8th Battalion, The Queens, (Royal West Surrey) Regiment

James Thewless was born in 1898 at Norwood to Alfred and Sophie Thewless. He was one of nine children and some years after his birth the family moved to 3 Station Road, Horley.

No service record is available for James but his medal card suggests that he enlisted at Guildford, probably in answer to Kitchener's famous appeal early in 1915.

He was sent to France on 14 October 1915 where 8th Queens were under command of 72nd Brigade, 24th Division. They had just been engaged in the Battle of Loos and James was part of a much needed draft of reinforcements.

At the start of 1916, the 24th Division, including the 8th Queens, moved north toward the Ypres area where, on the night of 29 April 1916, they were subjected to an intense German gas attack supported by infantry at Wulverghem.

On 24 July 1916, they were moved south again to the Battle of the Somme. By 1 September the 8th Queens were in positions consolidating possession of Delville Wood, the scene of bitter fighting from 15 July until its final capture on 25 August.

They suffered 143 casualties before they were finally withdrawn from the line on the night of 5/6 September 1916.

By early October 8th Queens were back in the line near Camblain-l'Abbe north west of Arras. They were well understrength and numbered just 437 men. The Battalion was spread across four trenches and it was a relatively 'quiet' time. Although the enemy artillery was generally silent, the German trench mortars were active most afternoons with Hartung Trench getting most of their attention.

It appears that James was wounded during this period and he died of his wounds on 7 October 1916, aged 18. He is buried in Quatre Vents Cemetery, Estree-Cauchy which is about 10 miles north west of Arras.

HERBERT TODD M.C & BAR
(CROIX DE GUERRE)

Captain, 4th (attached 8th) Battalion East Surrey Regiment

Herbert Stanley Todd was born in Twickenham on 1 April 1898, to Herbert and Ellen Todd. He was educated at Wellesley House, in Broadstairs, and Westminster School.

Ellen was the daughter of R V Evered of Oatlands, Horley.

Herbert joined the 16th (Public School's) Battalion, Middlesex Regiment in September 1914, and the battalion joined the BEF in France in November 1915. He was commissioned with the rank of 2nd Lieutenant on 8 August 1916, and posted to the front again, this time with the East Surrey Regiment; promoted Lieutenant, 5 February 1917; and Acting Captain, 1 October 1917. He served in Italy from November 1917 to February 1918, at which time he was invalided home, returning to France in August 1918.

He was awarded his first Military Cross for an action in 1917:

'For conspicuous gallantry in sector south of Tower Hamlets, leading his men after all the other officers had become casualties, he advanced with great dash and gallantry; reaching his objective, he consolidated in depth. He reorganised his company, and all through showed an utter disregard for personal danger. This, combined with his personal cheeriness had great effect on his men. During the whole of the operations this officer was suffering from fever.'

He won his second MC :

'For conspicuous gallantry and devotion to duty at St Pierre Vaast Wood on 1 September 1918. He was in command of one of two companies in the attack, and when the other Company Commander was wounded at the start, he supervised the advance of both for a distance of two miles, without any previous reconnaissance. He reached his objective up to time, reorganised and gained touch with the flanks, showing great resource against determined opposition.'

Herbert was also awarded the Belgian Croix de Guerre for gallantry at Ypres.

Captain Todd was killed in action leading D Company in an attack at Roussoy on 18 September 1918, aged 20, during which the Company lost all of its officers.

He was killed by a machine gun bullet to the head and was buried at Lieramont Cemetery. His Colonel wrote "He would undoubtedly have made a great name for himself as he had great personality and force of character"

He was later reburied at Peronne Communal Cemetery, Rue de Peupliers, Peronne.

Herbert Stanley Todd (Photo from Ruvignys Roll of Honour.)

CHARLES TOMSETT
Private 279403, 11th Battalion, Royal Fusiliers

Charlie (not Charles) Tomsett was born at Worth in 1887 to John and Ellen Tomsett. He was one of eight sons and the family lived at Green Lane, Worth. By 1901 Ellen was widowed and had moved with the family to East Park, Ifield.

In 1908 Charlie married Clara Jane Cook. By 1911 Charlie was a gardener and they were living at Ifield with their daughter Winifred, where they had three more children before he joined up. It is possible that they, or Clara when widowed, moved to Horley later but it is not known where they lived. On enlistment he gave his residence as Redhill.

Charlie's medal card suggests that he did not see active service before at least 1916. He was originally in the Royal Sussex Regiment and later transferred into the 3rd Battalion RF. 3rd RF spent a good part of the war in Egypt and Salonika and did not return to France until July 1918.

The 11th Battalion RF landed in France in July 1915 as part of 54th Brigade, 18th Division and fought in many of the major engagements throughout the remainder of the war.

As it cannot be established when Charlie was transferred from the 3rd to the 11th RF, it is difficult to discover how and when he died but his CWGC record seems to place him with the 11th when he was killed.

At the end of September 1918, the 54th Brigade were pushing the Germans opposite them back, and the German army was almost in a full retreat. The 11th Battalion RF, together with the rest of the Brigade, were in action at Vendhuile, north of St Quentin and were pushed ahead to mop up the village and establish a line on the west bank of the canal. Snipers and machine guns prevented the crossing of the bridges.

It appears that Charlie was killed soon after this action was fought.

Charlie Tomsett died on 3 October 1918, aged 31, and was buried nearby. Some months later graves from this area were bought together and reburials carried out at Grevillers British Cemetery just west of Bapaume.

CHARLES TRIBE

Private 32919, 7th Battalion, East Surrey Regiment

Charles Frederick Tribe was born in 1884 to William and Jane Tribe. He was one of nine children and the family lived at Blundells Cottages, Vicarage Road, (now Vicarage Lane), Horley. William was a Police Constable. At the time of the 1901 census Charles was living with his married brother in Eastbourne and was employed as a gardener.

In 1907, by now a dairyman, he married Clara Jane Kenward at St Bartholomews Church and they settled with their daughter, Ethel, at 37 Queens Road, Horley. In 1911 Charles was employed as a milkman. Jane later lived at 'Hill View', Church Road, Horley and Charles may also have lived there.

No service record survives for Charles but his medal card suggests that he saw no active service before 1916.

The 7th East Surreys landed in France in June 1915 as part of 37th Brigade, 12th (Eastern) Division and fought in many major engagements before its' disbandment in February 1918.

Between 17 May and 19 October 1917, the Division held positions east of Monchy le Preux, mounting several raids and small scale attacks and beating off some made against them, notably in the area of Hook Trench, Pick Avenue and Tites Copse. Much manual work took place, for the position held in May was of shell holes and disconnected parts of trenches, with few dugouts and no communications. When out of the line they took part in training at Beaurains.

In August 1918 the Battalion was ordered to carry out a large scale raid on the enemy line on the night of 9 August. The raid went in at 7.45pm and was entirely successful.

The raiding party returned at about 3.00am the following day. Two officers were wounded, 9 other ranks killed, 5 missing and 21 wounded.

It seems that Charles was one of the men killed in this raid.

Charles Tribe died on 9 August 1917, aged 33, and he is buried in Albuera Cemetery, Bailleul-Sire-Berthoult which is about four miles north east of Arras.

ARTHUR TURNER

Gunner 207748, 462nd Battery, Royal Field Artillery

Arthur Bert (not Burt) Turner was born in 1892 to Abraham and Philadelphia Turner who, by 1911, lived in Elm Cottage, Mill Lane, Horley. He was a farm labourer and enlisted at Horley.

No service record survives for Arthur and his medal card gives no useful information other than to omit any award of the 1914/15 star.

462nd Battery RFA were part of 179th Brigade, 39th Division. The 174th, 184th and the 179th Field Gun Brigades were all raised by The Thames Iron Works.

The 39th Division were ordered to France early in 1916. They crossed to Le Havre and by 11 March all units were concentrated near Blaringhem.

The Division was in action at many of the major battles throughout 1916 and 1917, including The Somme and the Third Battle of Ypres.

The colossal German offensive launched on 21 March 1918, following the largest bombardment ever seen on the Western Front, resulted in spectacular successes but failed to achieve an outright breakthrough for the German Army. Slowed by the innumerable defiant actions of outnumbered garrisons in isolated British redoubts, the end of the day, contrary to German expectations, saw the greatest gains achieved against Gough's Fifth Army on the front from St Quentin to the Oise. The night of 21–22 March was one of frenzied activity as near-reeling British Divisions readjusted to the incursions into their defensive zones and German forces were reinforced to inflict further damage.

It seems certain that Arthur Turner was killed in this action.

He died on 21 March 1918 and has no known grave. He is commemorated on the Pozieres Memorial which is about five miles north east of Albert.

Along with Joseph Reeves, Arthur has the distinction of being named on both Horley and Charlwood War Memorials.

ERNEST VALLANCE

Private 5904, 24th Battalion, Australian Infantry Force

Ernest Arthur Vallance was born at Dorking in 1886 to Peter and Harriett Vallance. He had two sisters and a brother and the family lived at 38 Orchard Road, Dorking.

At the time of the 1901 census, Ernest was to be found a prisoner at St Davids Reformatory School at Mold in North Wales.

He is not identifiable on the 1911 census and may already have emigrated to Australia where he married an Australian girl named Mary.

The 24th Battalion was raised in May 1915 and assigned to the 6th Brigade, 2nd Division. After arriving in Egypt, the battalion carried out its training before being sent to Gallipoli in early September as reinforcements for the forces that had landed there in April. The battalion remained at Gallipoli for three months, serving around the Lone Pine sector until December 1915. Following this, they returned to Egypt where they took part in the defence of the Suez Canal until March 1916, when they returned to France.

In May 1917 they took part in the Second Battle of Bullecourt.

At 3.34 am on the 3 May after sheltering in a sunken road, whilst a preparatory barrage raked the German defences, the 5th and 6th Brigades 'went over the top' towards the eastern edge of what was left of Bullecourt village. The British 62nd Division advanced towards the village itself. A creeping barrage gave the advancing troops cover. The Australian 5th Brigade were soon halted by heavy machine gun fire but the 6th Brigade had more luck. The lie of the land gave them more cover and they were able to surprise the Germans in their trenches. Some progress was made and the second line of the German defences was reached in some places. By late morning, lacking support on their left or right, 6th Brigade was ultimately forced to pull back by vigorous German counter attacks. The Division suffered 80% casualties in this attack.

Ernest Vallance was killed in this action. He died on 3 May 1917, aged 31. He has no known grave and is commemorated with 10,761 other Australian soldiers on the Villers Bretonneux Memorial, just east of Amiens.

ARTHUR VOICE

Painter M/22859, HMS Pembroke *Royal Navy*

Arthur Edward Voice was born in Horley in 1895 to Albert and Jane Voice. He had two older brothers and two older sisters and the family lived at 25 Albert Road, Horley.

Early in 1916 Arthur married Winifred Leppard and may have lived with her at Edmondbury, Meath Green, Horley.

No details of Arthurs enlistment are available and Royal Navy medal rolls give no useful information.

HMS *Pembroke* was the name of the Royal Naval barracks at Chatham. It seems likely that Arthur had been in the service for some time as he was already a classified tradesman...Painter 2nd class... unsurprising as he had been a house painter before joining up. So he is likely to have been on the regular establishment at Chatham or awaiting a posting, rather than 'passing through' on training.

On the night of 3 September 1917 the Naval base at Chatham was targeted in a night attack by the Gotha bombers of *Kagohl 3*, the *Englandgeschwader.* Five Gothas set out on the raid, but one had to return en route because of engine problems. The Gothas dropped 46 bombs, about half of which fell on or near the Base. The Chatham attack commenced at 11.10pm but, due to a communications failure, Chatham received no warning of the raid, which resulted in the Naval personnel being killed when a bomb hit the drill hall which was being used for accommodation purposes. The RFC flew 16 defensive sorties against the raid, with aircraft from Numbers 37, 39, 44 and 50 Squadrons involved, but without result.

131 men were killed and 90 injured in what was to be the worst 'single bomb' incident of World War I.

Arthur died in this bombing raid on 3 September 1917, aged 22 and is buried in Gillingham Cemetery which is in Woodlands Road.

A memorial cross in the cemetery is dedicated to the men killed in this raid.

WILLIAM WARNER

Private 47967, 25th (Tyneside Irish) Battalion, Northumberland Fusiliers

William Joshua Warner was born in Greatford, Lincolnshire in 1882 to John and Emma Warner and he had two older sisters. By 1901 he was living at Earlswood and earning his living as a carpenter.

In 1903 he married Emily Sargent from Horley and they lodged at 10 Common Road, Earlswood.

William enlisted at Redhill, though we do not know when, and was initially Sapper 178021 in the Royal Engineers. At some stage he appears to have transferred to the Northumberland Fusiliers.

The 25th (2nd Tyneside Irish) Battalion, Northumberland Fusiliers was a 'Pals Battalion', raised at Newcastle on 9 November 1914, by the Lord Mayor and City. In June 1915 the Battalion joined 103rd Brigade, 34th Division and proceeded to France in January 1916, where they concentrated at La Crosse, east of St Omer. They were in action during the Battles of the Somme, including the capture of Scots and Sausage Redoubts, The Battles of Bazentin Ridge and Pozieres Ridge. 103rd Brigade and the Divisional Pioneers also saw action in The Battle of Flers-Courcelette.

In 1917 the 34th Brigade, as part of the 3rd Army, were engaged at the Battle of the Scarpe. On Monday 9 April 1917 at 5.30 a.m Canadian Divisions opened their attack on Vimy Ridge. Wresting control of this height from the Germans would allow the 3rd Army under General Edmund Allenby to advance on Douai, an important road and rail junction. Allenby was also expected to take Monchy-le-Preux, a village lying a few kilometres to the east of Arras, which gave a commanding view over the Scarpe Valley and, because of this, could hinder the second arm of the offensive directed at Cambrai, another vital base for the German military apparatus.

William Warner was killed in this action on 9 April 1917, aged 25. He is buried at Roclincourt Valley Cemetery which is near the village of that name, about three miles north of Arras.

HENRY WEBBER

Lieutenant, 7th Battalion, South Lancashire Regiment.

Henry Webber was born at Tonbridge in 1849, the youngest of eight children, to William and Eliza Webber. He was educated at Tonbridge School and Pembroke College, Oxford where he distinguished himself at rowing and cricket, representing the college at both.

In 1874 he married Emily Morris from Lingfield and they lived in Horley from 1875, firstly at Greenfields, and then at The Elms in Horley Row.

Henry and Emily soon became involved in the social and spiritual side of life in Horley. They had four sons and five daughters though one, Marjorie, died in 1914.

Having established himself as a successful stockbroker he soon became an influential figure in the affairs of Horley. He was one of the original members of Surrey County Council when it was first formed in 1889, representing Horley, Charlwood, Burstow and Nutfield. He also became the first Chairman of Horley Parish Council when it came into being in 1894.

He became involved in the administration of the Cottage Hospital having suggested the purchase of the former Temperance Hotel to the Trustees in 1902 and maintained an interest in its welfare.

He was the Chairman of the Directors of Horley Gas Company formed in 1886 and was a County Magistrate as well as a Church Warden.

Henry was still a keen sportsman. As well as being a good shot he regularly rode to hounds with the Old Surrey and Burstow Hunt. He was always an excellent cricketer scoring 200 runs in a match when he was aged 59, having already played 18 holes of golf on the same day. He was a member of the MCC and the first Captain of Gatwick Golf Club, then situated within the horse racing track, besides being the first commissioner of Horley Scouts.

Above all, Henry Webber was a good Churchman and set a brilliant example to men of his own position in the parish and district by his regular attendance at St Bartholomews Church. He was a churchwarden there from 1881 to 1891 and later served as a sidesman.

Henry Webber, the oldest British Serviceman in a fighting unit to die in WWI. Killed near Mametz 21 July 1916.

When WWI started he relentlessly tried to join up as three of his four sons had. Then aged 65 he was repeatedly turned down as the War Office had an age limit of 60. He even recruited a company of 'Rough riders', fellow-horsemen like himself, and offered this complete unit to the Army, but again he was rejected. Eventually the South Lancashire Regiment accepted him as a junior Lieutenant.

He was accepted quite normally by the younger officers in the battalion; he performed his duties well and not many knew his true age, although the CO found that his own father and Webber had rowed together at Oxford in the same year, over half a century earlier. Webber hoped that he might meet and salute his three sons who all held ranks higher than his.

In May 1916 he arrived in France to join his Battalion preparing for the Somme offensive. Late on 21 July he was in command of a party of troops who had bought up supplies to the 7th Lancs position in a wood near Mametz.

Leaving his men to unload the horses, he went over to where the C.O. was talking to a group of officers. Into this routine, peaceful scene there suddenly dropped a single, heavy German shell. When the smoke and dust had cleared it was found that twelve men and three horses had been hit. Henry Webber lay unconscious, badly wounded in the head. He and the other wounded were rushed to a Dressing Station but, for Webber, it was too late. He never regained consciousness and died that night.

The news of the death of this old warrior was noted in high places. His family received special messages of sympathy from the King and Queen and from the Army Council – unusual tributes to a dead lieutenant of infantry. Webber's devotion to duty was further honoured when he was mentioned in the C in C's Despatches. His wife never recovered from the shock of his death and died two years later but ironically, his three sons all survived the war.

Henry Webber was killed on 21 July 1916, aged 67, and was, for nearly 100 years, believed to be the oldest British serviceman to be killed in World War One. He is buried in Dartmoor Cemetery at Becordel-Becourt which is about two miles south east of Albert. In 2014 it was established that an honorary Lieutenant Colonel Jasper Richardson, who was serving as a General Staff Officer (Agriculture), was killed by a shell near Bapaume in March 1918, aged 68. Richardson's duties did not normally bring him into a danger area and Henry Webber remains the oldest soldier to lose his life whilst on 'active' service.

The grave of Henry Webber in Dartmoor Cemetery. For many years this showed his age as 68 but it has now been corrected.
(Photo courtesy of David Hall)

JOSEPH WELLER

Leading Stoker 312171, HMS Formidable, *Royal Navy*

Joseph Albert Weller (not Albert Joseph as on the Memorial) was born in Horley in 1886 and was one of seven children born to Joseph and Mary Weller. He was probably known as Albert to differentiate him from his father. The family lived at Hope Cottage, Charlesfield Road, Horley.

Joseph joined the Royal Navy in 1907, signing on for 12 years and by 1911 was serving in the Mediterranean. On 21 October 1913 he was posted to HMS *Formidable* which was a pre-dreadnought battleship.

HMS Formidable *in which Joseph Weller lost his life, 1 January 1915.*

HMS *Formidable* was in the 5th Battle Squadron and spent 31 December 1914 participating in gunnery exercises off the Isle of Portland, supported by the light cruisers *Topaze* and *Diamond*. After the exercises, that night the fleet remained at sea on patrol even though submarine activity had been reported in the area. *Formidable* was steaming at 10 knots at the rear of the squadron off Portland Bill when at 2:20am on 1 January 1915 a torpedo from a German submarine, U-24, struck the number one boiler port side.

By 2:40am she had taken a list of 20° to starboard and Captain Noel Loxley gave the order to abandon ship. At about 3:05am *Formidable* was struck by a second torpedo on the starboard side. Amidst a 30 foot swell the boats were launched and the two light cruisers came alongside and managed to pick up 80 men in the deteriorating weather. By 4:45am, she seemed in imminent danger of capsizing and a few minutes later she rolled over onto many of the men in the water and sank quickly.

Captain Loxley remained on the bridge along with his fox terrier, Bruce, calmly overseeing the evacuation of the ship.

Joseph Weller was killed in this incident and died on 1 January 1915, aged 28. His body was never recovered and he is commemorated on the Chatham Naval Memorial.

WILLIAM WELLER

(believed to be) Private 55307, 8th Battalion, Royal Fusiliers

William John Weller was born in 1897 at Kingswood to Harry and Elizabeth Weller. He was one of eighteen children and the family lived at 11 Clears Cottages, Reigate. His connection to Horley is not known. On the 1911 census William's occupation is given as 'Golf Caddy'.

William enlisted at Reigate but we don't know exactly when. His medal card suggests that he did not see active service before 1916.

On 19 January the 8th Battalion began a period of training in open warfare at Busnes, then moved back into the front line at Loos on 12 February 1916. In June they moved to Flesselles and carried out a training exercise. They moved to Baizieux on 30 June and went into the reserve at Hencourt and Millencourt on 1 July. They relieved the 8th Division at Ovillers-la-Boisselle that night and attacked at 3.15am the following morning with mixed success.

On 7 July they attacked again and despite suffering heavy casualties in the area of Mash Valley, they succeeded in capturing and holding the first and second enemy lines close to Ovillers. They were withdrawn to Contay on 9 July but were back in action in The Battle of Pozieres on 3 August with a successful attack capturing 4th Avenue Trench and were engaged in sustained heavy fighting until they were withdrawn on 9 August.

The Battalion was then moved north and at the Third Battle of the Scarpe on 3 May 1917 the British attacked on a 12 mile front towards the village of Fresnay.

The attack in the small hours of the morning was beset by confusion caused by the darkness. The German artillery opened fire and concentrated upon the British infantry. The intensity of this fire, the heaviest that many an experienced soldier had ever witnessed, lasted without slackening for fifteen hours.

William Weller was killed in this action on 3 May 1917, aged 20. He has no known grave and is commemorated on the Arras Memorial in the Faubourg-d'Amiens Cemetery, which is in the Boulevard du General de Gaulle in the western part of the town of Arras.

ALBERT WHITE

Private 16630, 2nd/5th Battalion, Duke of Wellington's
(West Riding Regiment)

Albert James White was born in Horley in 1893 to James and Hannah White and lived with several siblings in Charlesfield Road, Horley. He became a typefounder at Monotype, Salfords and later worked at Bayhorne Farm.

His father, James, later moved to 32 Albert Road and Albert may have also lived there. His older brother, Charles, was also to die.

He joined up as soon as war broke out and enlisted in the Royal Dragoons, though in June 1915, was transferred into the West Riding Regiment. Albert was not a model soldier and his rank varied from Private to Corporal over his time in the army, though he never committed more than minor military offences. He spent the early war years in England before being posted to France in December 1916.

Albert arrived in France just in time to take part in the battles around Arras which were to be a diversionary tactic to assist the French army attacking further south.

On 23 April 1917 the second Battle of the Scarpe began and Albert was wounded on the following day. He was fortunate enough to be passed down the casualty line very efficiently and arrived back in England four days later to be hospitalised at Newcastle. His wounds kept him in hospital until August when he was given leave before returning to the depot. He returned to France in November 1917.

In the summer of 1918 following the collapse of the Russian front, Albert was gassed whilst fighting in the actions to contain the German assault and in the allied advance that followed.

By August 1918 the fighting had moved steadily eastwards again and it seems that Albert may have been fighting at the 3rd Battle of the Scarpe when he was killed.

Albert White was killed in action on 25 August 1918, aged 25, and is buried in Gomiecourt South Cemetery which is about four miles north west of Bapaume.

CHARLES WHITE

Lance Corporal, 1795, 28th Battalion, Australian Infantry Force

Charles White was born in Horley in 1889 to James and Hannah White and lived with several siblings in Charlesfield Road, Horley. His father, James, later moved to 32 Albert Road and Charles may have also lived there. His younger brother, Albert, was also to die.

Before the 1911 census was taken Charles had emigrated to Australia and after war broke out in 1914 he joined the Australian Army.

The 28th Battalion was raised at Blackboy Camp in Western Australia on 16 April 1915. The battalion left Australia in June, and, after two months spent training in Egypt, landed at Gallipoli on 10 September. The 28th had a relatively quiet time at Gallipoli and the battalion left in December, having suffered only light casualties.

After another stint in Egypt, the 7th Brigade proceeded to France as part of the 2nd Australian Division. The 28th Battalion took part in its first major battle at Pozières between 28 July and 6 August 1916. Later that year the 28th Battalion took part in confused and costly fighting to the east of Flers, in the Somme Valley.

For many of the major battles of 1917, the 28th found itself in supporting roles. At the second battle of Bullecourt, the 28th provided reinforcements who were nonetheless involved in heavy fighting. The 28th went on to attack as part of the third phase at the battle of Menin Road, capturing its objectives in seven minutes, and was in reserve during the capture of Broodseinde Ridge. The battalion was also in reserve for the battle of Poelcappelle on 9 October, but, with the attack floundering in the mud, they soon became embroiled in the fighting.

Charles White died in action to the east of Ypres shortly after this battle. He was killed on 2 November 1917, aged 28, and is buried in Menin Road South Cemetery which is on the east side of Ypres.

GEOFFREY WHITE VC

Lieutenant Commander, HM Submarine E14, Royal Navy

Geoffrey Saxton White was born in 1886 at Bromley, to William and Alice White, but was living at Park House, Charlwood, by 1901. The family were affluent and employed ten servants including maids, footmen and grooms.

Lieutenant Commander Geoffrey White V.C who died on board HM Submarine E14, 28 January 1918.

He attended Parkfield, Haywards Heath and Bradfield College before joining HMS *Brittania*. He passed out in 1901 and was promoted midshipman in September 1902.

During the next six years he served in the Channel Fleet and on the China Station on several ships, including the cruisers *Amphitrite* and *Glory* and the battleship *Venerable*.

By 1909 Geoffrey was a Lieutenant and was posted to HMS *Forth*, a depot ship serving B and C class boats where he trained for the submarine service before being given his first command, C27, in November that year.

In 1911 he married Sybil Thomas with whom he had two sons and a daughter.

Early in 1914 he was posted to a newly commissioned battleship, HMS *Monarch*, wherein he served until returning to submarines in September 1915, when he took command of the submarine D6 in the 11th Submarine Flotilla.

Later he took command of a more advanced submarine, the E14 which was commissioned on 18 November 1914. Her hull cost £105,700. This submarine enjoyed a rare distinction in that she had two commanding officers, each of whom won the Victoria Cross in the same area but three years apart.

In 1915, following a successful action in the Sea of Marmara, her captain, Lieutenant Commander Edward Courtney Boyle received the Victoria Cross.

Geoffrey White's award of this supreme recognition of bravery was for the incident recorded in the *London Gazette,* dated 24 May, 1919:

"For most conspicuous gallantry and devotion to duty as Commanding Officer of HM Submarine E14 on the 28 January, 1918.

HM Submarine E14 left Mudros on the 27 January, under instructions to force the Narrows and attack the German ship Goeben, which was reported aground off Nagara Point after being damaged during her sortie from the Dardanelles. The latter vessel was not found and E.14. turned back. At about 8.45 a.m. on the 28 January a torpedo was fired from E.14. at an enemy ship. 11 seconds after the torpedo left the tube a heavy explosion took place, caused all the lights to go out, and sprang the fore hatch. (Authors note: Probably a premature explosion of their torpedo.) *Leaking badly the boat was blown to 15 feet, and at once a heavy fire came from the forts, but the hull was not hit. E.14. then dived and proceeded on her way out.*

187

Soon afterwards the boat became out of control and as the air supply was nearly exhausted, Lieutenant-Commander White decided to run the risk of proceeding on the surface. Heavy fire was immediately opened from both sides, and, after running the gauntlet for half-an-hour, being steered from below, E14 was so badly damaged that Lieutenant-Commander White turned towards the shore in order to give the crew a chance of being saved. He remained on deck the whole time himself until he was killed by a shell."

Geoffrey White died on 28 January 1918, aged 31, and his body was not recovered. He is commemorated on the Portsmouth Naval Memorial.

In June 2012, after a three-year search, Turkish marine engineer Selçuk Kolay and filmmaker Savas Karakas discovered the wreck of E14 in 20m of water about 250m off Kum Kale. The ship is largely buried in sand, only 7m of the coral-encrusted bow, with a shell hole, remaining visible. The British government has asked the Turkish authorities to ensure that the wreck is respected as a war grave.

Submarine E14 sunk 28 January 1918.

GEORGE WHITE

Trumpeter L7796, 16th (attached 9th) Queens Lancers

George Garrett William White (registered at birth as Garrett George) was born in Horley in 1896 to George and Tamar White. He was baptised at St Bartholomews Church in March 1900. They also had four daughters and lived in Albert Road for some years during which time George attended Horley Infant School. By 1911 the family had moved to 8 Kings Terrace, Balcombe Road, Horley and George was employed as an Errand Boy.

George enlisted into the 16th Lancers fairly soon after his 18th birthday. He may have enlisted as a Trumpeter but his medal card shows that he was later classified as a Private.

The 1914 British cavalry regiment was composed of twenty-six officers and 523 other ranks. The other ranks included one warrant officer, 37 senior N.C.Os, 22 artificers, 6 trumpeters, and 457 privates.

The last 'Lance on Lance' cavalry action took place in September 1914 and as the machine gun began to dominate the battlefields of Flanders cavalrymen, were increasingly used as Infantry and took their places in the line.

George arrived in France on 29 November 1915 and would have joined his unit as part of 2nd Cavalry Brigade. The 16th Lancers were in and out of the line throughout 1916 but not engaged in any major actions.

In April 1917 they were in action during the battle of the Scarpe near Arras and later fought through the offensive around Cambrai.

On 21 March 1918 the Germans launched a ferocious assault on the British lines. At 4.40am a terrific German bombardment began. British communications were shattered and many of our guns were neutralised or destroyed over the next few hours of shelling.

George White was killed on this day, 21 March 1918, aged 22. He has no known grave and is commemorated on the Pozieres memorial which lies on the north side of the Albert – Pozieres road just south west of Pozieres.

RONALD WHITE

Lieutenant 908066, 78th Battalion (Manitoba Regiment)
Canadian Army and 2 Squadron, Royal Flying Corps

Ronald White as he appeared on his Royal Aero Club Aviators
Certificate.

Ronald John Saxton White was born in 1892 at Charlwood, to William and Alice White and lived at Park House, Charlwood.

The family were affluent and employed ten servants including maids footmen and grooms. He was the younger brother of Geoffrey White VC who also died.

Sometime before 1911 Ronald left England for the USA and settled in Omaha, Nebraska. He married Rose Catherine but no details exist to tell us what his occupation was.

It appears that soon after war was declared, Ronald decided to enlist in the Canadian Army. He joined the 78th Battalion – The Manitoba Regiment.

The battalion embarked at Halifax on 22 May 1916 aboard the *Empress of Britain*, disembarking in England a week later.

Its strength was 37 officers and 1097 other ranks. After a period of training in England the battalion arrived in France on 12 August 1916, becoming part of the 12th Canadian Infantry Brigade, 4th Canadian Division.

It is not known whether Ronald was actually in action in France with 78th Battalion but if so, it was not for very long.

By early 1917 he had transferred into the Royal Flying Corps and was learning to fly Caudron Biplanes at the Ruffy-Baumann Flying School at Acton, West London.

He gained his Royal Aero Club Aviators certificate (No 4749) in May 1917 and probably went on to do his military flying training at the Central Flying School before being posted to 2 Squadron RFC.

The average life expectancy of a pilot on the Western Front in 1917 was about three weeks and it seems likely that Ronald's was an average span.

Ronald White died of wounds, received in action, on 27 October 1917, aged 26. He is buried at St Pol Communal Cemetery which is on the east side of Saint Pol-sur- Ternoise.

RICHARD WILSON

Private G/4140 2nd Battalion, The Queens, (Royal West Surrey) Regiment

Richard John Wilson was born at Horley in 1895 and baptised in St Bartholomews Church. He was one of eight children born to Charles and Eliza Wilson and lived at 84 Albert Road. Richard attended Horley Infant school and is commemorated on the memorial plaque there. By 1911 he was an errand boy.

Richard, giving his occupation as a carman, joined up in January 1915 into the 3rd Queens but was later transferred to the 2nd Battalion.

His medal card shows that he was in a draft to France on 5 July 1915 and may well have been in the 30 man draft of reinforcements which reached the battalion in the front line on 21 July. Through the next few months, 2nd Queens were in and out of the line and subject to a steady stream of casualties.

On 5 November the battalion left their rest area billets near Essars and marched off to relieve troops of the South Staffordshire Regiment in the line near Givenchy, where they found the trenches to be in a terrible state and the front line especially bad.

Richard was wounded the following day, probably by sniper fire. He received a severe gunshot wound to the right shoulder which caused a lasting loss of feeling in his arm. He was sent down the line to a Casualty Clearing Station and was judged to need hospitalisation. He was sent home to England and after some time at the Regimental depot and following medical treatment and examinations at Shoreham and Croydon, he was discharged as medically unfit for further service in July 1917 and awarded a pension.

He married Carrie Brotherton (also known as Rose Ridley), who was also from Albert Road, in Lancashire late in 1917 and they had a daughter, Sadie. Richard died, possibly as a result of his injury in late 1918, aged 23.

His death does not appear to have been treated as relating to the war and he is not listed by CWGC. His exact place of burial is not known.

Rose remarried an Arthur Nicholson from Reigate in 1920. Charles and Eliza still lived in Albert Road and probably asked for Richard's name to be listed on our War Memorial as well as that of his brother Thomas, who also died.

THOMAS WILSON

Private L/8927, 2nd Battalion, The Queen's (Royal West Surrey) Regiment

Thomas William Wilson, born in 1889 at Ifield, was one of eight children born to Charles and Eliza Wilson. By 1891 the family were living at 84 Albert Road, Horley where they seem to have stayed.

Thomas became a regular soldier sometime before 1911, as the census in that year lists him as serving overseas with 2nd Queens.

His service record does not survive but 2nd Queens were in South Africa when war broke out. They were hurriedly shipped home arriving at Southampton on the *Kenilworth Castle* on 17 September.

By mid October, they were equipped for war service and, as part of 22nd Brigade, 7th Division, despatched to France and rushed into the line east of Ypres.

They fought their first major action at Gheluvelt to stop the German advance. This was significant as it was the nearest that the German army would come to breaking through the Allied lines at Ypres until 1918.

Early on 29 October the battalion moved into action near Veldhoek but was caught by heavy shellfire before they could take cover and sustained many casualties.

About 8.00am they were ordered to advance further along the Gheluvelt road to occupy another set of dugouts and from these they advanced in extended order to reinforce the Guards at Gheluvelt. They occupied a position facing the Gheluvelt – Menin road but the fire from the enemy trenches was so heavy that they were beaten back.

60 men were wounded on this day and it seems as though Thomas was amongst them. He was passed through the casualty lines and evacuated to England.

Thomas died of his wounds, aged 25, on 5 December 1914. He is buried in Manchester Southern Cemetery which is about two miles south of the city centre.

JAMES WILTSHIRE

Private 23568, 5th Battalion, King's Shropshire Light Infantry

James Albert Wiltshire (usually known as Albert) was born at Charlwood in 1892 to James and Alice Wiltshire and lived with them and his two sisters at Pound House Lane, near Povey Cross. His parents later lived in Bonehurst Road, Horley.

By 1911 Albert was employed at The Mill shop, Lee Street, as a delivery driver.

No service record survives for Albert and his medal card gives no useful information.

5th KSLI were part of the 42ndBrigade in the 14th (Light) Division and landed in France on 20 May 1915.

On 30 July, at Hooge, the Division became the first British Army unit to be attacked with Flamethrowers, although the 42nd Brigade were not in the thick of it.

The Division were still in the same area by late September and were part of the assault on the Bellewaarde Ridge at Hooge.

In the spring of 1916 the Division were moved south in preparation for the Battle of The Somme.

On 24 August, in high summer temperatures, the Division was set the task of clearing Delville Wood. This was a strategic high point, which, together with High Wood to the west, gave the holders a good view over the surrounding area.

Assisted by a creeping barrage they advanced through the remains of the wood and reached their objectives. Within three days the Division finally drove the Germans from their strong position in Edge Trench and established a barricade which left Delville Wood completely in British hands.

Casualties were high and it was almost certainly here that Albert received his fatal injuries. He was evacuated from the battlefield and died of his wounds at the hospital in Rouen on 5 September 1916, aged 24.

He is buried in St Sever Cemetery, Rouen, which is just south of the city centre.

ARTHUR WOODS

Private 8114, 1st Battalion, The Queens (Royal West Surrey) Regiment

Arthur John Woods was born in 1886 at Farnborough, Kent, to John and Jane Woods but by 1901 they were living at Broadstone Cottages, Cross Oak Lane and Arthur was employed at Monotype.

Arthur joined The Queens as a regular soldier in 1904.

After his three years service, although still on reserve, he worked for some time as a sailor between England and Western Australia.

Arthur was either recalled to the colours or, more likely, volunteered for re-enlistment as he was with 1st Queens in time to sail to France on board the SS *Braemar Castle* and land at Le Havre on 13 August 1914.

Together with the rest of the "old contemptibles" they were rushed towards Mons and were in the thick of the fighting there and during the subsequent retreat.

Having been constantly engaged throughout August and September, during which time they sustained a steady stream of casualties, the 1st Queens were eventually sent north to the Ypres sector where they arrived on 17 October and they were then faced with yet another series of long and arduous marches to bring them into the line near Langemark.

After beating off a series of German attacks, the Battalion was ordered south to the vicinity of Hooge where they received a welcome draft of reinforcements.

On 29 October the battalion was ordered to move along the Menin Road to take up positions near Gheluvelt.

Early on the 31st an attack was repulsed but the enemy dug in within 300 yards of the Queens lines and at 7am, they came under a very heavy bombardment. Soon after this the enemy advanced again to within 150 yards and 1st Queens were forced to fall back and regroup.

624 men were killed, wounded or missing in this action and Arthur Woods was amongst them. Arthur died on 31 October 1914, aged 28, and his body was never recovered.

He is commemorated on the Menin Gate at Ypres.

WILLIAM WOOLLHEAD

Chief Petty Officer, Mechanic 2nd Grade, F Squadron,
2nd Wing, Royal Naval Air Service

William Hugh Woollhead (spelt as Woolhead on the War Memorial) was born in 1893 at Hounslow, Middlesex, to Edwin and Laura Woollhead. One of six children, William and his family came to live at 4 Langshott Cottages, Horley, and by 1911 he was apprenticed to a boiler engineer.

No details survive of William's enlistment and we do not know when he joined up, though it may have been before war was declared. His training as a boiler engineer would have enabled him to learn the mechanics of aircraft engines quite easily and he seems to have made steady progress through the ranks.

The Naval Wing of the RFC became the Royal Naval Air Service (RNAS) in July 1914 under the control of the Admiralty and had 93 aircraft, six airships, 2 balloons and 727 personnel. On 1 August 1915 the Royal Naval Air Service officially came under the control of the Royal Navy.

2nd Wing were sent to support the allied landings at Gallipoli and were based at RNAS Mudros on the island of Lemnos just 60 miles West of the Dardanelles. When that campaign ended they were in a position to support Allied actions in Macedonia (Greece).

During 1917 the main fighting took place around Lake Doiran, where the line was adjusted several times by each side early in the year. In April 1917, the British attacked, gained a considerable amount of ground and resisted strong counter-attacks. In May, the Bulgarians attacked the British positions, but were firmly repulsed.

William's rank of CPO Mechanic could have meant that he served as ground crew or as an airborne observer.

The circumstances of William's death are not clear. The Royal Naval records show that he died "by means other than disease, accident or enemy action" which leaves little else but death from natural causes.

William died on 27 May 1917, aged 23, and he is buried in Struma Military Cemetery which is near the town of Strimoniko about 35 miles north east of Thessalonika, Greece.

LESLIE YARDLEY

Private 7560, 1st/13th Kensington Battalion, The London Regiment

Leslie Alfred Yardley was born at Islington in 1896 to Alfred and Clara Yardley. He was an only child and was still at school by the time of the 1911 census, which shows the family living in the City of London.

When his will was published, it gave Leslie's address as Fairlight, Woodham, Woking. His connection with Horley is not known.

Leslie enlisted at Somerset House in London and joined the 15th (County of London) Battalion (Prince of Wales's Own, Civil Service Rifles). This unit was raised in August 1914, so it seems as though Leslie was an early volunteer, and after a period of training they landed in France on 11 May 1915 as part of the 140th Brigade, in the 47th (2nd London) Division.

It is not known when Leslie was transferred to 1st/13th Battalion but it was probably owing to reorganisation and reinforcement bought about by the huge casualties sustained in the trenches. The 1st/13th was forced to undergo a restructuring during May 1915 and did not resume it's own identity until 11 August.

In February 1916 they came under the command of 168th Brigade, 56th London Division.

At the Somme on 1 July 1916, in rising temperatures under a clear blue sky, the Division was tasked with an attack south of Gommecourt. At 7.20am their assault was pressed home with huge losses and although early successes were secured, the day ended with little ground gained.

After being heavily reinforced the Brigade was again in a major action on 9 September, when tasked with an attack east of Guillemont near Leuze Wood towards a heavily defended German strongpoint, known as the Quadrilateral.

Leslie Yardley was killed in this attack and died on 9 September 1916, aged 20. He has no known grave and is commemorated on the Thiepval Memorial.

CHAPTER FIVE
WHEN THE WAR ENDED

On the 11 November 1918 the atmosphere throughout Britain was one of relief. People did not rejoice and cry "We've won the war". They were more likely to say, "The War is over – Thank God". One in ten of an entire generation of young men had been wiped out – the brightest and the best of Britain's youth were gone. Some 300,000 children had lost at least one parent and families were shattered by the scale of the losses which had reached into every corner of the country.

Few at the time could visualise the futility of the last four years. The British Army had gone into action in August 1914 just north of the town of Mons, in Belgium. The first man recorded as killed was Private J Parr of the Middlesex Regiment, who died on the 23 August 1914. He is buried in St Symphorien War Cemetery just east of Mons. In 1918 elements of our army were in exactly the same place and one of the last, if not the last, man to die is also buried there. Private G E Ellison of the 5th Royal Irish Lancers was recorded as being the last man to die before the Armistice at 11 am on 11 November 1918. His grave is just a few steps away from that of Private Parr.

The Armistice lead immediately to a flurry of diplomatic activity and delegations from all the combatant nations gathered in Paris to hammer out the terms of the Peace, that was to ensure that this would be the War to end all Wars. In fact, the French were allowed to place such hugely unreasonable demands on Germany for financial and geographical reparations, that they, unknowingly, laid the foundations for the next world shattering conflict that lay in wait twenty years hence.

The initial sum to be repaid by Germany was set at 226 billion Reichsmarks but was reduced to 132 billion Reichsmarks in 1953 (About £22 billion at that time).

The debt was not finally cleared until a payment of £59.5 million was made in October 2010.

England had been the centre of the Empire before World War I, as well as the great creditor nation of the world, providing financial, shipping and insurance services worldwide. The cost of the war amounted to about 136% of our Gross National product and was so great that the United Kingdom consumed just about all of its credit and became heavily indebted to the United States.

The demands by women for the right to vote had become increasingly strident in the years leading up to the war. It could no longer be denied. Women acquired that right throughout most of the countries of Europe following the war.

Working class people, as well as women, were fully employed throughout the war, and their status, once defined as subordinate to the aristocracy, was greatly enhanced. The distribution of income shifted in their favour. Relatively, the status of the aristocracy was diminished and politically this was reflected by the rise of the Labour Party as one of the two major parties. By 1919 the British working scene was returning to normality, with more than 2 million workers on strike during the year. Strikes continued throughout many industries and by 1921 unemployment reached 11.3%, the highest since records began. Coal, shipbuilding and the steel industries contracted and women were forced to concede their hard won jobs to returning men.

In France, the heavy losses at the front decimated an entire generation and, as in England, created a leadership vacuum when that generation came to middle age. France had fallen behind Germany and England in population during the 19th century and was, therefore, less able to sustain wartime losses.

France also suffered untold property damage since most of the war on the western front was fought on French soil.

The United States, removed by an ocean from the centre of conflict and joining late in the war, did not suffer the catastrophic losses of the major belligerents. US losses in life were great, more than 100,000, but this was small in comparison to the millions lost by the other major powers.

In Horley it was decided to organise a celebration of the Peace in the summer of 1919. Accordingly, the arrangements were placed in the hands of a large committee and, following a procession from the Munitions Store, a great tea party was enjoyed by more than 3000 men, women and children at Mr Apps Field on 19 July. This was followed by a programme of sports and entertainments which were judged to be a great success and enjoyed by all.

The Peace Procession at the junction of Russell Crescent and Victoria Road.

The British troops who remained under arms were anxious to be demobilised and this was to be decided according to industrial and economic priorities. Progress was slow and, as discontent began to spread through the ranks, the government became worried. Fearing a mutiny, Winston Churchill, the new Minister for 'War and Air' quickly revised the system to take account of wounds, age and length of service instead, and slowly, the rate of discharge increased.

Thousands of the soldiers returning home from World War I suffered greatly from the horrors they had witnessed. Although it was called shell shock at the time, many returning men suffered from what we know today as post-traumatic stress disorder.

Shell shock was a condition that was developed by many soldiers in the trenches during the war. Early symptoms included tiredness, irritability, giddiness, lack of concentration and headaches which frequently led to a complete mental breakdown.

Soldiers suffering from it were often treated as cowards and it was not until after the war that doctors were able to determine the cause. Higher ranking soldiers suffering from the condition were sent home, while enlisted men just had to continue fighting as best they were able. With doctors unable to define the reasoning behind shell shock, there was no apparent treatment. Doctors originally believed that it originated from the physical effects of heavy bombardment or being buried alive but it soon became apparent that soldiers who had not been exposed to shelling were developing similar symptoms. The British army reported 80,000 men as suffering from shell shock during the war. The effects went on for many years and over ten years later there were still

65,000 ex-soldiers receiving treatment in Britain. Some cases continued for up to 50 years after the war.

As the soldiers drifted home to a 'Land Fit for Heroes' their arrival, whilst giving joy to their own families, had the opposite effect on families who had lost husbands and sons.

In Horley, the scale of losses was felt throughout the town and the bereaved families were equally split between the mean working class cottages and the larger affluent homes.

Some idea of the impact on working class communities can be seen from the maps below.

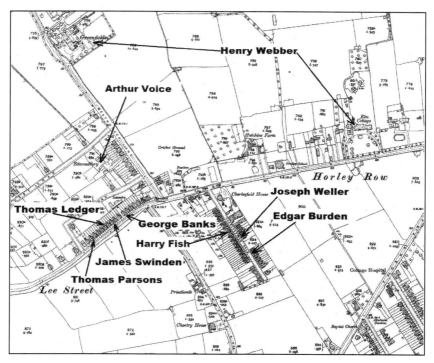

The small semi-detached cottages that lined Charlsfield Road and the northern side of Lee Street are typical of the housing that was built around the late Victorian period and can still be seen throughout Horley and parts of Redhill today. This small community around Harelands Corner lost a number of young men. Because of the difficulty in fixing exact addresses for men after 100 years, it is almost certain there were others from here as well. Remember too, that some men returned home carrying the effects of wounds and emotional trauma that would stay with them for years to come.

Albert Road and Lumley Road, which led into the town centre, can be seen at the bottom right of the above map and here the story was similar.

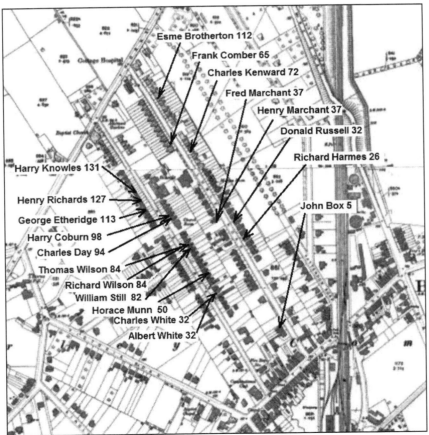

One of the mysteries which we face today is to explain quite why Horley War Memorial should include so many men from the closely packed housing at Earlswood which would appear to have been well to the north of Horley Parish. Indeed these houses were all just a few steps from St Johns Church, Earlswood. The following map shows where some of these men lived.

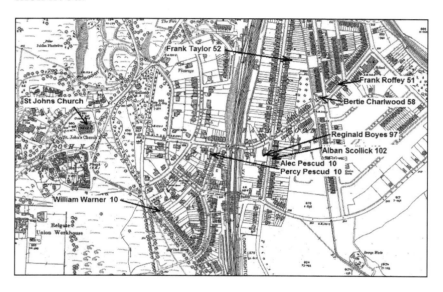

For every man who died, there was another who would never be the same again. The young lads who had marched to war with a smile on their lips and a cheerful grin were replaced by many who could only stagger along with a limp, and others whose lungs were so ravaged by the effects of gas that they would never work again.

Others would spend the rest of their lives haunted by what they had seen and a morbid dread of loud noises, dark nights and flashing lights.

Almost as soon as the war ended, communities throughout

the country began to give thought to the construction of war memorials and when the idea of building The Cenotaph in London was proposed, it generated so much publicity that the demand for local memorials began to grow.

The idea of an Unknown Soldier was first suggested by the Reverend David Railton from Margate, who had been an army chaplain near Armentierres during the war. He wrote to the Dean of Westminster with the idea and the government, quickly appreciating its propaganda value, pushed the scheme through, despite initial opposition from the King.

The battlefields were strewn with cemeteries and improvised graves and it was decided to send a number of parties to France and Belgium, where each was to recover one single body. Great care was taken to ensure that the bodies were taken from areas where they would be well decomposed so that no chance of identifying them remained.

They were received by trained morticians and all traces of remaining uniforms were removed.

On the stroke of midnight on 7 November, 1920, Brigadier General LJ Wyatt, General Officer Commanding British Troops in France and Flanders, entered a hut near the village of St Pol, near Ypres in Belgium. In front of him the remains of four bodies (some sources say six) were lying under Union flags.

The General raised his lantern and placed his hand on one of the coffins indicating his selection.

The body was placed inside an oak coffin and sealed with two wrought-iron straps topped with a seal. Inscribed on the seal were the words: 'A British Warrior Who Fell in the Great War 1914–1918. For King and Country.' A sword was also attached to the seal. This was a gift from the King and came from his private collection.

The coffin was transported across the English Chanel on board HMS Verdun and escorted by six destroyers. As they arrived at Dover a Field Marshalls salute of 19 guns was fired and a band played Land of Hope and Glory.

Crowds gathered at Dover to watch as the coffin was drawn to the station and loaded into the same van (number 132) that had been used to carry home the remains of Nurse Edith Cavell (executed by the Germans in Brussels in 1915 for assisting British soldiers to escape captivity) in May 1919. Thousands packed each station along the way to pay their respects as the train journeyed to London via the Canterbury, Faversham and Chatham route.

At 9.15am on the morning of 11 November 1920 the Unknown Warrior began the last lap of his Long, Long Trail. His flag draped coffin was mounted on a gun carriage and set off from Victoria Station at the head of 400 troops led by Field Marshall Haig, Earl Beatty and Air Marshall Trenchard. When it stopped, briefly, at the Cenotaph, the King laid a wreath upon it.

At 11 o'clock, accompanied by the mournful tolling of Big Ben, the coffin was carried through the north transept door of Westminster Abbey. There, the aisle was lined with 100 recipients of the Victoria Cross. The congregation was made up of 1,000 widows and mothers of the fallen.

After the coffin had been lowered into the grave and six barrels of Flanders earth poured over, it a large slab of Tournai marble was placed on top. By the end of the day, more than 200,000 people had visited the tomb. Within five days, more than a million people had paid their respects – the population of inner London at the time was four-and-a-half million.

Subsequently a new stone was laid on the Tomb bearing these words:

BENEATH THIS STONE RESTS THE BODY
OF A BRITISH WARRIOR
UNKNOWN BY NAME OR RANK
BROUGHT FROM FRANCE TO LIE AMONG
THE MOST ILLUSTRIOUS OF THE LAND
AND BURIED HERE ON ARMISTICE DAY
11 NOV: 1920, IN THE PRESENCE OF
HIS MAJESTY KING GEORGE V
HIS MINISTERS OF STATE
THE CHIEFS OF HIS FORCES
AND A VAST CONCOURSE OF THE NATION
THUS ARE COMMEMORATED THE MANY
MULTITUDES WHO DURING THE GREAT
WAR OF 1914–1918 GAVE THE MOST THAT
MAN CAN GIVE LIFE ITSELF FOR GOD
FOR KING AND COUNTRY
FOR LOVED ONES HOME AND EMPIRE
FOR THE SACRED CAUSE OF JUSTICE AND
THE FREEDOM OF THE WORLD
THEY BURIED HIM AMONG THE KINGS BECAUSE HE
HAD DONE GOOD TOWARD GOD AND TOWARD
HIS HOUSE

The Grave of The Unknown Warrior in Westminster Abbey.

In the immediate aftermath of the war, a housing boom erupted as 200,000 homes were built – effectively the beginning of council housing. Old age pensions were increased and wages throughout the country were standardised.

But the "Land Fit for Heroes" that Lloyd George had promised soon began to fade away and, as boom turned to bust, the people of Horley and throughout the country, tightened their belts and began the slow downhill slide towards the great depression.

In Horley, a local builder named George Strawson, who lived at the top of Charlesfield Road, became very concerned at the plight of ex-servicemen who could not find work and had little to do all day other than walk the streets or sit drinking in public houses. He had built the Strawson Hall close to where Consort Way now stands and it was used for local meetings and social events. Together with the Rev Henry Lewis (who was to chair the War Memorial Committee) and others, George founded the Red Triangle Club which met in the hall from 1919. The Red Triangle later became the symbol of the YMCA (Young Men's Christian Association). This gave ex-servicemen a focal point where they could meet with others in a similar situation to themselves and stay away from the pub – which was very pleasing to George Strawson as he was a confirmed teetotaller. The Strawson Hall was moved during the development of Horley and now sits in Albert Road.

Soldiers, crippled or blinded during their war service and unable to work, became a common sight begging on our streets and this poem by Margaret Postgate Cole is evocative of many.

THE VETERAN

We came upon him sitting in the sun
Blinded by war, and left. And past the fence
There came young soldiers from the Hand and Flower,
Asking advice of his experience.
And he said this, and that, and told them tales,
And all the nightmares of each empty head
Blew into air; then, hearing us beside,
"Poor chaps, how'd they know what it's like?" he said.
And we stood there, and watched him as he sat,
Turning his sockets where they went away,
Until it came to one of us to ask "And you're – how old?"
"Nineteen, the third of May."

CHAPTER SIX

THE HORLEY WAR MEMORIAL

When the war came to an end in November 1918 the townspeople of Horley must have heaved a collective sigh of relief that the slaughter was finally over. The bereaved families would have been trying to hold the fabric of their lives together without the support and income of their former breadwinner, whilst coping with all the suffering of their loss.

In February 1919 a public meeting was held at Albert Road School to discuss the possibility of building a Memorial to commemorate the dead men. It was resolved to ask the Parish Council to undertake the task and, in the time honoured manner of such bodies, the Council decided to 'set up a committee' which met for the first time in July 1919.

Their task was to find a suitable piece of land within the town, acquire the land, raise the funds and arrange for the construction of a War Memorial.

The committee proceeded to meet and the record of their discussions survives to this day.

For the first 18 months of their existence, they seem to have searched high and low for a suitable place for the Memorial but any land that was offered to them was too expensive for serious consideration.

They explored the possibilities of land owned by Mr J Stevens, the Cooks Company, Christ's Hospital and Mr J H Bridges but the owners were all either unwilling to sell or too expensive.

One of the sites considered was on the west side of

Bonehurst Road near the Cambridge Hotel but the amount asked for it was not acceptable.

The committee later favoured a site between the Station Hotel and the White Swan public house in what is now Station Approach but, again, the site was not affordable. They also looked at a site on the edge of Ringley Oak Farm where Church Road crosses Brighton Road but that was also rejected.

They began to suspect that they would fail in their task and sent a report to the Council laying out their difficulties. Their dilemma was finally resolved in April 1921. A small patch of land, like a triangular island, in front of the Thorns Hotel (now the Air Balloon) had previously been sought but the owners refused to sell it. The then chairman of the committee, Mr G Freeman, (who had lost his son, George, in 1916) said he would "have a word with them". As he was also a prominent member of the Parish Council, it is interesting to speculate on the nature of this 'word'. Nevertheless, he was persuasive and the land was subsequently offered free of charge. Perhaps he made them an offer they couldn't refuse!

Consequently, the committee accepted the offer of this land from Messrs Mellersh and Neale in front of The Thorns Hotel, at the junction of Victoria Road and Brighton Road. This small patch of land was originally a residue of the old Horley Common.

The committee also made extensive enquiries with regard to selecting a firm to build the Memorial. It did not take them long to settle on CE Ebbutt and Sons Ltd, the well-established monumental masons of Croydon. Several alternative designs were then submitted for discussion and, after some deliberation, a design was accepted which was to cost about £350 (£13,250 today). Later work, including preparation of the site and surrounding posts and chains, was to increase this amount to nearer £600 (£22,700).

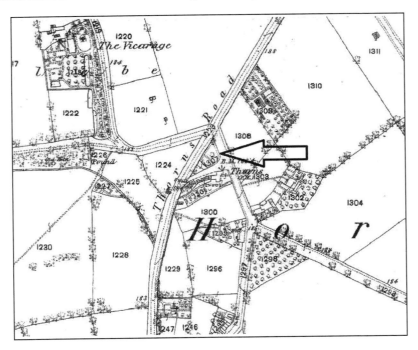

Whilst all this was going on, the committee were struggling to raise the necessary funds. 1500 flyers requesting donations were printed and distributed door to door. By November 1920 about £160 (£6050) had been raised. Then the committee had a really bright idea. They decided to hand the fundraising responsibilities to a team of women. Thus groups of door to door collectors were embodied to add to the money donated. One of these ladies was Mrs EM Sangster who lived in Lumley Road, Horley. Both her sons had died in the war but for some inexplicable reason neither Edward nor Hugh were named on the War Memorial. Whether or not she knew that this was to be so is not recorded.

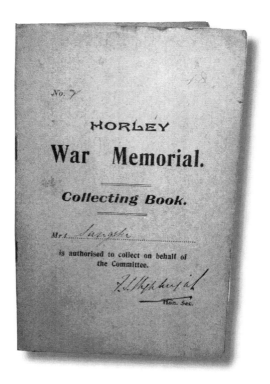

Mrs Sangster's collecting book. (Authors Photo)

Money was still very slow to come in and the givers of larger sums were all revisited in an effort to increase their already generous donations. By November 1921 the committee estimated that they were still £178 (£6,734) short of their requirements and as late as a fortnight before the unveiling ceremony they estimated that they still needed about £74 (£2,800) to clear all their debts.

The contributions of the larger donors were recorded and the record survives. Lloyds Bank and Barclays Bank in Horley acted as joint bankers for the fund and were represented on the War Memorial Committee by their respective managers, Archibald Langley and Kenelm Burgess Smith. Archibald

Langley would have been mindful that one of his own former staff members had been killed: Francis Ferris (originally from Wiltshire) had died near Arras in 1917, aged 26, whilst serving with 11th Royal Fusiliers.

The largest single donor was Mr George Carter Oliver JP who lived at "The Elms" in Horley Row, where Henry Webber had once lived. He was a boot and shoe manufacturer and when he died in 1934, his estate amounted to £158,206 (£9,575,000). He donated £25 (£1,036), a very generous sum for those days!

Others contributed sums of 3 or 5 guineas (£125 or £210) but the majority of donations varied between 1 and 5 shillings – 5 and 25 pence in today's money though worth about £2 or £10 in 1921.

When the final bill for £601-17-11d (£24,595) arrived from Ebbutts, the committee did not have sufficient funds to pay the balance owing, some money having already been paid 'on account'. They wrote to Ebbutts and asked if they could trim the bill in some way and, as to be expected, received a sharp response in the negative.

Fortunately an anonymous donation was made which covered the balance and left a surplus of £7-7s-1d (£350) and this sum was donated to Horley Cottage Hospital, where it eventually arrived in January 1924!

The total sum collected was £788-9s-5d (£37,950). The Committee incurred various expenses over its duration culminating in those for the unveiling ceremony itself and after these were deducted from the total amount raised, the bill from Ebbutts was settled and the small surplus was left over.

The list of names of the dead men must have been pulled together at some stage. What steps, if any, were taken to see that it was complete are not known.

January 21st. 1922.

F.J.Nightingale Esq.
Hon. Sec.
Horley War Memorial Committee,
Horley.

Dear Sir;
Your favour of the 20th instant to hand with cheques for £100. 0. 0 on account, for which we thank you and enclose receipt for same.

We are astounded by the request of your committee to "assist them in regard to the balance owing - by way of contribution to the memorial", as it is perfectly impossible for us to contribute to every memorial we erect, especially in view of the fact that we estimate on the lines of first class material and workmanship, small profits amd cash within one month, thus allowing our capital to turn itself over quickly.

All our accounts are subject to an increase of 5% if not paid within one month, as per enclosed blank statement form, but in your Committee's particular case we have never mentioned this, as our Mr Ebbutt understood your difficulties.

With reference to the items of account,we should feel honoured if you would invite two or three reliable firms of good standing to give your Committee an estimate of their charge for erecting a similar memorial to the memorial erected by us, as we know for certain that all the other estimates will exceed our special price of £395. 0. 0 even today when labour is cheaper than one year ago.

Reference to the inscription on same, we

The letter received from Ebbutts (Authors photo)

-2-

estimated for <del>for</del> cutting , drilling and filling with lead the imperishable raised lead letters @ 1/4 per letter and the trade price of these at the date of our estimate was 1/6 per letter, and is today @ 1/4 per letter, and cannot be guaranteed as imperishable at less cost than this.

The whole of the lettering and carving was at piece work rates and paid for by us to our employees before the end of June.

For the extra foundation 2ft high, we only charged you the actual cost of gravel, brieze and cement that we had to pay Messrs Hall & Co of Horley, and when we paid by cheque in July we did not receive one penny discount from Messrs Hall & Co., and we should be pleased if your Committee would kindly verify these facts. The labour was put in at cost, viz: 2/- per hour, which you will find was the Government rates for London in which district we are included for wages.

We commenced paying wages on this memorial the first week in February 1921, and we can only ask you once morein fairness to ourselves, to get outside estimates from other reliable firms to see that the small profit possible for us to have made over the memorial will not recompense us for having sunk £600. 0. 0 capital to be tied up for a period spread over 12 months, and how utterly impossible it is for us to"assist your Committee et as you suggest, but we should like to know exactly what the amount was that your Committee thought we might have been able to have contributed in view of the fact that there is still the amount of £101.17.11 outstanding.   Yours Faithfully,

David H. Ebbutt

The letter received from Ebbutts (Authors photo)

217

On 3 May 1921 the committee resolved:

"that the list of names to be inscribed on the memorial should be confined strictly to those of the Parish of Horley and that Rev HT Lewis and Messrs Cleather and Langley go through the list of names and verify same."

The Reverend Henry Lewis, vicar of St Bartholomews, was the committee chairman by this time. How many names were on the list that he and his two fellow committee members pruned is not known. The original list, in whatever form it existed, cannot be found.

The edited list was sent to Ebbutts on 19 August 1921. The letter which accompanied the list survives but the list itself does not, though there is no reason to think that it contained anything other than the 122 names which were subsequently inscribed. It would have been interesting to see the list, however, as there are some discrepancies in names and spellings and it would have been possible to determine whether they occurred in the construction or, as is most likely, were incorrectly listed.

As the project neared completion, the Committee turned its thoughts to a ceremony to mark the unveiling of the Memorial in February 1922.

How wonderful, they thought, if we could get the Prince of Wales (the future King Edward VIII) to unveil it. So they wrote to him and asked him – but he declined on 9 July 1921, pleading that if he agreed to all the similar requests he was receiving, then he would never have time for anything else!

The Duke of York (the future King George VI) appeared to be the next best personality, so they wrote to him and received a similar reply a few weeks later. When they were again disappointed by the great Naval hero Earl Beatty, something close to desperation was starting to set in, so it must have been a great relief when their fourth choice, Brigadier General GK Cockerill, CB, MP wrote back to them on 28 January 1922 – just four weeks before the scheduled unveiling on 25 February – and accepted their invitation.

The committee would have written to Cockerill in his capacity as their MP (for Reigate in those days) and almost certainly have been quite unaware of his military background and his clandestine work in Military Intelligence.

Cockerill (1867–1957) was a long-time intelligence officer, and one of the most innovative thinkers in British intelligence in World War I. Head of MO5 – which became MI5 – the Special Intelligence Section of the General Staff at the outbreak of the War, he organized postal censorship, and carried out a revolution at the lower and middle levels of the military bureaucracy. Despite great opposition from traditionally-minded generals, Cockerill affected the first extensive use of propaganda by the War Office at any time in the country's history. Cockerill's chief contribution was a refinement of the art of mass propaganda. He conducted this mainly through the propaganda leaflet, smuggled behind enemy lines and dropped over enemy troops from aeroplanes and large balloons. It became an increasingly potent weapon as the Great War proceeded.

A suitable ceremony was planned for the unveiling at 3.30pm on Saturday 25 February 1922 and a booklet was printed to contain the Form of Service and a Roll of Honour. It stated that this Memorial "is erected to the 123 men who gave their lives for their country in the Great War." This document was given an addendum to list the units of some of the men. This included one additional name (Bagg) and so, in fact, lists 124 men. The fact that the Memorial lists only 122 men seems to have been overlooked and that 4 men who are named on the Memorial are not on the Roll of Honour, smacks of carelessness or, if we are to be charitable, last minute confusion. Close comparison of this Roll of Honour with the men named on the Memorial shows several discrepancies and we shall look at these later on.

Crowds attending the Service of Dedication of Horley War Memorial on 25 February 1922.
(Courtesy of Horley Local History Society.)

The service opened with Hymn number 439 "The Son of God goes forth to war...." and moved through the Lord's Prayer to Psalm 23 "The Lord is My Shepherd".

After a short lesson (taken from the book of Wisdom, long

since removed from protestant Bibles) the congregation joined in the Nunc Dimittis and the Apostles Creed before launching themselves into Hymn 438 "How bright these glorious spirits shine..."

At the conclusion of this hymn the unveiling itself took place by General Cockerill and was followed by a Dedication by Rev HT Lewis, Vicar of Horley:

"In the Faith of Jesus Christ, we dedicate this Memorial Cross to the Glory of God and in memory of these, His servants, who have given their lives in the Great War, in the name of the Father, and of the Son, and of the Holy Ghost."

The Last Post was sounded and a two minute silence was observed, followed by The Reveille and as its last poignant notes died away amidst a flurry of damp handkerchiefs, the voices of the crowd moved into a lively rendition of Hymn 437 – "For all the Saints who from their labours rest..."

The vicar delivered a final blessing and then Mr Robert E Neale, the donor of the land, asked the chairman of Horley Parish Council to accept the land and the Memorial as a gift from the subscribers to the Town of Horley, forever. Mr EJ Wadham, on behalf of the Council, graciously accepted the same and a vote of thanks was proposed to General Cockerill.

The singing of the National Anthem bought the ceremony to a close.

The last minuted meeting of the committee was on 4 August 1922 and its final composition was as follows:

Chairman: Rev. H.T.Lewis
Joint Hon Treasurer: A.G.S.Langley

Joint Hon Treasurer: K. Burgess Smith
Hon Secretary: F.J.Nightingale
Asst Hon Secretary: A.V.De'Ath
Members: Dr S.A.Clarke, R.L.Norris, F.J.Cassini, J.W.Stevens,
J.J.Chiswell, E.C.Charleton, R.W.Brett, A.H.Eve, E.P.Cleather,
J.H.Mallinson, E.J.Flint, A.Henley

This photograph, looking south down the Brighton Road, shows the
War Memorial on its original site.
(Courtesy of Horley Local History Society.)

The War Memorial remained in situ outside the The Thorns
until 1953. Part of a base plinth was added after the Second
World War and another 46 names of the dead of that conflict
were inscribed.

By 1953 the traffic using the Brighton Road had increased
considerably and some major readjustments needed to be

made at the crossroads, to cope with the volume of traffic passing along the A23 and across the junction from Vicarage Lane into Victoria Road.

The owners of The Thorns Hotel also wanted to improve their car parking facilities so it was agreed to move the War Memorial diagonally across the road to a site in the recreation ground, where it remains to this day in its own Garden of Remembrance, carefully maintained by Horley Town Council.

By 1967 the Memorial was found to be in danger of collapse. The cross, weighing three tons, was out of alignment because the plinth had subsided and funds were raised locally to provide £1200 (over £18,000 today) for restoration which was successfully carried out.

In October 1999 new gates were added to the Garden of Remembrance. They were designed by Kieran Chart, a pupil of Oakwood School and built by Horley blacksmith, Brian Sims. The gates are designed around the words "Their Name Liveth for Evermore" and they were in place in time for the Remembrance Day ceremony on the 14 November.

The Garden of Remembrance continues to be kept in immaculate condition by the Town Council and remains the key focus of local Remembrance every November when a well-attended service is held there.

MEN OF HORLEY

A.E.NEWTON • C.A.NISBER • C.W.NORMAN • F.H.NORTHERN
J.A.NOWERS • A.O.OLLETT • R.P.OULSNAM • W.F.PADDOCK
J.PAGE • A.J.PALMER • F.A.PALMER • H.L.PALMER • C.C.PANNELL
A.B.PARROTT • H.H.PARSONS • J.W.PATRICK • F.P.PAYNTER
R.PEARCE • B.H.PENFOLD • S.W.PENTY • R.F.PERCIVAL • F.G.PERKINS
A.E.PERCE • J.L.S.PILLEY • W.FOSKITT • F.J.POTTER • D.B.POWELL
J.S.POWELL • E.J.PRIME • F.J.PRITCHARD • G.PURSLOW • G.C.READ
W.READMAN • G.A.REID • L.F.RHODES • A.R.RICHARDS
F.S.RICHES • C.B.ROBINSON • H.W.ROBINSON • R.F.ROTHWELL
J.B.ROWLEY • H.W.K.RUDD • A.A.S.RUST • R.S.SALMON
F.SANGSTER • C.SAUDERS • M.A.SCARBOROUGH • A.B.SCHOFIELD
C.J.SCOTT • H.A.SETCHELL • M.H.M.SIMS • QF.SIMS • J.L.SKINNER
W.G.SLICER • C.D.SMITH • D.J.SMITH • J.SMITH • O.SMURTHWAITE
R.M.SMYTHE • A.SOPWITH • W.R.SOULSBY • W.J.SPILLER
H.T.SPRINGTHORPE • R.C.SPRINKS • F.J.C.SQUIRE • H.STACEY
W.L.STEVENS • C.H.STONE • F.G.STRANACK • H.G.STRIDE
H.SUTHERLAND • C.H.SWANN • A.G.E.SYMS • R.A.TAIT
H.E.W.TEALBY • F.E.THOMES • H.M.THOMAS • E.A.THOMPSON
F.C.THOMPSON • W.J.THOMPSON • H.C.THORNS • F.S.TILLEY
G.H.TINKLER • H.A.TOMPKINS • C.C.TONGUE • G.DE.G.TOOLEY
H.G.TOWN • G.T.TOWNSEND • H.S.TROTTER • C.G.TYRRELL
R.M.UPTON • H.S.VINALL • W.H.B.WALES • H.W.WALKER
J.S.WATSON • C.S.WEBSTER • N.K.WELBAND • J.WELLS • G.L.WHITE
P.WHITE • H.T.WHITING • W.R.WHITTAKER • F.P.WHITTET
F.H.WICKS • S.A.B.WIGHTMAN • E.J.WILDE • M.B.WILKS
W.F.D.WILLIAMS • A.W.WILSON • G.E.WILSON • J.A.S.WOOD
H.L.WOODHOUSE • B.W.WRIGHT • H.W.ROUGHTON • H.C.CYEO
M.Y.E.WDALL • H.B.BARRETT • D.J.BROWNE • L.R.CLARK
I.D.FLEETWOOD • C.R.MANN • M.A.PRENTICE • W.V.STEED
F.M.S.TONKIN • G.W.BERRY • N.T.M.BURRELL • R.C.DAGNALL
A.R.HOLMES • L.B.OAKES • G.P. ROWE • M.J.F.TEASDALE
N.F.VENTHAM • G.N.BROMLEY MARTIN • A.M.CAMPLIN
D.S.EVANS • G.C.LAWRENSON • F.J.PINNELL • J.PROWNTREE
B.H.THOMAS • G.RYEOMANS • E.C.AITKEN • H.J.ALEXANDER
C.A.BAKER • C.BARTLETT • G.F.BLIGHT • W.BOOTH • A.L.S.BRAID
H.A.BRAND • P.H.BRICKELL • M.R.BRIERLEY • V.G.BROOKLESBY
L.V.BROWN • P.E.M.BROWN • D.H.BURGESS • G.F.BUFRIDGE
F.L.H.BURTON • W.BUTLER • C.S.CALDER • R.S.CANE
A.R.CANFOR • C.CARPENTER • E.F.CARPENTER • J.C.G.CARTER
P.L.CATCHPOLE • J.F.CHALKEY • F.L.CHAMP • G.T.CHANDLER
F.P.M.CHURCH • A.H.COPPACK • R.C.CORTI • O.W.COWHAM
R.C.CREWES • G.P.CROUCH • A.J.CULLEN • U.P.DAVIES
F.C.DENNING • H.G.DOWSETT • F.J.EGLINGTON • H.ELGAR
E.A.EMIES • A.R.ESPURY • E.M.YOUNG • B.E.FISH • J.A.FLECK
H.FLEMING • A.I.FROST • C.C.GOODMAN • L.A.GREEN
P.H.GRIFFIN • R.E.GROVES • I.HADDON • R.E.HALL • H.L.HALSE
A.D.HAMILTON • T.J.H.HAPRISON • N.W.HASELDINE • S.A.HAVES
K.E.HAWKINS • R.HOGBIN • W.D.HOLIDAY • P.L.HORNING
I.S.HOWLETT • E.C.HURST • B.H.CHUSK • S.J.HUTCHINGS
C.H.I.SLEY • W.A.IVES • G.K.JENNINGS • J.A.B.JONES • C.H.KEANEY
J.KILBY • C.E.KING • N.H.KIPLING • S.W.LAMBRICK
F.G.R.LAWTON • N.G.LEFTWICH • F.R.C.LeMONQUAIS
T.C.LIDSTONE • S.T.LOCKWOOD • A.LYTH • A.L.MABBOTT
G.O.C.MAIDMENT • R.McCONKEY • A.MANN • K.M.MARSDEN
B.S.MARTELL • F.R.MARTYR • C.C.MATHER • H.MELDRUN
A.M.G.MERRILL • R.V.MILLEST • A.J.MUNGER • J.F.S.MURRAY
G.NORMAN • L.A.NORMAN • H.R.NOTT • F.E.OLDHAM
S.A.OSBORNE • H.L.PADFIELD • H.C.PANTER • F.H.W.PASCOE
A.J.PEARCE • L.G.PEASTON • G.PENNELL • D.F.PENNEY
F.D.PEWTRESS • W.POOK • A.C.PRATT • L.C.PRICE • F.PROCTER
S.H.RADCLIFFE • F.E.RAYNER • R.W.REED • W.REID
D.R.REWCASTLE • E.V.RICHER • S.C.RIDDICK • W.F.ROPER
S.W.ROWLES • I.PRYAN • E.SAINT • D.ST LEGER • E.Y.SAXBY
E.D.SELFE • A.C.SHARP • E.V.SIMS • A.G.SMITH • I.E.J.SMITH

J.A.G.SMYTH • B.L.SORRELL • C.F.STARLING • J.H.STILLMAN
G.C.STORKEY • A.J.TAYLOR • G.E.R.THOMAS • C.G.TREBY
F.A.TRUFITT • E.F.TUMBER • N.D.TURTLE • A.H.VOYSEY
C.F.WARD • R.A.P.WARLTERS • S.J.WATTS • V.V.WEARING
S.B.WEATHERSTON • C.F.WEBB • F.B.WEBB • H.J.WEST • L.H.W.HIPP
G.R.WHITE • H.J.WHITE • H.N.WHITE • J.E.WHITEOAK
S.C.WHITLOCK • H.H.WICKS • A.J.WILKINSON • A.C.WILLEY
D.C.WILSON • W.J.WINDSON • H.L.WINTER • A.J.WINTERBOURNE
R.WOOD • L.C.W.WORRALL • E.C.B.WRIGHT • A.J.YOUNG
M.FAINSLIE • J.ANDREW • F.AUSTIN • P.BALMER • H.BATESON
H.BENTHAM • H.BIRKETT • T.M.BIRTLE • G.S.BLACKBURN
R.A.BLACKLOCK • E.P.BOWER • T.C.BROCKBANK • B.R.BYERS
P.F.CANNON • W.D.CHISHOLM • P.CLARK • A.CLARKE • J.G.COE
C.CONSTANTINE • E.CORKILL • C.COTTON • H.S.CROWE
R.CURSON • T.CUTHBERTSON • R.DAVISON • J.F.DODD • P.H.DON
A.E.F.DRAPER • H.R.DUDLEY • H.W.EDWARDS • B.P.EMSLEY
R.H.FISHER • L.McL.FORD • P.N.FRY • W.E.GALLOWAY
R.P.GARNER • F.W.GIDLEY • A.W.GORDON • W.G.GRAINGER
H.GRAY • A.GRENSTED • A.E.GRIEVE • J.GRIEVE • W.HAIGH
R.S.HAWORTH • W.R.C.HAWORTH • J.HEATON
•F.P.HERD.L.PHILL•W.E.HIPWELL•H.HODGSON•B.G.HUMPHRYS
F.JACKSON • R.S.JACKSON • C.JARAH • H.W.JOEL • C.S.JONES
G.JONES • R.F.JONES • S.JONES • T.K.KENWORTHY • J.KINCAID
W.F.KING • A.LEIGHTON • G.LEE.ROUGETEL • R.V.LISTER
C.J.G.LIVESEY • H.G.E.LUCHFORD • J.LYONS • J.MACKENZIE
W.E.McLAUGHLIN • G.C.S.MANN • T.L.MARTIN • F.G.MAYOR
R.E.MAYOR • J.MEEK • A.A.MILROY • L.MOLDEN • L.E.MOORE
W.MURDOCH • J.NEWTON • E.J.NUTTALL • A.E.O'NEIL
D.T.PARRY • C.F.PEARSON • C.H.PEARSON • K.PEARSON
J.A.PEEBLES • A.M.PENBERTHY • A.PHILLIPSON • L.POLLOCK
H.C.PONTING • W.POYNTER • H.PRINCE • W.C.RAVENSCROFT
J.W.RAWLING • N.S.REAM • J.M.ROBERTS • T.W.ROBERTS
W.A.ROBINSON • W.RODGERS • R.G.ROSS • T.L.ROWLAND
J.F.SAMPSON • E.B.SCHOFIELD • W.SCOTT • S.S.CURR
C.B.SHEPERD • A.SHEPPEY • R.W.SIDDALL • E.SMITH • H.SNAITH
J.E.STANSFIELD • G.STERLING • J.P.SUGEDIN • J.SWINBURN
H.N.TAYLOR • J.H.TEMPLE • G.W.THOMAS • H.VENTHAM
A.G.WALKDEN • C.G.S.WARD • G.W.WATSON • E.A.WEAVER
W.V.WHITTLEY • R.B.WILSON • G.W.ACWORTH • G.ARNOLD
P.R.BIANCHFLOWER • F.H.BOWETT • H.E.BREWSTER
T.B.BROOKS • G.H.BROWN • D.C.BRUNNING • C.A.BUTTON
O.W.N.CARNE • C.H.CARPENTER • C.R.CARRUTHERS
A.C.CHITTY • N.K.COLES • H.H.COPPEN • N.N.DANIEL
C.L.DAVIES • D.C.DAVIES • E.J.DAVIES • J.C.DAVIES • J.W.DAVIES
T.DAVIES • W.N.DAVIES • A.DRAYCOTT • W.S.DUTCH
H.E.DUTTON • C.G.EASTGATE • H.EDWARDS • J.EVANS
W.H.EVANS • J.E.M.EVERETT • R.M.FILSHIE • A.C.FLORANT
C.W.GALVIN • E.V.GARRAD • C.N.GEAN • E.W.GEORGE
T.M.GEORGE • D.P.GORDON • W.S.WRIGHT • O.S.GREEN
W.J.GREEN • D.J.GRIFFITHS • H.N.O.GUTHRIE • H.G.HALL
J.HARRIS • L.V.HEARD • W.J.HOWELLS • J.C.JACKSON • E.L.JONES
E.T.JONES • T.JONES • W.W.KEY • G.KING • D.J.V.KNOTT • R.J.LAMB
G.H.LANE • H.B.LANEY • A.C.LEE • R.A.LEWIS • J.V.LUKE
A.C.MACDONALD • A.H.MAHR • M.J.MARSDEN • M.T.MASON
J.H.MATHIAS • J.McLINTOCK • F.MOORE • D.N.MORTON
F.K.MOTT • S.G.MULLIGAN • R.C.O'DONOGHUE • A.COWEN
H.J.OWEN • W.D.OWEN • J.T.PARISH • S.T.PARKYN • R.J.PARSLEY
L.B.PARSONS • E.J.POND • R.C.A.POOLE • F.T.PRICE • C.G.T.PRIST
H.W.PROCTOR • A.P.RANKINE • L.A.RAYNER • D.S.REES
J.REES • A.H.REYNOLDS • E.F.REYNOLDS • T.F.RICHES
S.D.ROBINSON • A.RONALDSON • J.D.RUCHMER
H.W.SAMPSON • J.H.SCARLES • A.I.SMITH • J.W.SMITH
L.E.K.STEPHENS • D.THOMAS • D.C.S.THOMAS • H.S.THOMAS
K.G.THOMAS • N.L.THOMAS • R.E.THOMAS • S.THOMAS

S.M.THOMAS • T.S.THOMAS • H.W.THOMPSON • H.D.VALENTINE
R.R.WEAR • I.S.G.WHITE • W.F.WHITE • A.O.WILLIAMS
H.D.WILLIAMS • T.H.WILLIAMS • K.P.WINDOW • W.G.WITTY
T.E.ADCOCK • A.V.ALLDEN • E.R.L.ANDREWS • F.F.APPLEGARTH
J.ARCHBOLD • L.R.ARMITAGE MC • A.H.ARMSTRONG
L.A.D.ARNOT • C.A.A.SHMAN • C.H.LASKEY • H.E.BACKHOUSE
L.A.BALL • W.G.BALL • N.W.BANNISTER • R.E.BARKER
T.A.BARNES • F.C.BARRETT • H.C.BARROW • S.J.BAYLEY
W.R.BEALL • R.D.BEAVIS • A.D.BEBEE • W.F.BELCHER
S.W.J.BENNETT • W.A.BENNETT • L.BINNEY • G.W.BIRKBECK
J.B.BISHOP • W.R.BISHOP • W.E.T.BOLITHO DSO • J.A.BOOTE
F.G.L.BORROW • A.BOTHWELL MC • W.H.BOULTON • H.BOUNDS
C.R.BOUSTEAD • E.P.BOUSTEAD • E.A.BOWYER • F.BOYSON
F.S.BROOKBANKS • I.J.BROOKE • H.F.G.BROOKSBANK
V.BROTHERTON • C.BROWN • F.A.BROWN • F.R.BROWN
G.F.BROWN • H.N.BROWN • W.BROWN • L.BROWNSCOMBE
E.A.BURTON • P.C.BUSS • F.H.BUTLER • J.G.BUTLER • A.R.BUXTON
W.P.CARR • R.H.CARRICK • H.W.CARTER • J.N.CARTWRIGHT
W.H.CATER • C.E.CHAPLIN • P.G.CHARLESWORTH • J.E.CHARMAN
H.CHILTON • G.D.CHISHOLM • L.F.CHRISTMAS • A.F.CLARKE
W.R.CLEPHAN MC • F.W.T.CLERKE • J.COATES • R.COBB • F.J.COLE
C.P.COLEMAN • A.E.COLMER • E.W.COOPER • H.C.OSSONS
C.C.CRAGGS • E.CRESSWELL • L.G.CRIMES • W.J.CRISP
T.A.K.CUBITT MC • H.W.CUMMINS • G.G.CURREY • M.A.DALE
H.G.DARBOUR • C.W.DAVIDSON • J.G.DAVIES • N.T.DAVIES
W.J.DAVIES • H.DAVIS • W.C.DAVIS • H.S.DAVY • A.DENTON
F.G.DE HERIZ • J.M.DE PARAVICINI • N.W.DERRY • L.G.DEUCE
R.DICKINSON • R.F.DICKSEE • W.H.P.DICKSON • A.R.DILLIWAY
A.W.DIPPER • R.F.DRAPER • E.E.DRESSER • C.G.DUCKWORTH
P.W.EAST • H.W.ELLIOTT • J.ELLIOTT • E.ELLIS • I.ELLIS • S.ELLIS
F.J.ELTON • J.M. EMERSON • R.J.ENNIS • A.E.G.EPPS • C.W.H.EVANS
H.G.EVANS • P.G.W.EVANS • H.FELL • THE EARL OF FEVERSHAM
L.V.FITZPATRICK • V.W.FLETCHER • E.FLINT • E.J.FLOUNDERS
G.L.A.FOGDEN • F.W.L.FORFEITT • C.FOSTER • P.E.C. FOX
J.FRANCIS • C.J.FRANK • J.H.FRIEND • E.X.GALL • W.S.GARBUTT
C.E.GARNHAM • J.R.GIBBONS • D.GIBBS • H.F.M.GILLAM
B.ST.J.GLANFIELD • W.GODDARD • H.A.GOLBY • T.GOLDSWORTHY
A.C.COSTELOW • E.T.GRAIGER • H.N.GRANT • J.F.GREEN
M.V.P.GREEN • S.F.GREEN • H.C.GREENHALGH • W.E.GREW
E.S.HAIN • T.HALL • E.J.HALLUM • C.J.HARBORD • F.W.F.HARRIS
F.G.HARRISON • J.S.HATCH • R.HAY • S.J.HAWKES • L.F.L.HAYDON
C.HEATHER • C.D.HEATON • N.HEAVEN • L.A.WEDGE • T.H.HELME
W.H.F.PENSTALL • W.HEARRING • G.R.HESELTON • J.HODGKINSON
G.C.HOEHN • W.J.HOLMES • H.H.HOOPER • W.J.HORNSEY
R.W.HORTON • J.H.HOSKINS • E.HOPE • N.M.HUGHES
L.A.HUGHMAN • F.H.HUMBY • E.J.HUTCHINGS
G.D.HUTCHINSON • H.HUTSON • W.A.IMBER • F.IVE • A.JACKSON
L.JACKSON • R.JARVIS • O.G.JARY • H.JEFFERSON • H.D.JOAD
N.R.JOHNSON • S.JOHNSON MC • A.M.JONES • E.D.JONES
I.D.JONES • J.M.JONES • M.F.JONES • T.M.JONES • W.B.JONES
A.JORDAN • S.F.JOWETT • E.KAY • J.H.M.KEIGHLEY
F.H.KENDRICK • H.C.KEW • R.D.KING • HON.A.M.KINNAIRD
P.F.KINGTON • G.B.KNIGHTS • W.C.LANCASTER • E.A.M.LANE
G.W.LATTER • P.C.LAVANCHY • J.M.LAVERACK • N.W.LAWSON
F.T.LEATHARD • A.LEE • S.A.LEITH • A.G.H.LEONARD • W.T.LEWIS
H.C.LITCHFIELD • B.G.LODGE • A.D.LOOKER • W.A.H.LOUNDS
C.R.LYDEKKER • E.LYON • A.MAIS • J.F.MALLETT • A.MALYN
W.G.MANSELL • J.W.MARYON • G.E.MATHERS • H.C.MATTHEWS
E.J.McCARTHY • A.B.MacCREATH AM • P.N.L.McINNEA
G.H.MELLOR • W.MEPHAM • W.N.MILES • W.H.MILLER
B.J.MILLWARD • L.MOROK • J.G.MORLEY • W.H.MORRIS
A.J.MOUTAIN • A.C.MURRELL • L.INEAVE

In memory of our colleagues who gave their lives.
1914-18 / 1939-45

CHAPTER SEVEN

IDENTIFICATION OF OTHER LOCAL MEMORIALS

Despite searching high and low, it has not been possible to find the various lists of names from which the War Memorial Committee selected the names for inscription on the War Memorial.

The Committee seemed to keep a good record of it's meetings and general activities so it is surprising that no casualty lists, amended or otherwise, survive.

No doubt, the joint treasurers had precise knowledge of the funds deposited within their respective banks, but even the surviving documents relating to the financial state of the accounts are little more than odd scraps of paper. Perhaps the missing lists of names were also written on various pages which have now been lost.

We do know, from the painstakingly kept minute book of the committee, the exact wording that the committee decided to apply to their list.

"That the list of names to be inscribed on the memorial should be confined strictly to those of the Parish of Horley and that Rev HT Lewis and Messrs Cleather and Langley go through the list of names and verify same."

The Military authorities kept careful records. War Diaries were maintained by each unit down to Battalion level, even under the difficult circumstances that prevailed in the trenches. Perhaps a pencil copy was made and typed up when conditions made it possible and this document would have been preserved and protected in the same way as code books and special orders. As soon as a unit was relieved from their spell in the trenches a roll call would take place and, under the supervision of an officer, the surviving men would report their comrades as 'missing', 'wounded' or 'dead'. The batallion report, together with the reports from the field and base hospitals, would form the basis for the initial reporting of casualties. This would start the chain of events and notifications which would end with the arrival of a telegraph boy on a doorstep in Horley, where he would hand over the dreaded news to a devastated parent or wife.

Any pension due to the bereaved family would have been administered by the military authorities. The families were not obliged to report the death of their men to any local body. Quite often, the vicar may have become aware of the death and offered comfort to the bereaved, whether they were part of his flock or not. In many cases it would have been the same vicar who had confirmed the man's personal details on his attestation papers.

There are a number of local sources which we can look at, in an attempt to reconstruct a full list of local men from which the War Memorial committee may have made their selection. The exact dates on which the church memorials were erected are not known.

These are as follows:

1. A list of names forming the basis for the 'Parsons plaque' followed by an appeal for more names which appeared in the Parish magazine in 1918.
2. The finished Parsons plaque (post 1919) in St Bartholomews Church.

3. The 1922 Roll of Honour used at the Dedication ceremony.
4. A Memorial tablet in St Emanuels Church at Sidlow Bridge.
5. A copy of the names on a plaque which was once displayed in the church of Christ the King, Salfords.
6. A small plaque in Horley Baptist Church.
7. A Memorial plaque originally erected in Horley Infant School.
8. The War Memorial at Charlwood.
9. A Roll of Honour in St Johns Church, Earlswood.

THE PARSONS PLAQUE IN ST BARTHOLOMEWS CHURCH

An extract from St Bartholomews Parish magazine in late 1918 may hold the clues as to how the names of the war dead were collected.

Major Bernard Parsons, DSO, survived the Great War (serving with The Hampshire Regiment) and his parents, Mr and Mrs BW Parsons of Horse Hills, decided to offer to meet the costs of an oak Memorial plaque within the church, to serve as a monument to those who had not been as fortunate as their son.

Soon after the war ended a Roll of Honour was published in the Parish Magazine. It listed the names of 103 men and said that the vicar would be glad to know, as soon as possible, of any omissions in the list, as their names were to be perpetuated in an oak Memorial Tablet. This appeal apparently generated at least 38 more names and the completed tablet lists 123 men – coincidentally the same number mistakenly given on the Roll of Honour used at the dedication ceremony.

Is it possible that these names formed the basis for the list used by the War Memorial Committee? It is certainly tempting to think so but a careful analysis of the names still leaves some uncertainty.

Some men named on this original list found their way onto the Parsons plaque but were subsequently left off the War Memorial. They were: Mark Dowlen, William Dowlen, Albert Eames, William Eames, Henry Lucas and William Henry Frederick Weller.

Of the names across both memorials, 38 were not on the published appeal list and so must have become known following the appeal. Of these 38 names, the following 20 were subsequently inscribed on the plaque:

Edwin Bagg, George Banks, George Barton, Thomas Bowen, Thomas Brocklehurst, Harry Coburn, Frederick Dann, Carl Hanson, William Hanson, John Humphrey, Benjamin Killick, Ernest Leach, Ernest Lindley, Stuart McMurray, Alec Shoubridge, Frederick Sired, Ernest Smith, James Swinden, Arthur Turner and Alfred Tyrrell.

The addition of these men brings us to the total number of names listed on the Parsons plaque – 123.

This plaque was in the form of a large oak tablet and was completed in time for a day of Memorial Services "on behalf of those who have fallen in the Great War", which was held on Sunday, 12 October 1919, when the plaque was dedicated to their memory. By this time, the War Memorial Committee were still seeking a suitable site and slowly raising funds.

The names on this plaque are not quite in alphabetical order and it is unclear as to why. Perhaps the names were painted in the order in which they were listed, though the painter could have been expected to question this. It is clear that he started by dividing the space available into three equal columns. In some cases, it was necessary to shorten names to fit them into a column width and in some instances the size of the lettering is slightly reduced to fit the name in.

As the lists approach the bottom of the third column we reach the name of Leslie Yardley and he, being at the end of the alphabet, should have been the last man.

Ten names have then been added and the lettering becomes increasingly compressed, so that by the time the sixth of these is added, it is level with the names at the bottom of the preceding columns. Of the final four names, two are compressed at the bottom of column three and two more are painted side by side in the space below columns one and two.

A contemporary photograph produced in the form of a post card exists but is undated. (This postcard is reproduced here courtesy of Richard Cooper.) It was probably taken when the plaque was dedicated on 12 October 1919, or it may have been taken on the following Remembrance or Armistice Day. It is clear from this photo that the final two names, those of Arthur Burt Turner and Thomas Bowen, have been painted in more recently than the others.

The names which were painted in completely out of sequence (seven of them after this photo was taken) are listed here with other added lettering:

Percy Pescud, Arthur Burt Turner, Thomas Bowen, Lt Carl Frederick Hanson, 2nd Lt William George Hanson, Harry George Coburn, Ernest Cecil Leach Lce Cpl 17th MR, Stuart McMurray, Ernest William Lindley (RFC) and Edwin Albert Bagg (CPO).

The first of these late names listed as 'add-ons' on the plaque is Percy Pescud. His name was on the 'appeal' list and he also appears on the War Memorial so the fact that his name appears out of sequence here is probably a signwriters error.

Of these late names the last three are not on the War Memorial and we should be able to say that: a) If they were known before August 1921 (when the list of names to be inscribed on the War Memorial was sent to Ebbutts) they must have been judged by the Committee to have been not "of the parish of Horley", or b) the church only became aware of them after August 1921 and they were added to the plaque after that date.

These three names were all added after the remaining

names on the plaque were painted in out of sequence, because they are fitted in along the bottom.

1. CPO Edwin Albert Bagg. His name must have been known early in 1922, because he is listed on the Roll of Honour published for use at the War Memorial dedication ceremony on 25 February 1922. His family resided for some years in Meath Green and his mother lived, at one time, in Lumley Road. He died on HMS "E18", a submarine, when it was lost in the Baltic Sea on 11 June 1916. He was married and living in Gosport when he died and this may have led to his exclusion from the War Memorial.
2. 2nd Lieutenant Ernest Lindley. He died on 18 February 1917 whilst serving in the Royal Flying Corps. The CWGC site shows that his parents lived at 'Woodfields', Russells Crescent, though the family lived in Croydon for most, perhaps all, of his life. Meeting on the 5 August 1921, the War Memorial Committee rejected a written request from his father to include his name on the War Memorial. Presumably he was not judged to be "of the Parish of Horley".
3. 2nd Lieutenant Stuart McMurray. He died on 8 August 1917 whilst serving with the RFC. The CWGC site shows his parents as living in Sydenham though they may have lived locally before or during the war.

In addition to these three men, the following 16 names were all placed on the Parsons plaque but were not inscribed on the War Memorial, though it seems certain that the names must have been known before August 1921.

1. Frederick Thomas Dann. Fred served in 4th Grenadier Guards and died in the Ypres sector on 13 April 1918. His connection with Horley cannot be traced, although, as he enlisted at Redhill, he may have come to live in Horley after the 1911 census.

2. Mark Dowlen. Mark served in 2nd Queens (RWS) and died in the Ypres sector on 6 November 1914 aged 26. He and his brother William (below) both lived at the Mill House, Lee Street, Horley. He is commemorated on Charlwood War Memorial.

3. William Dowlen. William served in 1st Queens (RWS) and died in the Ypres sector on 13 April 1918. He is commemorated on Charlwood War Memorial.

4. Albert Eames. Albert served in the Army Cyclists Corps and died near Ypres, aged 23, on the 25 February 1916. He and his brother William, below, lived at Gatwick Brickworks, Hookwood, where the present Tesco superstore now stands. He is commemorated on Charlwood War Memorial.

5. William Eames. William served in 1st East Surreys and died in the Ypres sector on 20 April 1915 aged 21. He also lived at Gatwick Brickworks, Hookwood. He is commemorated on Charlwood War Memorial.

6. Francis Honour. Francis served in 23rd Field Company, Royal Engineers and died at the Somme on the 30 October 1916 aged 20. He lived at 3 Brookside, Hookwood. He is commemorated on Charlwood War Memorial.

7. F W Lovell. This may refer to Frederick William Lovell who served in the 190th Brigade RFA and died on the Somme sector 25 September 1916, aged 19. It has not been possible to identify this man, though he may be related

to a family of Lovells who lived in Yattendon Road, Horley in 1911. He is one of only two men on the plaque who are not listed with their Christian names, which suggests that he was not personally known to the church. The other man is C Steer.

8. Henry Lucas. Henry served in the 8th Queens (RWS) and died on the Somme, aged 38, on the 17 August 1916. He lived at Lemberg Cottage, Hookwood. He is commemorated on Charlwood War Memorial.

9. Frank Miller. Frank served in C Battery, 183rd Brigade RFA and died on the Somme on 13 October 1916, aged 20. He was born at Charlwood but lived in Church Road, near the junction with Brighton Road. Frank was baptised at St Bartholomews but still did not make his way onto Horley War Memorial. He is commemorated on Charlwood War Memorial.

10. Donald Farquharson Roberts, MC. Donald was a Captain in 4th East Surreys. He was born at Tooting and lived mainly near Bedford. He died 20 November 1917 near Cambrai, aged 25. It has not been possible to trace his connection with Horley.

11. Edward Sangster. Edward served in 2nd Royal Sussex and died, aged 19, at Ypres on 6 November 1914. The Sangster family lived in Crawley for many years but Hugh Sangster (below) certainly gave Horley as his residence when he enlisted. The family came to live at 19 Lumley Road. He is commemorated on Charlwood War Memorial.

12. Hugh Sangster. Hugh served in 2nd Battalion, The Rifle Brigade, and died near Arras, aged 19, on 17 October 1918. He is commemorated on Charlwood War Memorial.

13. Edward Sargent. Edward served in 4th Royal Sussex

and died at Jerusalem on 6 November 1917. He lived at Charlwood and is commemorated on Charlwood War Memorial.

13. Frederick Sired. Frederick served 2nd/5th Kings Own Royal Lancs and died, aged about 23, near Arras on 29 August 1918. He lived at Crawley but his family may have moved nearer to Horley later. He is commemorated on Charlwood War Memorial.

14. Alfred Tyrrell. Alf served with 1st East Surreys and died at the Somme, aged 19, on 29 July 1916. He lived at 35 Lumley Road, Horley and was christened in St Bartholomews Church but by the end of the war his family had moved to Banstead.

15. William Henry Frederick Weller. It has proved impossible to positively identify this man. He is thought to be a different man from the William John Weller listed on the Horley War Memorial, since middle names, if known, are included on the plaque. Both men are listed on the 1922 Roll of Honour. There were Wellers at Charlwood and he may be related to this family.

It appears that most of these men lived in the Hookwood area and, despite being less than a mile from St Bartholomews Church, this placed them technically in the parish of Charlwood. Many of them are commemorated on the Charlwood War Memorial.

Whether or not the others should have found a place on the Horley War Memorial is a matter of debate. Certainly Frank Miller, Alfred Tyrrell, the Dowlen brothers and the Sangster brothers appear to have been hard done by.

The exclusion of these 19 men reduced the list to 104 so we should expect to find 18 men listed on the Horley War

Memorial, who, for some reason, are not listed on the Parsons plaque.

Charles Atkins	Lived Salfords
John Box	Lived Smallfield
Reginald Boyes	Lived Salfords
Albert Charlwood	Lived Earlswood
Arthur Cheesman	See Detail in chapter 4
James Cornford	Lived Salfords
Thomas Holmes	Lived Salfords (Petridge Wood)
Henry Lisles	Lived Earlswood
William Maynard	Lived Earlswood (Shocks Green)
George Morgan	Lived Massetts Road, Horley
Archibald Remnant	Lived Salfords
Alfred Roser	Lived at Ockley, Father lived in Horley
George Steer	Lived Salfords or Earlswood
Albert Strudwick	Lived Earlswood
Frank Taylor	Lived Earlswood
George Terry	Lived Earlswood
William Warner	Lived Earlswood
William (John?) Weller	Lived Reigate?

Some of these men lived so close to St John's Church, Earlswood that they must have been well to the north of the Horley Parish boundary and some of them are also recorded on a Roll of Honour inside St Johns Church.

Quite why George Morgan was excluded is not known. It is most peculiar that the men from the Hookwood and Povey Cross area, which was very close to St Bartholomews church, were left off the War Memorial, but that men from far to the north of the Parish boundary at Earlswood were included.

THE 1922 ROLL OF HONOUR

And what about the 124 names on the Roll of Honour used at the Dedication ceremony in February 1922? How did they differ from the names on the War Memorial and the Parsons plaque?

The men named on the 1922 Roll of Honour but not inscribed on the War Memorial are as follows:

Edwin Bagg, F W Lovell, Donald Roberts, Edward Sangster, Hugh Sangster and William H F Weller.

The Roll of Honour is interesting because it is the only original source that links some men with their units. 76 out of 124 men have a unit indicated. Some entries give simply a Regiment's name, or in the case of several men, a ship's name, and others give a Battalion, suggesting that the War Memorial Committee had more information on some men than on others.

Quite why it was not thought necessary to ensure that this published list agreed exactly with the names on the War Memorial, we shall never know.

Perhaps the truth is, that, as with the financial accounts of this committee, the list was handwritten, added to and deleted from, to exclude men from outside the Parish. Without the benefit of an Excel spreadsheet it must have been difficult to keep track of who was who, and to avoid confusion between men with similar names – Bugden and Budgen or Coomber and Comber – and unrelated men with the same surname.

Certainly in the case of the two men named Cooper, it is possible that the War Memorial Committee belatedly realised that duplication had been made.

The name Frank Cooper appears on the appeal list in late

1918. The name of Francis Hezekiah Cooper clearly appeared subsequently in response to the appeal. Both names appear on the Parsons plaque (1919) and the War Memorial (names fixed in August 1921) but only the name of Francis Hezekiah Cooper appears on the Roll of Honour in February 1922. It is certainly possible that the name of Frank Cooper was left off the Roll of Honour because the committee had belatedly discovered that they were one and the same.

The table on the following pages shows the correlation between the names on the War Memorial, the Parsons Plaque list and the Roll of Honour. The letter Y (for Yes) indicates inclusion.

SURNAME	CHRISTIAN NAME	WAR MEMORIAL	PARSONS PLAQUE	ROLL OF HONOUR
Apps	Thomas	Y	Y	Y
Atkins	Charles	Y	–	Y
Bagg	Edwin	–	Y	Y
Bailey	Charles Henry	Y	Y	Y
Banks	George	Y	Y	Y
Barton	George William	Y	Y	Y
Bingham	Charles Sydney	Y	Y	Y
Borer	Frederick Ernest James	Y	Y	Y
Borer	Norman Jonathan Henry	Y	Y	Y
Bourne	Sidney	Y	Y	Y
Bowen	Thomas	Y	Y	Y
Box	John	Y	–	–
Boyes	Reginald John	Y	–	Y
Bradley	Thomas McKenzie	Y	Y	Y
Brocklehurst	Thomas Pownall	Y	Y	Y

SURNAME	CHRISTIAN NAME	WAR MEMORIAL	PARSONS PLAQUE	ROLL OF HONOUR
Brooker	George McForland	Y	Y	Y
Brotherton	Esme	Y	Y	Y
Buckell	Harry Thomas	Y	Y	Y
Budgen	William	Y	Y	Y
Bugden	Harry Robert	Y	Y	Y
Burbridge	Arthur Allen	Y	Y	Y
Burden	Edgar	Y	Y	Y
Charlwood	Albert	Y	–	–
Cheesman	Arthur Edward	Y	–	Y
Chessall	Arthur Rowland Holmes	Y	Y	Y
Coburn	Harry William George	Y	Y	Y
Comber	Frank	Y	Y	Y
Coomber	Charles	Y	Y	Y
Cooper	Francis Hezekiah	Y	Y	Y
Cooper	Frank	Y	Y	–
Cornford	James Edward	Y	–	Y
Coutts	Albert Edward	Y	Y	Y
Croxford	William Charles	Y	Y	Y
Dann	Frederick Thomas	–	Y	–
Day	Charles Robert	Y	Y	Y
Dowlen*	Mark	–	Y	–
Dowlen*	William	–	Y	–
Drewell	Robert John	Y	Y	Y
Eames*	Albert Edward	–	Y	–
Eames*	William C	–	Y	–
Elson	Charles	Y	Y	Y
Etheridge	George Alfred	Y	Y	Y
Fish	Harry Edward	Y	Y	Y
Flowers	George	Y	Y	Y

SURNAME	CHRISTIAN NAME	WAR MEMORIAL	PARSONS PLAQUE	ROLL OF HONOUR
Freeman	George Cyril	Y	Y	Y
Grahame	John Gordon	Y	Y	Y
Hansen	Carl Frederick	Y	Y	Y
Hansen	William George	Y	Y	Y
Hards	William Walter Jordan	Y	Y	Y
Harmes	Richard	Y	Y	Y
Henning	John Sidney	Y	Y	Y
Hoare	William	Y	Y	Y
Holmes	Thomas George	Y	–	Y
Honour*	Francis George	–	Y	–
Hughes	Wilfred Sydney	Y	Y	Y
Humphrey	John	Y	Y	Y
Humphrey	Michael James	Y	Y	Y
Kenward	Charlie	Y	Y	Y
Killick	Benjamin Harvey	Y	Y	Y
Killick	Sidney	Y	Y	Y
Knowles	Harry	Y	Y	Y
Lambert	Edward Albert	Y	Y	Y
Leach	Ernest Cecil	Y	Y	Y
Ledger	Thomas	Y	Y	Y
Liles	Henry Walker	Y	–	–
Lindley	Ernest William	–	Y	–
Lockyer	Edward John	Y	Y	Y
Lovell	F W	–	Y	Y
Lucas	Edward George	Y	Y	Y
Lucas	Henry	–	Y	Y
Luscombe	Alfred Geoffrey	Y	Y	Y
Manners	Douglas William M	Y	Y	Y
Marchant	Frederick George	Y	Y	Y

SURNAME	CHRISTIAN NAME	WAR MEMORIAL	PARSONS PLAQUE	ROLL OF HONOUR
Marchant	Henry	Y	Y	Y
Martin	John James	Y	Y	Y
Maynard	William	Y	–	Y
McMurray	Stuart	–	Y	–
Miller*	Frank	–	Y	–
Mills	Frank	Y	Y	Y
Morgan	George Alfred	Y	–	Y
Mott	Francis Stanley	Y	Y	Y
Munn	Horace Frank	Y	Y	Y
Nixon	Robert William	Y	Y	Y
Parsons	Thomas	Y	Y	Y
Payne	Edwin	Y	Y	Y
Peach	Ernest Alfred	Y	Y	Y
Peppiatt	George William	Y	Y	Y
Perry	Kenneth George	Y	Y	Y
Pescud	Alec Joseph	Y	Y	Y
Pescud	Percy Robert	Y	Y	Y
Reeves*	Joseph Basil	Y	Y	Y
Remnant	Archibald	Y	–	Y
Richards	Henry George	Y	Y	Y
Roberts	Donald Farquaharson	–	Y	Y
Roffey	Frank	Y	Y	Y
Roser	Alfred	Y	–	Y
Russell	Donald	Y	Y	Y
Sangster*	Edward	–	Y	Y
Sangster*	Hugh Alec	–	Y	Y
Sargent*	Edward	–	Y	–
Scollick	Alban Vincent	Y	Y	Y
Shoubridge	Alec John	Y	Y	Y

SURNAME	CHRISTIAN NAME	WAR MEMORIAL	PARSONS PLAQUE	ROLL OF HONOUR
Sired*	Frederick	–	Y	–
Smith	Ernest Cecil Peirson	Y	Y	Y
Sotham	Ralph Clifford	Y	Y	Y
Southgate	Sydney George	Y	Y	Y
Standing	Charles William	Y	Y	Y
Steer	Christopher	Y	Y	Y
Steer	George Walter	Y	–	Y
Stevenson	Albert Frederick	Y	Y	Y
Still	William Alfred	Y	Y	Y
Stringer (Hawk)	Bertie	Y	Y	Y
Strudwick	Albert Daniel	Y	–	Y
Swain	Thomas Arthur	Y	Y	–
Swinden	James Sidney	Y	Y	Y
Taylor	Frank Lennox	Y	–	Y
Terry	George	Y	–	Y
Thewless	James	Y	Y	Y
Todd	Herbert Stanley	Y	Y	Y
Tomsett	Charlie	Y	Y	Y
Tribe	Charles	Y	Y	Y
Turner*	Arthur Bert	Y	Y	Y
Tyrell	Alfred	–	Y	–
Vallance	Ernest Arthur	Y	Y	Y
Voice	Arthur Edward	Y	Y	Y
Warner	William Joshua	Y	–	Y
Webber	Henry	Y	Y	Y
Weller	Joseph Albert	Y	Y	Y
Weller	William John	Y	Y	Y
Weller	William Henry Frederick	–	–	Y

SURNAME	CHRISTIAN NAME	WAR MEMORIAL	PARSONS PLAQUE	ROLL OF HONOUR
White	Albert James	Y	Y	Y
White	Charles	Y	Y	Y
White	Geoffrey Saxton	Y	Y	Y
White	Ronald John Saxton	Y	Y	Y
White	George Garrett William	Y	Y	Y
Wilson	Richard John	Y	Y	Y
Wilson	Thomas William	Y	Y	Y
Wiltshire	James Albert	Y	Y	Y
Woods	Arthur John	Y	Y	Y
Woollhead	William Hugh	Y	Y	Y
Yardley	Leslie Alfred	Y	Y	Y
		122	123	124

The men on the above list with an * beside their surname are commemorated on the Charlwood War Memorial. Note that both Joseph Reeves and Arthur Turner are named on both Memorials.

HORLEY BAPTIST CHURCH

A plaque in Horley Baptist Church lists the following men :

Bourne S, Cooper F H, Eames A E, Eames W C, Munn H F, Standing C W and Whibley R.

Sidney Bourne is also named at Sidlow church.

Of these men, only the Eames brothers and R Whibley are not named on the Horley War Memorial. The Eames brothers are named on the Charlwood War Memorial.

These men are all detailed elsewhere with the exception

of R Whibley and it has proved impossible to trace him with any certainty. No likely entry exists on CWGC or census lists. There was a family with this name living in Oakfield Road in 1911 but there does not appear to be a family member who fits this name.

He may well have been Ernest R Whibley but called himself by his middle name, Ralph. If so, he came from Southborough, Kent and died in France from wounds on the 22 November 1918 whilst serving in the 70th Battery, Royal Field Artillery. His connection with Horley is not known.

SALFORDS CHURCH

At Christ The King Church, Salfords, the plaque removed from the original building was riddled with woodworm and has been destroyed. Fortunately a good copy was made by hand and we know that it listed the following men:

1.	Charles Atkins	On HWM Lived at Salfords.
2.	Reginald Boyes	On HWM Lived at Earlswood. He is also listed on the Roll of Honour in St Johns Church, Earlswood.
3.	Bertie Charlwood	On HWM Lived at Earlswood. He is also listed on the Roll of Honour in St Johns Church, Earlswood.
4.	Arthur Cheesman	On HWM Probably Vicars brother.
5.	James Cornford	On HWM Lived Axes Lane, Salfords.
6.	Alfred Elsey	Served in 1/16th Bn London Regiment and died, aged 33, near Arras, on 28 August 1918. Lived at Earlswood.

7.	Maurice Elsey	Served in 1st Bn Royal Fusiliers and died, aged 21, near Corbie, Somme on 8 August 1918.
8.	George Freeman	On HWM Lived Picketts Lane.
9.	John Monroe Gage	Served as a Captain in the RAMC attached to 57th Bde, RFA. Died on 29 November 1918, aged 31, near Thessaloniki, Greece.
10.	Robert Gatland	Identified as Charles Robert Gatland. Served 6th Kings (Liverpool) Regt and died 26 September 1918 near Loos. Lived Salfords.
11.	Thomas Holmes	On HWM Lived Petridge Wood, Earlswood.
12.	Albert Lambert	On HWM Lived Little Lake Farm, Salfords.
13.	H W Lyle	Surname should be Liles as on HWM. Lived at Earlswood.
14.	William Maynard	On HWM Lived at Shocks Green, Earlswood. He is also listed on the Roll of Honour in St Johns Church, Earlswood.
15.	J T Morley	Joseph Timothy. Served with 7th Queens (RWS) and died, aged 25, on 28 September 1916 at The Somme. Lived in Masons Bridge Road, Earlswood.
16.	George Peppiatt	On HWM He may have lived at Redhill as his wife gave it as her address to CWGC.

17.	Christopher Steer	On HWM Lived in New House Lane.
18.	Albert Strudwick	On HWM Lived at Earlswood.
19.	Frank Taylor	On HWM Lived at Earlswood and is also on the Roll of Honour in St Johns Church, Earlswood.
20.	George Terry	On HWM Lived at Earlswood.
21.	William Warner	On HWM Lived at Earlswood.

In the case of the Salfords Memorial, a lot of the men lived well to the north of the Horley Parish boundary. It has not been possible to establish beyond doubt why they were commemorated in Salfords and yet, mostly, excluded from the Roll of Honour in St Johns Church, Earlswood.

It may simply be that some of these men preferred to attend the church at Salfords and were remembered there but why they were missed off the St Johns Roll of Honour is peculiar.

EMANUEL CHURCH, SIDLOW BRIDGE

At Emanuel Church, Sidlow the following men are named on a memorial tablet:

1.	Sidney Bourne	On HWM Lived in Lonesome Lane.
2.	Thomas Brocklehurst	On HWM Lived at Kinnersly Manor.
3.	William Brown	Served in 2nd Queens (RWS) and died near Loos on 16 May 1915. It has not been possible to trace an address for this man.

4.	Walter Chaplin	Served in 2/4th Queens (RWS) and Lived at Norwood Hill. He died on 3 August 1918 probably on the Hospital ship HMT *Warilda* torpedoed between Le Havre and Southampton.
5.	George Fairall	Served in 101st Company, Labour Corps and died, aged 39, on 3 December 1918 near Mons. Lived at Norwood Hill.
6.	Walter Falsham	Identified as Walter Fasham. Born in Kent but lived at Norwood Hill. Served in 8th Queens (RWS) and died near Ypres, aged 31, on 1 May 1916. He is commemorated on Charlwood War Memorial.
7.	Stephen Goacher	Served in 2/4th Queens (RWS) and died at Gallipoli, aged 24, on 11 August 1915. He lived at Irons Bottom.
8.	Harry Huggett	Served 2nd Grenadier Guards and died, aged 20, near Ypres on 14 June 1916. Lived at Dovers Green.
9.	John Huggett	Served 8th Royal Fusiliers and died, aged 27, on 9 April 1917, near Arras. He lived at Dovers Green.
10.	Ernest Jeal	Served 2nd South Lancs and died of wounds, aged 20, on 24 November 1918 at a Casualty Clearing Station north east of Lille. Lived at Sidlow.

11.	Harvey Killick	On HWM Lived at Duxhurst.
12.	Sidney Killick	On HWM Lived at Duxhurst.
13.	Lt TAG Rouse-Boughton-Knight	Thomas Andrew Greville. Old Etonian. Served 1st Bn Rifle Brigade and died on the Somme, aged 19, on 18 October 1916. It has not been possible to link this man with Sidlow or Horley.
14.	Arthur Pelham MM	Served in 1st Queens (RWS) and died, aged 39, on 27 December 1916. Lived at Meadvale, Redhill and is buried in Sidlow Churchyard.
15.	John Wadham	Served in Kings Royal Rifle Corps and died, probably from wounds, aged 19, on 28 September 1918 near Bailleul south west of Ypres. Lived at Dovers Green.
16.	Charles Rapley	Served in 2nd Coldstream Guards and died at The Somme, aged 28, on 16 September 1916. Lived in St Johns Road, Redhill.
17.	Edwin Woods	Served in 49th Remount Squadron, RASC and died, aged 26, on 4 January 1919 in Greece. Lived at Sidlow Bridge.

Certainly some of the above men lived very close to the Parish borders and could have expected a place on the Horley War Memorial. It seems as if the War Memorial Committee applied the boundary meticulously, especially on the western side of the Parish. In some cases it may be that the Committee were never informed of a man's death.

The Horley Infant School Plaque

HORLEY INFANT SCHOOL PLAQUE

This plaque (kindly photographed by staff at Lumley Road School) was found in the attic at Horley Infant School at Lumley Road. The school has now re-hung the plaque on prominent display. It was constructed for the first Horley Infant School in Albert Road to commemorate former pupils who lost their lives during the war.

It is an important local item as it confirms the names of many men listed on Horley and Charlwood War Memorials.

The men listed on either Memorial are detailed below.

1.   C H Brooker   Charles Brooker. Unable to trace a military record or details of his death but he lived at Bayhorne Farm in 1891.

2.	F Cooper	Note that the F Cooper on this plaque is thought to be Francis Hezekiah Cooper who is known to have lived in Yattenden Road in 1901.
3.	F Coomber	This entry is thought to refer to the Frank Comber who lived in Charlsfield Road. Frank Coomber (RAMC) survived the war. The name on the Parsons plaque is spelt as Comber and Frank Comber is detailed in Chapter 4.
4.	A V Lewis	Albert Lewis. Served in the 2/8th Royal Warwickshire Regt and died 20 July 1916 at Aubers. His parents lived at Reigate after the war.
5.	R Martin	Richard Martin. This man cannot be identified militarily. He is shown as living near Coppingham in 1881 and later lived near Forest Row.
6.	W McKiddie	Only one man appears with this name on the CWGC list and he served with 1/5th Sherwood Foresters and died 12 May 1917. He appears to have come from Derbyshire so it is not possible to identify this man with any certainty.
7.	G Pescud	Note that the entry for G Pescud should probably read A Pescud. Gilbert Pescud did attend the school but survived the war. His brother Alec Pescud was killed and is detailed in Chapter 4.

8.	E Thewless	This could be Edward Thewless, the older brother of James Thewless, who is listed on Horley War Memorial. No record exists of Edward Thewless dying in WW1 though he is thought to have served in the Royal Field Artillery.
9.	O Tyrrell	Identified as A O Tyrrell. Detailed in the Parsons plaque section earlier in this chapter.
10.	F Washer	Frank Washer. Served in the Army Service Corps attached to the 196th Battery RGA and died 24 November 1918 at Struma, Greece. He lived at 53 Lumley Road but his parents later moved to Redhill. He is also listed on the Roll of Honour in St Johns Church, Earlswood.
11.	J Washer	This may refer to either James or Jesse Washer, brothers of Frank Washer. Neither man is listed on the CWGC site.
12.	A Webb	Albert Webb. Served in 11th Cameronians and died 19 September 1918 whilst serving in Greece. Buried at Doirans Cemetery. He lived at Chiswick Farm in Meath Green Lane in 1901.

THE CHARLWOOD WAR MEMORIAL

The Charlwood War Memorial (Authors Photo)

For the sake of clarity all the men named on Charlwood War Memorial are listed here, together with an indication of where else they are commemorated.

Many of these names may be familiar to anyone researching local Horley families. Again, a Y indicates inclusion.

SURNAME	CHRISTIAN NAME	HORLEY WAR MEMORIAL	PARSONS PLAQUE	SIDLOW CHURCH
Herbert G	Andrews			
Norman F	Andrews			
Alfred E	Barnes			
Donald F	Beckhusen			
William	Bishop			
Bertram E	Brown			
Charles J W	Brown			
Thomas W	Brown			
Thomas W	Chantler			
W James	Charman			
Percy C J	Cook			
Denis	Daly			
Ernest	Dancy			
Mark	Dowlen		Y	
William	Dowlen		Y	
David	Duffell			
Albert E	Eames		Y	Y
William C	Eames		Y	Y
William J	Edwards			
Leonard W	Ellis			
Walter	Fasham			
Charles E	Francis			
J Felix	Frith			
Albert A W S	Giles			
Herbert	Guyatt			
Frank	Harold			

SURNAME	CHRISTIAN NAME	HORLEY WAR MEMORIAL	PARSONS PLAQUE	SIDLOW CHURCH
Fred	Hemsley			
A Monro	Hepburn			
Albert	Hitchcock			
Francis G	Honour			
John	Hoy			
George T	Humphrey			
Charles	Illman			
George T	Illman			
John A	Innes			
Job	Jenkins			
Leonard	Jordan			
Alfred	King			
Frederick W	King			
William	Lingard			
Henry	Lucas			
Robert O	Martin			
Hugh	McKean			
George	McQueen			
Frank	Miller		Y	
Jack	Monk			
James H	Newell			
George S	Pelham			
Albert C	Pescud			
Joseph B	Reeves	Y	Y	
Edward G	Sangster		Y	
Hugh A M	Sangster		Y	
Edward	Sargent		Y	
Frederick A	Sired		Y	
Walter	Skinner			

SURNAME	CHRISTIAN NAME	HORLEY WAR MEMORIAL	PARSONS PLAQUE	SIDLOW CHURCH
Charles	Tullett			
Phillip J	Tullett			
Arthur B	Turner	Y	Y	
Edward J	Warren			
Jesse	Warren			
Edward V	Wicks			
Harry	Wicks			

These men have not been individually researched for this book because, despite the fact that many of them will have enlisted with addresses such as "Charlwood, Horley, Surrey", they are almost all 'of Charlwood' as opposed to 'of Horley'. The exceptions are those indicated on the above list and all of these men are detailed elsewhere in this book.

ST JOHN THE EVANGELIST CHURCH, EARLSWOOD

The hand written Roll of Honour in St Johns Church is a lengthy one and is beautifully decorated, laid out and drafted. It is unusual because it is written in descending rank order, then alphabetically, and is headed by Sergeant Arthur George Knight VC. Knight had emigrated from Earlswood to Canada and won his VC for an act of individual bravery whilst serving with the CEF on 2 September 1918 at Villers-les-Cagnicourt, France.

The St Johns plaque is mentioned here only because so many of the men listed on Horley War Memorial are clearly from the Earlswood area and are listed on it. It names nearly 200 men and, unusually, one woman. Probationer Nurse Frances Mary Bates died from pneumonia whilst nursing at the Cambridge

Military Hospital, Aldershot. It is generally accepted that nurses who died from this are thought to have contracted the illness from the patients that they were nursing. She is buried in Reigate Cemetery in Chart Road, Reigate.

Of the men listed on the Horley War Memorial, Reginald Boyes, Bertie Charlwood, William Maynard, Alec Pescud, Percy Pescud, Frank Roffey, Alban Scollick, Albert Strudwick and Frank Taylor are all named on this Roll of Honour at St Johns, Earlswood.

CHAPTER EIGHT

THE COLLATION OF NAMES INCLUDING MEN NAMED IN EXTERNAL SOURCES

It is worth reflecting on the fact that a man could have been born in and lived in Horley all his life and joined the forces before the outbreak of war. If his remaining family then died or, more usually, simply moved away from the town, then the War Memorial Committee may never have been made aware of his death and he may well deserve a place on the Horley War Memorial.

Many other men were born elsewhere but had made their homes in Horley and gave this as their address on enlistment.

Thanks to the excellent Commonwealth War Graves Commission website and the information on Ancestry.com, it is possible to compile a list naming some of these men. It is very probable that this list is incomplete. Many men gave an approximation of either or both their places of birth or place of residence. Instead of 'Salfords', for instance, they may have said 'Redhill' and so would not show up in the relevant searches.

Most servicemen listed on the CWGC site were 'claimed' by relatives and the relevant entry includes, in most cases, their addresses. It is not possible to state conclusively that the men concerned actually lived there, as parents or spouses may have moved in the preceding years.

In the following list men from nearby locations such as Charlwood or Smallfields have been excluded wherever possible, even though their entry included Horley as a supplementary address.

The following tables show the Men of Horley who can be identified as having given their lives in the Great War of 1914–1918.

The first table shows where the initial sources for the naming of each man come from. These are abbreviated as follows:

WM = Horley War Memorial

PP = The 'Parsons' memorial plaque in St Bartholomews Church.

RoH = The Roll of Honour used in February 1922.

B = The memorial plaque in Horley Baptist Church.

Sid = The memorial plaque in Emanuel Church, Sidlow Bridge.

Sal = The memorial plaque in the Church of Christ the King, Salfords.

HIS = The memorial plaque in Horley Infant School, Lumley Road.

CWGC = The Commonwealth War Graves Commission website.

SDGW = Ancestry records taken from 'Soldiers who Died in the Great War'.

Although it is not cited in this table, almost all of these men are listed on the Commonwealth War Graves Commission website and many are also listed in 'Soldiers Died in the Great War'.

The second table repeats the same list of names and shows the approximate age of each man at the time of his death and an indication of where he died and where he is buried or commemorated.

Forename	Surname	Served In	Died	Source Info from
Thomas	Apps	10th Bn, Queens (R W S)	11/11/1918	WM, PP, RoH, HIS
Charles	Atkins	Anson Bn RN Div RNVR	07/11/1917	WM, RoH, Sal
Edwin	Bagg	HM Submarine E18	11/06/1916	PP, RoH,
Charles H	Bailey	4th Bn Grenadier Guards	03/10/1915	WM, PP, RoH, HIS
George	Banks	34th Siege Bty, RGA	20/01/1919	WM, PP, RoH,
George W	Barton	1st Bn, Royal Dublin Fus	29/06/1915	WM, PP, RoH,
Charles	Bartrum	Middlesex Regiment	29/07/1917	CWGC, SDGW
Frank Arthur	Batcup	The Queen's (RWS)	16/10/1915	CWGC, SDGW
James	Bates	Royal Army Service Corps	09/01/1918	CWGC, SDGW
Charles Sydney	Bingham	88th Coy, Machine Gun Corps	26/04/1917	WM, PP, RoH,
Frederick E	Borer	16th Bn Machine Gun Corps	04/04/1918	WM, PP, RoH, HIS
Norman J	Borer	HMS Bulwark	26/11/1914	WM, PP, RoH, HIS
Sidney	Bourne	6th Bn, Queens (RWS)	03/07/1916	WM, PP, RoH, B, Sid, HIS
Thomas	Bowen	7th Bn, Kings Shropshire Light Inf	03/04/1916	WM, PP, RoH,
John	Box	RASC	28/07/1919	WM
Reginald John	Boyes	1st Bn, Queens Own (RWKent) Regt	03/10/1917	WM, RoH, Sal
Thomas McK	Bradley	110th Siege Battery, RGA	21/03/1918	WM, PP, RoH,
Thomas P	Brocklehurst	2nd Bn, Queens (RWS)	01/07/1916	WM, PP, RoH, Sid

Forename	Surname	Served In	Died	Source Info from
George MacF	Brooker	18th Bn, Middlesex Regt	08/03/1918	WM, PP, RoH,
Charles H	Brooker	unknown	unknown	HIS
Esme	Brotherton	1st Bn London Regt, Royal Fusiliers	16/08/1917	WM, PP, RoH,
William	Brown	2nd Queens (RWS)	16/05/1915	Sid
Harry Thomas	Buckell	130th Bty, RFA	01/09/1915	WM, PP, RoH,
William Robert	Buckland	Coldstream Guards	16/09/1914	SDGW
William	Budgen	9th Bn, East Surrey Regt	02/09/1916	WM, PP, RoH, HIS
Harry Robert	Bugden	A Bty, 86 Bde, RFA	08/11/1917	WM, PP, RoH,
Arthur Allen	Burbridge	16th Bn Royal Sussex Regt	19/09/1918	WM, PP, RoH, HIS
Edgar	Burden	5th Bn, Ox & Bucks Light Inf	25/09/1915	WM, PP, RoH, HIS
Walter	Carey	The Rifle Brigade	17/09/1916	CWGC, SDGW
Walter	Chaplin	2/4th Queens (RWS)	03/08/1918	Sid
Albert	Charlwood	7th Bn, Queens (RWS)	16/07/1916	WM, Sal
Percy James	Charman	Royal Army Service Corps	06/02/1917	CWGC, SDGW
Arthur Edwin	Cheesman	1/5th The Buffs (R W Kent) Regt	26/09/1916	WM, RoH, Sal
Arthur Rowland	Chessall	1/15th Bn, London Regt (CS Rifles)	07/10/1916	WM, PP, RoH,
Harry George	Coburn	26th Bn, Middlesex Regt	07/01/1919	WM, PP, RoH,
Frank	Comber	2/4th Bn, Queens (RWS)	27/12/1917	WM, PP, RoH,

Forename	Surname	Served In	Died	Source Info from
Charles	Coomber	2nd Bn East Surrey Regt	28/03/1915	WM, PP, RoH,
Francis H	Cooper	1st Bn Northamptonshire Regt	16/08/1916	WM, PP, RoH, B, HIS
Frank	Cooper	unknown	unknown	Wm, PP
James Edward	Cornford	2nd Bn, Queens (RWS)	29/09/1915	WM, RoH, Sal
Albert Edward	Coutts	1st Bn, Queens Own (RWKent)	26/10/1917	WM, PP, RoH, HIS
W A	Craddock	Royal Field Artillery	21/04/1918	CWGC
William Charles	Croxford	9th Bn, Welsh Regt	15/10/1918	WM, PP, RoH,
Hubert Percy	Cunningham	Royal Field Artillery	13/06/1917	CWGC
Tom Wilfred	Dale	The Queen's (RWS)	27/06/1917	CWGC, SDGW
Frederick T	Dann	4th Grenadier Guards	13/04/1918	PP
Alfred	Dawson	Royal Fusiliers	31/07/1917	CWGC
Charles Robert	Day	C Battery, 189th Bde RFA	22/07/1917	WM, PP, RoH, HIS
Mark	Dowlen	2nd Queens (RWS)	06/11/1914	PP, CHA
William	Dowlen	1st Queens (RWS)	13/04/1918	PP, HIS, CHA
Robert John	Drewell	97th Field Coy, Royal Engineers	22/03/1918	WM, PP, RoH
William C	Eames	1st East Surreys	20/04/1915	PP, B, HIS, CHA
Albert Edward	Eames	Army Cyclists Corps	25/02/1916	PP, B, HIS, CHA
Alfred	Ellis	The Queen's (RWS)	07/11/1914	CWGC, SDGW

Forename	Surname	Served In	Died	Source Info from
Alfred	Elsey	1/16th Bn London Regiment	28/08/1918	Sal
Maurice	Elsey	1st Bn Royal Fusiliers	08/08/1918	Sal
Charles	Elson	7th Bn, Queens (RWS)	01/07/1916	WM, PP, RoH,
George Alfred	Etheridge	8th Bn Machine Gun Corps	25/03/1918	WM, PP, RoH, HIS
Harold	Evered	Middlesex Regiment	28/08/1917	CWGC, SDGW
George	Fairall	101st Company, Labour Corps	03/12/1918	Sid
Walter	Fasham	8th Queens (RWS)	01/05/1916	Sid, CHA
Francis Wm	Ferris	Royal Fusiliers	03/05/1917	CWGC, SDGW
Harry Edward	Fish	HMS Russell	27/04/1916	WM, PP, RoH, HIS
George	Flowers	HMS Good Hope	01/11/1914	WM, PP, RoH,
George Cyril	Freeman	6th Bn Royal Berks Regt	01/10/1916	WM, PP, RoH, Sal
John Monroe	Gage	RAMC attchd 57th Bde, RFA	29/11/1918	Sal
Charles Robert	Gateland	6th Kings (Liverpool) Regt	26/09/1918	Sal
Albert Arthur	Giles	Mercantile Marine Reserve	30/12/1917	CHA, CWGC
Stephen	Goacher	2/4th Queens (RWS)	11/08/1915	Sid
Gerald Robert	Goosey	London Regiment	25/09/1915	CWGC
John Gordon	Grahame	Hon Artillery Company	24/04/1915	WM, PP, RoH,
Carl Frederick	Hansen	165th MGC attd 9th Kings	31/07/1917	WM, PP, RoH,

Forename	Surname	Served In	Died	Source Info from
William George	Hansen	9th Bn, The Kings Liverpool Regt	25/09/1916	WM, PP, RoH,
William Walter	Hards	HM Submarine E50	31/01/1918	WM, PP, RoH, HIS
Richard	Harmes	127th Bty, RFA	23/06/1916	WM, PP, RoH, HIS
Charles F	Harris	East Surrey Regiment	03/10/1915	CWGC
John Sidney	Henning	5th Bn Canadian Mounted Rifles	02/10/1916	WM, PP, RoH,
William	Hoare	1st Bn, Lincolnshire Regt	28/12/1914	WM, PP, RoH,
Thomas Geo	Holmes	100 Squadron RFC	05/05/1917	WM, RoH, Sal
Francis Geo	Honour	23rd Field Company, Roy Engineers	30/10/1916	PP, HIS, CHA
C P	Hornung	Royal Fusiliers	07/02/1916	CWGC
Harry	Huggett	2nd Grenadier Guards	14/06/1916	Sid
John	Huggett	8th Royal Fusiliers	09/04/1917	Sid
Israel	Hughes	The Queen's (RWS)	09/08/1916	CWGC, SDGW
Wilfred Sydney	Hughes	HMS Racoon	19/01/1918	WM, PP, RoH,
John	Humphrey	22nd Bn, Royal Fusiliers	01/06/1916	WM, PP, RoH,
Michael James	Humphrey	16th Bn, London Regt	30/11/1917	WM, PP, RoH,
H	Izzard	Middlesex Regiment	22/04/1916	CWGC
Ernest	Jeal	2nd South Lancs	24/11/1918	Sid
A J	Jupp	Royal Field Artillery	13/08/1918	CWGC

Forename	Surname	Served In	Died	Source Info from
Charlie	Kenward	7th Bn, Queens (RWS)	14/07/1916	WM, PP, RoH, HIS
John William	Kew	The Queen's (RWS)	26/04/1918	CWGC, SDGW
George Robert	Kew	Bedfordshire Regiment	24/04/1918	CWGC, SDGW
Benjamin H	Killick	7th Bn, Queens (RWS)	01/07/1916	WM, PP, RoH, Sid, HIS
Sidney	Killick	8th Bn, Queens (RWS)	01/05/1916	WM, PP, RoH, Sid, HIS
David William	Kimber	Durham Light Infantry	23/04/1917	CWGC
William	Knowles	Royal Fusiliers	18/10/1917	CWGC
Harry	Knowles	2nd Bn Royal Sussex Regt	25/09/1915	WM, PP, RoH,
Edward Albert	Lambert	1st/4th Bn, Duke of Wellingtons Rgt	30/03/1918	WM, PP, RoH, Sal, HIS
Ernest Cecil	Leach	7th Bn, Middlesex Regt	08/08/1916	WM, PP, RoH,
Thomas	Ledger	3/4th Bn, Queens (RWS)	30/01/1916	WM, PP, RoH,
Albert	Lewis	2/8th Royal Warwickshire Regt	20/07/1916	HIS
Henry Walker	Liles	23rd Bn, Northumberland Fus	11/06/1917	WM, Sal
Ernest William	Lindley	Royal Flying Corps	18/02/1917	PP
Edward John	Lockyer	6th Bn, Queens (RWS)	19/04/1916	WM, PP, RoH, HIS
F W	Lovell	190th Bde RFA	25/09/1916	PP, RoH,
Edward George	Lucas	13th Bn, Kings Royal Rifle Corps	17/09/1918	WM, PP, RoH, HIS
Henry	Lucas	8th Queens (RWS)	17/08/1916	PP, RoH,

Forename	Surname	Served In	Died	Source Info from
Alfred Geoffrey	Luscombe	HMS Blackmorevale	01/05/1918	WM, PP, RoH,
Douglas W M	Manners	2nd Bn, Royal Sussex Regt	27/11/1916	WM, PP, RoH, HIS
Henry	Marchant	6th Reserve Brigade RFA	10/09/1917	WM, PP, RoH,
Frederick Geo	Marchant	2nd Bn, Seaforth Highlanders	25/04/1915	WM, PP, RoH,
Robert Owen	Martin	Grenadier Guards	23/08/1918	CHA, CWGC
John James	Martin	54th Company, MGC	11/08/1917	WM, PP, RoH
Richard	Martin	unknown	unknown	HIS
S P	Matthews	Canadian Mot M/Gun Bgd	22/02/1919	CWGC
William	Maynard	1st Bn, Queens (RWS)	25/09/1915	WM, RoH, Sal
W	McKiddie	1/5th Sherwood Foresters	12/05/1917	HIS
Stuart	McMurray	Royal Flying Corps	08/08/1917	PP
George	McQueen	The Queen's (RWS)	06/09/1916	CHA, CWGC
Frank	Miller	183rd Brigade RFA	13/10/1916	PP, HIS, CHA
Frank	Mills	unknown	unknown	WM, PP, RoH,
George Alfred	Morgan	"D" Battery, 80th Brigade RFA	17/05/1916	WM, RoH
J T	Morley	7th Queens (RWS)	28/09/1916	Sal
Francis Stanley	Mott	24th Bn, Royal Fusiliers	23/07/1916	WM, PP, RoH,
Horace Frank	Munn	1st Bn, Queens (RWS)	21/12/1916	WM, PP, RoH, B, HIS

Forename	Surname	Served In	Died	Source Info from
D	Nicholson	The Queen's (RWS)	16/03/1917	CWGC
Hugh Quidmpton	Nickalls	Royal Flying Corps	29/07/1917	CWGC
Robert William	Nixon	Labour Corps	14/07/1918	WM, PP, RoH,
Frederick	Page	Hampshire Regiment	19/04/1917	CWGC, SDGW
Thomas	Parsons	Army Service Corps attchd RGA	25/10/1917	WM, PP, RoH,
Thomas	Payne	Royal Fusiliers	26/10/1917	CWGC, SDGW
Edwin	Payne	4th Bn, Canadian Mounted Rifles	18/06/1917	WM, PP, RoH,
Ernest Alfred	Peach	A Bty, 158 Brigade, RFA	12/06/1918	WM, PP, RoH, HIS
Arthur	Pelham	1st Queens (RWS)	27/12/1916	Sid
George Wm	Peppiatt	8th Bn, London Regt (PO Rifles)	19/05/1917	WM, PP, RoH, Sal
Kenneth Geo	Perry	11th Bn Royal Sussex Regt	01/11/1916	WM, PP, RoH,
Alec Joseph	Pescud	22nd Bn, Royal Fusiliers	11/02/1916	WM, PP, RoH, HIS
Percy Robert	Pescud	9th Bn, East Surrey Regt	26/09/1915	WM, PP, RoH, HIS
Benjamin	Potter	S.S. "Lusitania" (Liverpool)	07/05/1915	CWGC
Charles	Rapley	2nd Coldstream Guards	16/09/1916	Sid
Charles Henry	Reed	The Queen's (RWS)	16/05/1915	CWGC, SDGW
Joseph Basil	Reeves	17th Bn, Royal Fusiliers	13/11/1916	WM, PP, RoH, CHA
Archibald	Remnant	9th Field Coy, Royal Engineers	30/04/1917	WM, RoH,

Forename	Surname	Served In	Died	Source Info from
Henry George	Richards	29th Bn, Middlesex Regiment	06/10/1917	WM, PP, RoH,
Donald Farq.	Roberts	4th East Surreys	20/11/1917	PP, RoH,
James William	Robinson	Hampshire Regiment	26/08/1914	CWGC, SDGW
Frank	Roffey	2/4th Bn, Queens (RWS)	27/12/1917	WM, PP, RoH,
Alfred	Roser	7th Bn, The Kings Regiment	27/09/1918	WM, RoH
T A G	Rouse-B-Knight	1st Bn Rifle Brigade	18/10/1916	Sid
Charles William	Russell	Army Service Corps	17/04/1916	CWGC, SDGW
Donald	Russell	3rd Bn, Grenadier Guards	14/09/1916	WM, PP, RoH, HIS
R	Sanders	The Queen's (RWS)	07/10/1916	CWGC
Edward	Sangster	2nd Royal Sussex	06/11/1914	PP, Roh, CHA
Hugh Alec	Sangster	2nd Battalion The Rifle Brigade	17/10/1918	PP, RoH, HIS, CHA
Edward	Sargent	4th Royal Sussex	06/11/1917	PP, CHA
Herbert Harold	Sawyers	Royal Sussex Regiment	25/01/1915	CWGC
Edward William	Schofield	Queen's Own (RWK) Regt	12/03/1917	CWGC, SDGW
Alban Vincent	Scollick	1/3rd Kent Field Coy, RE	28/10/1915	WM, PP, RoH,
Alec John	Shoubridge	4th Dragoon Guards	24/04/1915	WM, PP, RoH,
Frederick	Sired	2/5th Kings Own Royal Lancs	29/08/1918	PP, CHA
Frank Stuart	Slater	The Queen's (RWS)	24/08/1917	CWGC, SDGW

Forename	Surname	Served In	Died	Source Info from
R G	Slater	Royal Navy	07/10/1919	CWGC
George William	Smith	The Queen's (RWS)	31/10/1914	SDGW
G C	Smith	Royal Air Force	16/05/1918	CWGC
Ernest Cecil	Smith	HMS 'Queen Mary'	31/05/1916	WM, PP, RoH,
John	Smyth	The Rifle Brigade	15/09/1916	CWGC, SDGW
Ralph Clifford	Sotham	1 Squadron RFC	09/01/1918	WM, PP, RoH,
Sydney George	Southgate	3rd Bn, Northamptonshire Regt	22/11/1918	WM, PP, RoH,
Charles William	Standing	12th Bn, East Surrey Regt	16/08/1918	WM, PP, RoH, B, HIS
Christopher	Steer	2nd Bn, Worcester Regt	18/04/1918	WM, PP, RoH, Sal
George Walter	Steer	1st Bn, East Surrey Regt	28/06/1918	WM, RoH,
Albert Frederick	Stevenson	RN Barracks Chatham	20/09/1918	WM, PP, RoH,
H S	Stewart	Corps of Royal Engineers	18/09/1916	CWGC, SDGW
William Alfred	Still	10th Bn, Sherwood Foresters	22/09/1918	WM, PP, RoH, HIS
Albert Arthur	Stoner	Royal Horse Artillery	05/07/1916	CWGC, SDGW
Bertie	Stringer (Hawk)	7th Bn, East Kent Regt	03/05/1917	WM, PP, RoH,
Albert Daniel	Strudwick	8th Bn, Queens (RWS)	05/07/1918	WM, RoH, Sal
Thomas Arthur	Swain	2nd Bn, Seaforth Highlanders	23/10/1916	WM, PP,
James Sidney	Swinden	2nd Bn, Cheshire Regt	15/04/1918	WM, PP, RoH,

Forename	Surname	Served In	Died	Source Info from
Percival Frank	Targett	Royal Sussex Regiment	07/08/1918	CWGC
Frank Lennox	Taylor	2nd Bn, Queens (RWS)	24/11/1915	WM, RoH, Sal
John	Tennant	The Queen's (RWS)	25/09/1915	CWGC, SDGW
George	Terry	HMS 'Bulwark'	26/11/1914	WM, RoH, Sal
James	Thewless	8th Bn, Queens (RWS)	07/10/1916	WM, PP, RoH,
William	Tickner	Royal Fusiliers	29/09/1918	CWGC, SDGW
Herbert Stanley	Todd	8th Bn, East Surrey Regt	18/09/1918	WM, PP, RoH, .
Arthur	Tomsett	Buffs (East Kent Regiment)	03/05/1917	CWGC, SDGW
Charlie	Tomsett	11th Bn, Royal Fusiliers	03/10/1918	WM, PP, RoH,
Charles	Tribe	7th Bn, East Surrey Regt	09/08/1917	WM, PP, RoH, HIS
Arthur Bert	Turner	462 Battery, RFA	21/03/1918	WM, PP, RoH, HIS, CHA
G E	Twigg	King's Royal Rifle Corps	05/08/1915	CWGC
Alfred	Tyrell	1st East Surreys	29/07/1916	PP, HIS
Ernest Arthur	Vallance	24th Bn Australian Infantry Force	03/05/1917	WM, PP, RoH,
Rowland	Vigar	The Queen's (RWS)	12/02/1916	CWGC
Arthur Edward	Voice	RN Barracks Chatham	03/09/1917	WM, PP, RoH, HIS
John	Wadham	Kings Royal Rifle Corps	28/09/1918	Sid
William Joshua	Warner	25th Bn, Northumberland Fusiliers	09/04/1917	WM, RoH, Sal

Forename	Surname	Served In	Died	Source Info from
Frank	Washer	ASC attd196th Battery RGA	24/11/1918	HIS
J	Washer	unknown	unknown	HIS
Albert	Webb	11th Cameronians	19/09/1918	HIS
Henry	Webber	7th Bn, South Lancs, Regt	21/07/1916	WM, PP, RoH,
William John	Weller	8th Bn, Royal Fusiliers	03/05/1917	WM, PP, RoH,
Joseph Albert	Weller	HMS 'Formidable'	01/01/1915	WM, PP, RoH, HIS
William H F	Weller	unknown	unknown	RoH
Ernest R	Whibley	70th Batty, Royal Field Artillery	22/11/1918	B, CWGC
Albert James	White	2/5th Bn, Duke of Wellingtons	25/08/1918	WM, PP, RoH, HIS
Charles	White	28th Bn, Australian Infantry Force	02/11/1917	WM, PP, RoH, HIS
Geoffrey Saxton	White	HM Submarine E14	28/01/1918	WM, PP, RoH,
George G. Wm	White	16th (attchd 9th) Lancers	21/03/1918	WM, PP, RoH, HIS
Ronald J Saxton	White	2 Squadron RFC	27/10/1917	WM, PP, RoH,
Richard J	Wilson	2nd Bn, Queens (RWS)	1918	WM, PP, RoH, HIS
Thomas Wm	Wilson	2nd Bn, Queens (RWS)	05/12/1914	WM, PP, RoH, HIS
James Albert	Wiltshire	5th Bn, Kings Shropshire Light Inf.	05/09/1916	WM, PP, RoH,
Stanley	Wood	The Rifle Brigade	12/09/1918	CWGC, SDGW
Arthur John	Woods	1st Bn, Queens (RWS)	31/10/1914	WM, PP, RoH,

Forename	Surname	Served In	Died	Source Info from
Edwin	Woods	49th Remount Squadron, RASC	04/01/1919	Sid
William Hugh	Woollhead	F Squadron 2nd Wing, RNAS	27/05/1917	WM, PP, RoH,
Walter	Wright	The Queen's (RWS)	01/07/1916	CWGC, SDGW
Leslie Alfred	Yardley	1st/13th Bn, The London Regt	09/09/1916	WM, PP, RoH,

Forename	Surname	Age	Served In	Died	Area of death	Buried or Commemorated at
Thomas	Apps	23	10th Bn, Queens	11/11/1918	UK	St Barts, Horley
Charles	Atkins	26	Anson Bn RN Div RNVR	07/11/1917	Ypres Salient	Mendinghem Mil Cem
Edwin	Bagg	37	HM Submarine E18	11/06/1916	Baltic	Portsmouth Naval Mem
Charles H	Bailey	21	4th Bn Grenadier Guards	03/10/1915	Loos	St Sever Cem, Rouen
George	Banks	38	34th Siege Bty, RGA	20/01/1919	Namur	Belgrade Cemetery
George W	Barton	28	1st Bn, Royal Dublin Fus	29/06/1915	Gallipoli	Helles Memorial
Charles	Bartrum	20	Middlesex Regiment	29/07/1917	Arras	Arras Memorial
Frank Arthur	Batcup	22	The Queen's (RWS)	16/10/1915		Etaples Mil Cem
James	Bates	25	Royal Army Service Corps	09/01/1918	UK	Hawley (Holy Trinity) Churchyard
Charles S	Bingham	36	88th Co, M/Gun Corps	26/04/1917	Arras	Duisans Cem, Etrun
Frederick E	Borer	19	16th Bn Machine Gun Corps	04/04/1918	Arras	Pozieres Memorial
Norman J	Borer	18	HMS Bulwark	26/11/1914	Sheerness	Portsmouth Naval Mem
Sidney	Bourne	20	6th Bn, Queens Regt	03/07/1916	Somme	Thiepval Memorial
Thomas	Bowen	34	7th Bn, Kings Shrops L I	03/04/1916	Ypres Salient	Menin Gate, Ypres
John	Box	32	RASC	28/07/1919	UK	St Barts, Horley
Reginald John	Boyes	29	1st Bn, Queens (R W Kent)	03/10/1917	Ypres Salient	Poelcappelle Cem
Thomas McK	Bradley	21	110th Siege Battery, RGA	21/03/1918	Arras	Arras Memorial
Thomas P	Brocklehurst	29	2nd Bn, Queens (RWS)	01/07/1916	Somme	Dantzig Alley Cem Mametz

Forename	Surname	Age	Served In	Died	Area of death	Buried or Commemorated at
George MacF	Brooker	26	18th Bn, Middlesex Regt	08/03/1918	Ypres Salient	Potijze Chateau Cem
Charles H	Brooker		unknown	unknown		
Esme	Brotherton	27	1st Bn London Regt, (R F)	16/08/1917	Ypres Salient	Menin Gate, Ypres
William	Brown		2nd Queens (RWS)	16/05/1915	Loos	Le Touret Memorial
Harry Thomas	Buckell	19	130th Bty, RFA	01/09/1915	Ypres Salient	Birr Cross Roads Cem
William Robert	Buckland	30	Coldstream Guards	16/09/1914	Aisne	Vendresse British Cem
William	Budgen	27	9th Bn, East Surrey Regt	02/09/1916	Somme	Thiepval Memorial
Harry Robert	Bugden	20	A Bty, 86 Bde, RFA	08/11/1917	Ypres Salient	Vlamertinghe New Cem
Arthur Allen	Burbridge	20	16th Bn Royal Sussex Regt	19/09/1918	Arras	Vis-en-Artois Mem
Edgar	Burden	19	5th Bn, Ox & Bucks Light Inf	25/09/1915	Ypres Salient	Menin Gate, Ypres
Walter	Carey	33	The Rifle Brigade	17/09/1916	Somme	Hawthorne Ridge 2 , Auchonvillers
Walter	Chaplin	24	2/4th Queens (RWS)	03/08/1918	At Sea	Hollybrook Mem, Soton
Albert	Charlwood	25	7th Bn, Queens (RWS)	16/07/1916	Somme	La Neuville Cem, Corbie
Percy James	Charman	40	Royal Army Service Corps	06/02/1917	Somme	Suzanne Mil Cem
Arthur Edwin	Cheesman	39	1/5th The Buffs (RWK)	26/09/1916	Iraq	Amara War Cemetery
Arthur R	Chessall	38	1st/15th Bn, London (CSR)	07/10/1916	Somme	Thiepval Memorial
Harry George	Coburn	30	26th Bn, Middlesex Regt	07/01/1919	South Russia	Haidar Pasha Mem
Frank	Comber	25	2/4th Bn, Queens (RWS)	27/12/1917	Jerusalem	Jerusalem Mil Cem
Charles	Coomber	33	2nd Bn East Surrey Regt	28/03/1915	Ypres Salient	Voormezeele No 3 Cemetery

Forename	Surname	Age	Served In	Died	Area of death	Buried or Commemorated at
George MacF	Brooker	26	18th Bn, Middlesex Regt	08/03/1918	Ypres Salient	Potijze Chateau Cem
Francis H	Cooper	31	1st Bn Northants Regt	16/08/1916	Somme	Thiepval Memorial
Frank	Cooper		unknown	unknown		
James Edward	Cornford	24	2nd Bn, Queens (RWS)	29/09/1915	Loos	Loos Memorial
Albert Edward	Coutts	26	1st Bn, Queens Own (RWK)	26/10/1917	Ypres Salient	Tyne Cot Memorial
W A	Craddock	36	Royal Field Artillery	21/04/1918	UK	St Michaels Church, South Malling
William C	Croxford	33	9th Bn, Welsh Regt	15/10/1918	Somme	Hermies Hill Cemetery
Hubert Percy	Cunningham	23	Royal Field Artillery	13/06/1917	Ypres Salient	Railway Dugouts Burial Ground
Tom Wilfred	Dale	20	The Queen's (RWS)	27/06/1917	Ypres Salient	Menin Gate, Ypres
Frederick T	Dann	22	4th Grenadier Guards	13/04/1918	Ypres Salient	Ploegsteert Memorial
Alfred	Dawson	26	Royal Fusiliers	31/07/1917	Ypres Salient	Tyne Cot Memorial
Charles R	Day	23	C Battery, 189th Bde RFA	22/07/1917	Ypres Salient	Chester Farm Cem
Mark	Dowlen	26	2nd Queens (RWS)	06/11/1914	Ypres Salient	Menin Gate, Ypres
William	Dowlen	21	1st Queens (RWS)	13/04/1918	Ypres Salient	Ploegsteert Memorial
Robert John	Drewell	22	97th Field Coy, (RE)	22/03/1918	Somme	Pozieres Memorial
Albert Edward	Eames	23	Army Cyclists Corps	25/02/1916	Ypres Salient	Ypres Reservoir Cem
William C	Eames	21	1st East Surreys	20/04/1915	Ypres Salient	Menin Gate, Ypres
Alfred	Ellis	22	The Queen's (RWS)	07/11/1914	Ypres Salient	Menin Gate, Ypres

Forename	Surname	Age	Served In	Died	Area of death	Buried or Commemorated at
Alfred	Elsey	33	1/16th Bn London Regt	28/08/1918	Arras	Bucquoy Road Cem
Maurice	Elsey	21	1st Bn Royal Fusiliers	08/08/1918		Corbie Communal Cemetery Ext
Charles	Elson	39	7th Bn, Queens (RWS)	01/07/1916	Somme	Dantzig Alley Cem Mametz
George Alfred	Etheridge	22	8th Bn Machine Gun Corps	25/03/1918	Somme	Pozieres Memorial
Harold	Evered	38	Middlesex Regiment	28/08/1917	UK	St Barts, Horley
George	Fairall	39	101st Co, Labour Corps	03/12/1918	Mons	Solesmes British Cem
Charles	Day	23	C Battery, 189th Bde RFA	22/07/1917	Ypres Salient	Chester Farm
Walter	Fasham	31	8th Queens (RWS)	01/05/1916	Ypres Salient	Bailleul Communal Cemetery Ext N
Francis Wm	Ferris	26	Royal Fusiliers	03/05/1917	Arras	Arras Road Cemetery, Roclincourt
Harry Edward	Fish	21	HMS *Russell*	27/04/1916	At Sea	Chatham Naval Mem
George	Flowers	40	HMS *Good Hope*	01/11/1914	At Sea	Portsmouth Naval Mem
George Cyril	Freeman	25	6th Bn Royal Berks Regt	01/10/1916	Somme	Blighty Valley Cem
John Monroe	Gage	31	RAMC attchd 57th Bde, RFA	29/11/1918	Salonika	Kirechkoi-Hortakoi Military Cemetery
Charles R	Gatland	18	6th Kings (Liverpool) Regt	26/09/1918	Loos	Loos Memorial
Albert Arthur	Giles	40	Mercantile Marine Reserve	30/12/1917		Gamboa British Cem

Forename	Surname	Age	Served In	Died	Area of death	Buried or Commemorated at
Stephen	Goacher	24	2/4th Queens (RWS)	11/08/1915	Gallipoli	Helles memorial
Gerald Robert	Goosey	24	London Regiment	25/09/1915	Loos	Loos Memorial
John Gordon	Grahame	29	Hon Artillery Company	24/04/1915	Ypres Salient	Voormeleeze No 3 Cem
Carl Frederick	Hansen	24	165th MGC attd 9th Kings	31/07/1917	Ypres Salient	Potijze Chateau Cem
William G	Hansen	22	9th Bn, The Kings Liverpool Regt	25/09/1916	Somme	Thiepval Memorial
William W	Hards	26	HM Submarine E50	31/01/1918	At Sea	Chatham Naval Mem
Richard	Harmes	19	127th Bty, RFA	23/06/1916	Somme	Sucrerie Cem, Colincamps
Charles F	Harris	19	East Surrey Regiment	03/10/1915	Arras	Cabaret-Rouge British Cem, Souchez
John Sidney	Henning	23	5th Bn Canadian (Mt Rifles)	02/10/1916	Vimy Ridge	Vimy Memorial
William	Hoare	32	1st Bn, Lincolnshire Regt	28/12/1914	Ypres Salient	Le Touquet, Paris Plage Cemetery
Thomas Geo	Holmes	23	100 Squadron RFC	05/05/1917	Arras	Douai British Cem
Francis Geo	Honour	20	23rd Field Co, RE	30/10/1916	Somme	Dernancourt Cem Ext
C P	Hornung	18	Royal Fusiliers	07/02/1916	Loos	Cambrin Churchyard Ext
Harry	Huggett	20	2nd Grenadier Guards	14/06/1916	Ypres Salient	White House Cem, St Jean-les-Ypres
John	Huggett	27	8th Royal Fusiliers	09/04/1917	Arras	Faubourg D'Amiens Cem
Israel	Hughes	28	The Queen's (RWS)	09/08/1916	Ypres Salient	London Rifle Brigade Cem
Wilfred	Hughes	24	HMS Racoon	19/01/1918	At Sea	Chatham Naval Mem

Forename	Surname	Age	Served In	Died	Area of death	Buried or Commemorated at
John	Humphrey	20	22nd Bn, Royal Fusiliers	01/06/1916	Vimy Ridge	Barlin Cem Ext
Michael James	Humphrey	26	16th Bn, London Regt	30/11/1917	Somme	Moeuvres Cem Ext
H	Izzard	28	Middlesex Regiment	22/04/1916	UK	Cambridge City Cem
Ernest	Jeal	20	2nd South Lancs	24/11/1918	Lille	Tourcoing (Pont-Neuville) Com Cem
A J	Jupp	40	Royal Field Artillery	13/08/1918	Somme	Villers-Bretonneux Military Cemetery
Charlie	Kenward	19	7th Bn, Queens (RWS)	14/07/1916	Somme	Thiepval Memorial
John William	Kew	38	The Queen's (RWS)	26/04/1918	Jerusalem	Jerusalem War Cem
George Robert	Kew	19	Bedfordshire Regiment	24/04/1918	Somme	Pozieres Memorial
Benjamin H	Killick	19	7th Bn, Queens (RWS)	01/07/1916	Somme	Dantzig Alley Cemetery, Mametz
Sidney	Killick	27	8th Bn, Queens (RWS)	01/05/1916	Ypres Salient	Bailleul Cem Ext
David William	Kimber	32	Durham Light Infantry	23/04/1917	Arras	Arras Memorial
William	Knowles	34	Royal Fusiliers	18/10/1917	Ypres Salient	Tyne Cot Memorial
Harry	Knowles	29	2nd Bn Royal Sussex Regt	25/09/1915	Loos	Loos Memorial
Edward Albert	Lambert	32	1st/4th Bn, Duke of Wellingtons Regt	30/03/1918	Ypres Salient	Menin Road South Cemetery
Ernest Cecil	Leach	25	7th Bn, Middlesex Regt	08/08/1916	Somme	Delville Wood Cem
Thomas	Ledger	34	3/4th Bn, Queens (RWS)	30/01/1916	UK	Cambridge City Cem
Albert	Lewis	28	2/8th Royal Warwicks Rg	20/07/1916	Loos	Aubers Ridge Brit Cem

Forename	Surname	Age	Served In	Died	Area of death	Buried or Commemorated at
Henry Walker	Liles	35	23rd Bn, Northum. Fus	11/06/1917	Arras	Duisans British Cem
Ernest W	Lindley	20	Royal Flying Corps	18/02/1917	Arras	Browns Copse Cem, Rouex
Edward John	Lockyer	21	6th Bn, Queens (RWS)	19/04/1916	Loos	Loos Memorial
F W	Lovell	19	190th Bde RFA	25/09/1916	Somme	Heilly Station Cem, Mericourt – l'Abbe
Edward G	Lucas	23	13th Bn, Kings Royal (RC)	17/09/1918	Arras	St Sever Cem, Rouen
Henry	Lucas	38	8th Queens (RWS)	17/08/1916	Somme	Peronne Road Cemetery, Maricourt
Alfred G	Luscombe	33	HMS *Blackmorevale*	01/05/1918	At Sea	Plymouth Naval Mem
Douglas W M	Manners	20	2nd Bn, Royal Sussex Regt	27/11/1916	Somme	Thiepval Memorial
Henry	Marchant	38	6th Reserve Brigade RFA	10/09/1917	Ypres Salient	Seaforth Cemetery, Cheddar Villa
Frederick Geo	Marchant	35	2nd Bn, Seaforth Highl.	25/04/1915	Ypres Salient	St Sever Cem, Rouen
Robert Owen	Martin	20	Grenadier Guards	23/08/1918	Arras	Bucquoy Road Cemetery, Ficheux
John James	Martin	20	54th Company, MGC	11/08/1917	Ypres Salient	Menin Gate Memorial
Richard	Martin		unknown	unknown		
S P	Matthews	37	Canadian Mot M/Gun Bgd	22/02/1919	Namur	Belgrade Cemetery
William	Maynard	28	1st Bn, Queens (RWS)	25/09/1915	Loos	Loos Memorial
W	McKiddie		1/5th Sherwood Foresters	12/05/1917	Loos	Maroc Brit Cem, Grenay
Stuart	McMurray	25	Royal Flying Corps	08/08/1917	Bethune	Lillers Communal Cem

Forename	Surname	Age	Served In	Died	Area of death	Buried or Commemorated at
George	McQueen	37	The Queen's (RWS)	06/09/1916	UK	Wandsworth (Earlsfield) Cemetery
Frank	Miller	20	183rd Brigade RFA	13/10/1916	Somme	Thiepval Memorial
Frank	Mills		unknown	unknown		
George Alfred	Morgan	20	"D" Battery, 80th Brig RFA	17/05/1916	Somme	Cite Bonjean Mil Cem
Joseph T	Morley	25	7th Queens (RWS)	28/09/1916	Somme	Thiepval Memorial
Francis S	Mott	20	24th Bn, Royal Fusiliers	23/07/1916	Somme	Lapugnoy Mil Cem
Horace Frank	Munn	22	1st Bn, Queens (RWS)	21/12/1916	Somme	Sailly-Saillisel Cem
Richard	Martin		unknown	unknown		
David	Nicholson	26	The Queen's (RWS)	16/03/1917	Germany	Cologne Southern Cem
Hugh	Nickalls	21	Royal Flying Corps	29/07/1917	Arras	Arras F/Svs Mem
Robert W	Nixon	52	Labour Corps	14/07/1918	UK	B'ham Lodge Hill Cem
Frederick	Page		Hampshire Regiment	19/04/1917	Dieppe	Mont Huon Military Cemetery, Le Treport
Thomas	Parsons	32	Army Service Corps attchd RGA	25/10/1917	Etaples	Etaples Military Cem
Thomas	Payne	28	Royal Fusiliers	26/10/1917	Ypres Salient	Tyne Cot Memorial
Edwin	Payne	22	4th Bn, Canadian (MR)	18/06/1917	Etaples	Etaples Military Cem
Ernest Alfred	Peach	30	A Bty, 158 Brigade, RFA	12/06/1918	Bethune	Houchin Cemetery
Arthur	Pelham	39	1st Queens (RWS)	27/12/1916	UK	Emanuel Churchyard, Sidlow Bridge

Forename	Surname	Age	Served In	Died	Area of death	Buried or Commemorated at
George Wm	Peppiatt	26	8th Bn, Lond Rgt (P O Rif)	19/05/1917	Arras	Achiet-Le-Grand Cem Ext
Kenneth Geo	Perry	33	11th Bn Royal Sussex Regt	01/11/1916	Somme	Puchevillers Cemetery
Alec Joseph	Pescud	20	22nd Bn, Royal Fusiliers	11/02/1916	Bethune	Veille-Chappelle Cem Lacouture
Percy Robert	Pescud	22	9th Bn, East Surrey Regt	26/09/1915	Loos	Loos Memorial
Benjamin	Potter	39	S.S. "Lusitania" (Liverpool)	07/05/1915	At Sea	Tower Hill Memorial
Charles	Rapley	28	2nd Coldstream Guards	16/09/1916	Somme	Thiepval Memorial
Charles Henry	Reed		The Queen's (RWS)	16/05/1915	Loos	Le Touret Memorial
Joseph Basil	Reeves	24	17th Bn, Royal Fusiliers	13/11/1916	Somme	Munich Trench, Beaumont Hamel
Archibald	Remnant	23	9th Field Co, R E	30/04/1917	Arras	Aubigny Comm Cem
Henry George	Richards	42	29th Bn, Middx Regt.	06/10/1917	Horley	St Barts, Horley
Donald Farq.	Roberts	25	4th East Surreys	20/11/1917	Somme	Cambrai Mem, Louverval
James William	Robinson	28	Hampshire Regiment	26/08/1914	Marne	La Ferte-Sous-Jouarre Memorial
Frank	Roffey	22	2/4th Bn, Queens (RWS)	27/12/1917	Jerusalem	Jerusalem Mil Cem
Alfred	Roser	36	7th Bn, The Kings Regiment	27/09/1918	Somme	Queant Comm Cem
T A G	Rouse-B-Knight	19	1st Bn Rifle Brigade	18/10/1916	Somme	Perronne Road Cem, Maricourt
Charles W	Russell	45	Army Service Corps	17/04/1916	UK	St Barts, Horley

Forename	Surname	Age	Served In	Died	Area of death	Buried or Commemorated at
Donald	Russell	23	3rd Bn, Grenadier Guards	14/09/1916	Somme	Guards Cem, Lesbouefs
R	Sanders	23	The Queen's (RWS)	07/10/1916	UK	St Barts, Horley
Edward	Sangster	19	2nd Royal Sussex	06/11/1914	Ypres Salient	Menin Gate Memorial
Hugh Alec	Sangster	19	2nd Bn, Rifle Brig	17/10/1918	Arras	Duisans British Cem
Edward	Sargent	27	4th Royal Sussex	06/11/1917	Jerusalem	Jerusalem Mil Cem
Herbert Harold	Sawyers	21	Royal Sussex Regiment	25/01/1915	Loos	Le Touret Memorial
Edward W	Schofield	21	Queen's Own (RWK) Regt	12/03/1917	UK	Tunbridge Wells Cem
Alban Vincent	Scollick	27	1/3rd Kent Field Coy, RE	28/10/1915	Gallipoli	Helles Memorial
Alec John	Shoubridge	21	4th Dragoon Guards	24/04/1915	Ypres Salient	Duhallow Cemetery
Frederick	Sired	23	2/5th Kings Own Royal Lancs	29/08/1918	Arras	Vis-en-Artoise Memorial
Frank Stuart	Slater	22	The Queen's (RWS)	24/08/1917	Ypres Salient	Bertenacre Mil Cem, Fletre
R G	Slater	17	Royal Navy	07/10/1919	UK	East Sheen Cemetery
George W	Smith	27	The Queen's (RWS)	31/10/1914	Ypres Salient	Menin Gate Memorial
G C	Smith	19	Royal Air Force	16/05/1918	Germany	Niederzwehren Cem
Ernest Cecil	Smith	20	HMS 'Queen Mary'	31/05/1916	At Sea	Portsmouth Naval Mem
John	Smyth	21	The Rifle Brigade	15/09/1916	Somme	Thiepval Memorial
Ralph Clifford	Sotham	23	1 Squadron RFC	09/01/1918	Arras	Arras F/Svs Memorial
Sydney George	Southgate	18	3rd Bn, Northants Regt.	22/11/1918	UK	St Barts, Horley
Charles W	Standing	19	12th Bn, East Surrey Regt	16/08/1918	Ypres Salient	Tyne Cot Memorial

Forename	Surname	Age	Served In	Died	Area of death	Buried or Commemorated at
Christopher	Steer	26	2nd Bn, Worcester Regt	18/04/1918	Ypres Salient	Mendinghem Mil Cem
George Walter	Steer	20	1st Bn, East Surrey Regt	28/06/1918	Ypres Salient	Ploegsteert Memorial
Albert Fred	Stevenson	19	RN Barracks Chatham	20/09/1918	UK	St Barts, Horley
H S	Stewart	34	Corps of Royal Engineers	18/09/1916	Somme	Guards Cem, Lesbouefs
William Alfred	Still	19	10th Bn, Sherwood Foresters	22/09/1918	Somme	Thilloy Road Cemetery
Albert Arthur	Stoner	20	Royal Horse Artillery	05/07/1916	Somme	Norfolk Cemetery, Becordel-Becourt
Bertie Stringer (Hawk)		26	7th Bn, East Kent Regt	03/05/1917	Arras	Arras Memorial
Albert Daniel	Strudwick	23	8th Bn, Queens (RWS)	05/07/1918	Loos	Bully-Grenay Com. Cem
Thomas A	Swain	26	2nd Bn, Seaforth Highlanders	23/10/1916	Somme	Guards Cemetery, Lesbouefs
James Sidney	Swinden	22	2nd Bn, Cheshire Regt	15/04/1918	Salonika	Doiran Memorial
Percival Frank	Targett	21	Royal Sussex Regiment	07/08/1918	Arras	St Sever Cem, Rouen
Frank Lennox	Taylor	26	2nd Bn, Queens (RWS)	24/11/1915	Loos	Loos Memorial
John	Tennant	21	The Queen's (RWS)	25/09/1915	Loos	Guards Cem, Cuinchy
George	Terry	32	HMS 'Bulwark'	26/11/1914	Sheerness	Portsmouth Naval Mem
James	Thewless	18	8th Bn, Queens (RWS)	07/10/1916	Arras	Quatre Vents Cem
William	Tickner	38	Royal Fusiliers	29/09/1918	Ypres Salient	Tyne Cot Memorial
Herbert S	Todd	20	8th Bn, East Surrey Regt	18/09/1918	Somme	Peronne Comm. Cem

Forename	Surname	Age	Served In	Died	Area of death	Buried or Commemorated at
Arthur	Tomsett	41	Buffs (East Kent Regiment)	03/05/1917	Arras	Arras Memorial
Charlie	Tomsett	31	11th Bn, Royal Fusiliers	03/10/1918	Somme	Grevillers Brit Cem
Charles	Tribe	33	7th Bn, East Surrey Regt	09/08/1917	Arras	Albuera Cemetery
Arthur Bert	Turner	26	462 Battery, RFA	21/03/1918	Somme	Pozieres Memorial
G E	Twigg	25	King's Royal Rifle Corps	05/08/1915	Armentieres	Chapelle-d'Armentieres Old Mil Cemetery
Alfred	Tyrell	19	1st East Surreys	29/07/1916	Somme	Thiepval Memorial
Ernest Arthur	Vallance	31	24th Bn Australian Infantry Force	03/05/1917	Arras	Villers Bretonneux Memorial
Rowland	Vigar	39	The Queen's (RWS)	12/02/1916		Wimereux Comm Cem
Arthur Edward	Voice	22	RN Barracks Chatham	03/09/1917	UK	Gillingham Cemetery
John	Wadham	19	Kings Royal Rifle Corps	28/09/1918	Ypres Salient	Bailleul Cemetery Ext
William J	Warner	25	25th Bn, Northumberland Fusiliers	09/04/1917	Arras	Roclincourt Valley Cemetery
Frank	Washer	20	ASC attd196th Battery RGA	24/11/1918	Salonika	Struma Mil Cem
J	Washer		unknown	unknown		
Albert	Webb	23	11th Cameronians	19/09/1918	Salonika	Doiran Cemetery
Henry	Webber	67	7th Bn, South Lancs, Regt	21/07/1916	Somme	Dartmoor Cemetery
William John	Weller	28	8th Bn, Royal Fusiliers	03/05/1917	At Sea	Chatham Naval Mem
Joseph Albert	Weller	20	HMS 'Formidable'	01/01/1915	Arras	Arras Memorial

Forename	Surname	Age	Served In	Died	Area of death	Buried or Commemorated at
William H F	Weller		unknown	unknown		
Ernest R	Whibley	19	70th Batty, RFA	22/11/1918	Cambrai	Caudry Brit Cem
Albert James	White	25	2/5th Duke of Wellingtons Regt	25/08/1918	Somme	Gomiecourt South Cemetery
Charles	White	28	28th Bn, Australian Infantry Force	02/11/1917	Ypres Salient	Menin Road South Cemetery
Geoffrey S	White	31	HM Submarine E14	28/01/1918	At Sea	P'mouth Navla Mem
George G Wm	White	22	16th (attchd 9th) Lancers	21/03/1918	Somme	Pozieres Memorial
Ronald J S	White	26	2 Squadron RFC	27/10/1917	In the Air	St Pol Comm. Cem
Richard J	Wilson	23	2nd Bn, Queens (RWS)	1918	UK	unknown
Thomas Wm	Wilson	25	2nd Bn, Queens (RWS)	05/12/1914	Ypres Salient	Manchester South. Cem
James Albert	Wiltshire	24	5th Bn, Kings Salop L I	05/09/1916	Somme	St Sever Cem, Rouen
Stanley	Wood	18	The Rifle Brigade	12/09/1918	Arras	Vis-en-Artois Mem
Arthur John	Woods	28	1st Bn, Queens (RWS)	31/10/1914	Ypres Salient	Menin Gate Memorial
Edwin	Woods	26	49th Remount Squadron, RASC	04/01/1919	Salonika	Mikra British Cemetery, Kalamaria
William Hugh	Woollhead	23	F Squadron 2nd Wing, RNAS	27/05/1917	Salonika	Struma Mil Cem
Walter	Wright	33	The Queen's (RWS)	01/07/1916	Somme	Thiepval Memorial
Leslie Alfred	Yardley	20	1st/13th Bn, The London Regt	09/09/1916	Somme	Thiepval Memorial

Perhaps we should finally remember the men buried under CWGC headstones in St Bartholomews Churchyard, for whom Horley will forever be their last resting place:

Apps, T. Private. G/21577. Died on Armistice Day, 11 November 1918, Aged 23. He served in The Queen's (Royal West Surrey Regiment) and is buried in the south of the churchyard. On Horley War Memorial.

Box, J Private. M/352155. Died on 28 July 1919. He served in the Royal Army Service Corps and is buried to the south-west of the Church. On Horley War Memorial.

Evered, Harold. Private. PS/404 He died on 28 August 1917. He served in the Middlesex Regiment and is buried to the west of the Church. He was born at Putney but lived at Oatlands, Horley. He left over £4000 in his will which would be worth nearly £250,000 today.

Groves, H G. Private. 15209. Alias Ridout.

Nalder, G. Private. 26057. He died on 2 December 1919 aged 29. He served in the Essex Regiment and is buried south west of the Church. He came from Newbury, Berkshire and joined up in 1915 but was discharged as physically unfit in February 1919 because he suffered from tuberculosis and this lead to his death. He had no obvious connection with Horley so perhaps he was hospitalised here.

Richards, H G Private. 71932. He died on 6 October 1917 aged 42. He served in the Middlesex Regiment and is buried on the east boundary of the churchyard. On Horley War Memorial.

Ridout, John Henry Alfred. Private15209. He died on 8 November 1919 aged 38. He served in the Dorsetshire Regiment as Private H G Groves and is buried south-west of the Church. The address given for him on his probate document was 'Thornboro', Queens Road, Horley. His wife gave CWGC an address in South Croydon.

Russell, Charles William. Private. R4/108634. He died on 17 April 1916 aged 45. He served in the Army Service Corps and is buried south-west of the Church. He was serving in England when he died and almost certainly died from natural causes. Born in London but lived at 46 Charlesfield Road, Horley.

Sanders, R. Private. 3516. He died on 7 October 1916 aged 23. He served in The Queen's (Royal West Surrey Regiment) and is buried in the south corner of the churchyard. He was born at Charlwood but his mother lived at 2 Swindon Villas, Lee Street, Horley and probably he did as well. He is not listed on the Horley or the Charlwood War Memorials.

Skinner, A. Squadron Quartermaster Sergeant 858. He died 2 October 1914. He served in the Army Pay Corps and is buried near the south-east boundary of the churchyard. He was born in Pimlico, London and no connection with Horley can be traced so perhaps he was hospitalised here.

Southgate S G.Private. 59929. He died on 22 November 1918. He served in the Northamptonshire Regiment and is buried in the east corner of the churchyard close to the lych-gate. On Horley War Memorial.

Stevenson, Albert Frederick.Able Seaman J/43488(PO). He died on 20 September 1918 at Chatham and is buried to the south of the Church. On Horley War Memorial.

These men, and all the other Men of Horley 1914–1918 who died across the battlefields of Europe and the wider world, must surely have received their rewards in heaven and perhaps they encountered a benevolent St Peter as did the soldier in this anonymous poem:

A soldier stood at the pearly gate,
His face was scarred and old.
He stood before the man of fate
For admission to the fold.

"What have you done" St Peter asked,
"To gain admission here?
""I've been a soldier, sir" he said,
"For many and many a year"

The pearly gate swung open wide
As Peter touched the bell.
"Inside", he said, "and choose your harp".
"You've had your share of Hell".

CHAPTER NINE
METHODOLOGY AND CONCLUSIONS

The starting point for this research was to photograph the names on the Horley War Memorial. The names were then listed on a spreadsheet and a Word document was opened for each man. Because of the similarity of several names a careful cross check was carried out to ensure that names were spelled correctly in transcription.

The Horley Local History Society provided a useful file of documents and press cuttings about the War Memorial and loaned a large file put together by an anonymous donor, which contained printed details of a rough guess at the identity of each man taken from the Commonwealth War Graves Commission website.

The first task was to match the name from the War Memorial with the identity of an individual on the 1911 census. If this did not disclose an obvious match the search was moved back to 1901 or even 1891, as the vast majority of men who died in WW1 were born between 1880 and 1900. Many names were spelled incorrectly on census records and this necessitated checking parentage back further to ensure that the correct man was identified.

Despite the care taken it is still possible that errors have crept in and this, if so, is much regretted.

The ability to search widely on the internet made the whole exercise possible. Both the Ancestry and the CWGC websites proved invaluable. The CWGC site enables a search by name, location or death dates but can stretch into hundreds of servicemen for common names. Most importantly, the CWGC details sometimes include a line at the bottom of an entry saying for instance:

"only son of Mr and Mrs Jones of Lee Street, Horley and husband of Mrs Jones of High Street, Redhill."

This entry, where it occurs, almost always pinpoints the man sought, both from the point of view of his family and his unit. Unfortunately there are many men whose families have not claimed them in this way. The information regarding the cemetery in which a soldier is buried, frequently gives details of the conditions nearby during the fighting and tells whether the graves were gathered in from smaller cemeteries in the same locality.

Once the unit is known it is fairly easy to piece together the story of each man through the war years.

Ancestry carries some Service Records from the Great War. These archives were stored in London during WW2 and the vast majority were destroyed in the London Blitz. Those that remain are mostly for soldiers serving at the beginning of the 1914-18 war and they are few in number and some are badly scorched. If the man sought has a complete service record, it shows where he lived, where he enlisted, his family details, postings, punishments and illnesses. It will usually end simply KiA... killed in action. Any letters from next of kin to the military authorities may also be included.

The other principal point of reference is the soldier's Medal Card. This will give a soldier's name (sometimes with middle names), service numbers (many soldiers may have two because the numbering system was changed mid-war) and an entry showing which medals a man was entitled to. Campaign medals were not issued in WW1. Almost all soldiers will have been entitled to the British War Medal and the Victory Medal. Only those who saw active service in 1914 will have been awarded the 1914 Star and those who began active service in 1915 will have been awarded the 1914–15 Star.

These three medals became known irreverently as Pip, Squeak and Wilfred (after three cartoon characters in the Daily Mirror) and are still so called today.

The award of a 1914 or 1914–15 star will confirm that a soldier served in a battle zone in those years. There is also a box, frequently empty, which gives us 'theatre of war first served in', and another box underneath which sometimes gives a date for 'date of entry therein'.

All too often the medal card will be endorsed with the words "Missing believed killed" or, more usually and dispassionately, "KiA" – killed in action – and sometimes these entries will be dated.

The other reference work available via Ancestry is a

publication called 'Soldiers Died in the Great War' and this may be referred to by the initials SDGW. This publication can usually be found in book form in the 'Reference' section of a public library and it is also available to buy on disc.

Regrettably the word 'soldier' is used as a generic term for all of these men. The vast majority of course were soldiers and the search for sailors or airmen can be more complicated. Neither the Royal Navy nor the Royal Flying Corps (later RAF) has an easily searchable medal card system, though the relevant information can usually be traced elsewhere.

Once the man is satisfactorily traced via the census and can be coupled with his military entity, the task of researching individual units can begin.

Sailors and Airmen are easy to deal with. A ship usually has a well documented history and an internet search will quickly provide the basic details for a narrative leading up to the time of a man's death. Likewise an RFC Squadron, a relatively small unit, will be generally well documented and easily researched.

A soldier is, however, at the sticky end of a long and tenuous command structure and it is usually quite impossible to say how exactly a man met his fate.

The British Army as a whole was split into Army Groups identified numerically as, for instance, Third Army or Fourth Army. These were further split into Divisions comprising Headquarters troops, Infantry, Cavalry, Engineers, Artillery, Pioneers and Labour troops. Divisions were subdivided into Brigades, each containing four battalions of Infantry. A battalion usually had a nominal strength of about 1000 men (though perhaps only 3-400 in the field) and would usually be subdivided into four Companies. Each company was subdivided into platoons and these were split into smaller groups called sections. Second line battalions raised recruits in England and shipped drafts of replacements to the front line battalions as fast as they were able to train them.

Most actions were fought as Divisions but occasionally only some of the Brigades would be used whilst the others remained as a reserve. When researching our men, it has usually been possible to focus down to Brigade level and sometimes, particularly where a war diary or published narrative exists, it has been possible to pinpoint the action at battalion level and much closer to our man.

The acquisition of a copy of the Dedication Ceremony of 1922 revealed the original Roll of Honour which contained the units of about 70 of our 122 men.

One or two men have proved very difficult to track because it has been impossible to identify them beyond all reasonable doubt.

The one document which cannot be found anywhere in Horley is the list of names drawn up by the War Memorial Committee and which was edited by the Rev Henry Lewis and two other committee members before it was sent to the masons for engraving onto the Memorial. It is not included in the file of documents held at the Surrey History Centre, which includes the minute book of the committee and other useful documents. Without this, it is impossible to ascertain where errors in spellings occurred and, in some circumstances, this may have led to errors of identification.

The final list of names shown in the analysis in Chapter 8 gives a better idea of the total losses suffered by Horley in 1914–1918.

Of these men, the following brief statistics can be stated.

Age	<20	20-29	30-39	40-49	50-59	60+	unknown
Number	26	127	48	7	1	1	10
Average Age was 26 years 5 months (10 unknown)							

Year of death	1914	1915	1916	1917	1918	1919	unknown
Number	12	26	61	52	57	6	6

Service	RN/MN	RFC/RAF/RNAS	CAV	ENG	ARTLY	INF	unknown
Number	16	8	2	6	18	164	6

Abbreviations:

RN/MN = Royal Navy or Merchant Navy

RFC/RAF/RNAS = Royal Flaying Corps, Royal Air Force, Royal
 Naval Air Service.

CAV = Cavalry Regiments

ENG = Royal Engineers

ARTLY = All Artillery Formations

INF = All Infantry regiments including Labour Corps and
 Pioneers.

The total number of men listed is 220 and this figure could vary depending on how one defines Horley. Many of the men listed lived, no doubt, outside the Horley parish, which was the definition applied by the War Memorial Committee for inclusion on the town's Memorial.

But why then, were all the men from Earlswood included? The answer is still uncertain. When the list of men from that area is examined it can be seen that almost all of them, irrespective of their precise address, were listed on the old plaque at Salfords

Church. Possibly they preferred to attend this church rather than St Johns or perhaps they were members of some other organisation that met there. There are some obvious exceptions to this theory. The Pescud brothers lived in Queens Road, Horley for many years and attended Horley Infant School. William Warner was certainly 'of Earlswood' but he married a Horley girl and her family may have asked for him to be named. Archibald Remnant's family lived at Salfords but no firm reason can be ascertained as to why Alban Scollick and Frank Roffey are included on Horley War Memorial.

If the rules could be bent for some of these men, why are there so many glaring exclusions. Frank Miller, although born in Charlwood, seems to have lived all his short life in Church Road and is not on the Horley War Memorial. Ernest Jeal who lived at Kinnersley Cottages, Sidlow is missed off the War Memorial but Tom Brocklehurst who lived at Kinnersley Manor, is on there. Also missing are the Sangster brothers who lived in Lumley Road and whose mother collected door to door for the War Memorial Fund. Three of these men are listed on Charlwood War Memorial but not at Horley. Certainly the men living between Povey Cross and Hookwood and the Dowlen brothers from Lee Street thought of themselves as residents of Horley but they, too, are commemorated in Charlwood.

Conversely, Geoffrey Saxton White VC and his brother Ronald who lived at Charlwood Park, south west of Povey Cross and most certainly in the parish of Charlwood are named on Horley War Memorial.

To be charitable we should say that the War Memorial Committee had a very hard task. Most of their time was taken up with trying to find a suitable site for the Memorial and perhaps they relied on the Reverend Lewis to collect the names via St Bartholomews Church. As we have seen, there were lots of reasons why they may never have been made aware of a man's death.

Hopefully the list in Chapter 8 will enable all of these Men of Horley 1914–1918 to be remembered.

At the front of this book is the poem *In Flanders Fields* written by John McCrae near Ypres in 1915. After his death in 1918, a collection of his poems was published and widely read and admired.

Many poets felt obliged to put pen to paper and 'reply' to the sentiments expressed in 'Flanders Fields' and this version by an American poet, Miss Moira Michael, seems to set an appropriate ending for this book.

WE SHALL KEEP THE FAITH

Oh! You who sleep in Flanders' fields,
Sleep sweet – to rise anew,
We caught the torch you threw,
And holding high we kept
The faith with those who died.

We cherish too, the poppy red
That grows on fields where valour led.
It seems to signal to the skies
That blood of heroes never dies,
But lends a lustre to the red
Of the flower that blooms above the dead
In Flanders' fields.

And now the torch and poppy red
Wear in honour of our dead.
Fear not that ye have died for naught
We've learned the lesson that ye taught
In Flanders' fields.

THE SCALE OF CASUALTIES

These tables show some British Army statistics of the Great War.

The British Army of 1914 was very small in comparison with the mighty armies of our continental neighbours France and Germany. It was considered as 'contemptibly small' by Kaiser Wilhelm II. Necessarily rapid expansion ensured that from mid-1916 it faced the main body of the enemy on equal or better terms and, in addition, fielded winning forces in many other theatres. By 1918, the scale, firepower and tactical sophistication were all very much greater than in the early days. The statistics of it all would fill a very large book: here are a few key facts.

HOW BIG WAS THE BRITISH ARMY OF 1914–1918?

8.7 million men served at some time

Men from the UK in army in 1914:	733,514	
plus recruited from England :	4,006,158	
plus recruited from Scotland:	557,618	
plus recruited from Wales and Monmouth:	272,924	
plus recruited from Ireland:	134,202	
plus Empire contingents sent to serve overseas:		
From Canada:	418,035	of total 628,964 in arms
From Australian and Tasmania:	330,000	of total 416,809 in arms

From New Zealand:	**100,471**	of total 220,099 in arms
From South Africa:	**74,196**	of total 136,070 in arms
From Newfoundland:	**10,610**	of total 11,922 in arms
From West Indies:	**16,000**	this total to the end of 1917
From other Dominions:	**31,000**	
Total British Army servicemen available for deployment:	**7,165,280**	
From the Indian Army and other 'coloured troops':	**1,524,187**	
Total force available for deployment:	**8,689,467**	

WHERE DID THESE MEN SERVE?

5.4 million men served in France and Flanders and this became known as the Western Front.

Theatre of war:	Peak strength	Total employed
France and Flanders:	2,046,901	5,399,563
Mesopotamia:	447,531	889,702
Egypt and Palestine:	432,857	1,192,511
Salonika:	285,021	404,207
Italy:	132,667	145,764
Gallipoli:	127,737	468,987
Other theatres:	293,095	475,210

HOW MANY SOLDIERS OF THE BRITISH ARMY DIED IN THE GREAT WAR?

According to figures produced in the 1920's by the Central Statistical Office, total British Army casualties were as follows:

Total killed in action, plus died of wounds, disease or injury, plus missing presumed dead:	**956,703**	of which Royal Navy and RFC/RAF casualties were 39,527
of which, from the British Isles were:	**704,803**	
and from Canada, Australia, India and other places:	**251,900**	
Total British Army deaths in France and Flanders:	**564,715**	of which 32,098 died of disease or injury
Total British Army deaths on the Gallipoli front:	**26,213**	
Total British Army deaths on all other fronts:	**365,375**	

HOW MANY SOLDIERS OF THE BRITISH ARMY DO NOT HAVE A KNOWN GRAVE?

In March 2009, the totals from the Commonwelath War Graves Commission for the First World War are as follows. These figures include all three services:

Buried in named graves : 587,989
No known graves, but listed
on a memorial to the missing : 526,816, of which

– buried but not identifiable by name : 187,861
– therefore not buried at all : 338,955
The last figure includes those lost at sea.

So it is fair to say that about half are buried as known soldiers, with the rest either buried but unidentifiable or lost.

HOW MANY SOLDIERS OF THE BRITISH ARMY WERE WOUNDED IN THE GREAT WAR?

The enormous firepower of the armies of 1914–1918 guaranteed a high proportion of wounded to men in action. According to figures produced in the 1920's in the Official History of the Medical Services, total British Army wounded were as follows:

Total British Army wounded in action, plus other casualties (e.g. accidental): if a man was wounded twice he appears here twice:	2,272,998	Royal Navy and RFC/RAF casualties were 16,862
Proportion returned to duty:	64%	
Proportion returned to duty but only for lines of communication, garrison or sedentary work:	18%	
Proportion discharged as invalids:	8%	i.e. approximately 182,000
Proportion died of wounds received:	7%	

HOW MANY SOLDIERS OF THE BRITISH ARMY WERE SICK IN THE GREAT WAR?

In every previous war, deaths and casualties to sickness far outstripped those from military action. By 1914 and beyond, medical advances and an increasingly well-organised medical chain of evacuation made sure this was not the case. The number of men evacuated to England from France and Flanders, who were suffering from an illness:

Year	Officers	Other ranks
1914	892	25,013
1915	5,558	121,006
1916	12,818	219,539
1917	15,311	321,628
1918	15,311	265,735

The proportion of men suffering from illnesses was very much higher in Palestine, Mesopotamia, Gallipoli and East Africa.

These statistics and much of the information used here was taken from 'The Long, Long, Trail' website at www.1914-1918.net, by kind permission of the owner Mr Chris Baker. This website will greatly assist readers as it contains a mass of information about World War I.